ASP.NET Core 9 Web API Cookbook

Over 60 hands-on recipes for building and securing enterprise
web APIs with REST, GraphQL, and more

Luke Avedon

Garry Cabrera

ASP.NET Core 9 Web API Cookbook

Portfolio Director: Ashwin Nair

Relationship Lead: Suman Sen

Program Manager: Aparna Nair

Content Engineer: Runcil Rebello

Technical Editor: Sweety Pagaria

Copy Editor: Safis Editing

Proofreader: Runcil Rebello

Indexer: Tejal Soni

Production Designer: Prashant Ghare

Growth Lead: Priyadarshini Sharma

First published: April 2025

Production reference: 3201125

Published by Packt Publishing Ltd.

Grosvenor House

11 St Paul's Square

Birmingham

B3 1RB, UK

ISBN 978-1-83588-034-0

www.packtpub.com

Contributors

About the authors

Luke Avedon has been contributing to the software development lifecycle for nearly a decade. In recent years, he has focused exclusively on .NET development. He helped to design and implement an ASP. NET Core API for a leading healthcare company, serving as the backbone for a system supporting nearly one billion USD in revenue. Luke has also developed secure solutions for integrating vendor APIs and upgrading legacy .NET APIs to help comply with Department of Defense GCC high-security standards. Additionally, he contributed to the development of large-scale AI models for a major technology company, gaining valuable insights into the intersection of AI and software engineering.

Garry Cabrera has seven years of expertise in building robust backend APIs for major financial institutions, including Credit Suisse and Bank of America. Though he specializes in .NET and Java development, Garry's technical versatility extends to Python and Groovy, enabling him to adapt solutions to diverse requirements. His deep knowledge of relational databases—SQL Server, MySQL, and Oracle—combined with proficiency in ORMs such as Hibernate, allows him to create efficient and scalable data access layers. Garry's integration expertise with Apache Camel and SSIS has proven invaluable in establishing seamless data flows across complex enterprise systems.

Learn more on Discord

To join the Discord community for this book – where you can share feedback, ask questions to the authors, and provide solutions to other readers – scan the QR code or visit the link:

https://packt.link/aspdotnet9WebAPI

About the reviewer

Gulab Chand Tejwani is a seasoned professional in digital marketing, data analysis, and full-stack web development. Founder of Technet Consultancy in 2011, he specializes in project management and innovative tech solutions. With over 20 years of experience in Microsoft technologies, he holds certifications such as PMP, MCT, and MCPS. Tejwani has also contributed as a director at Learnotics LLP and TechnoSmart Academy, mentoring emerging talents. He holds an MCA from IGNOU and an MBA in IT from Sikkim Manipal University. Fluent in various tech domains, he continues to inspire through his expertise.

Table of Contents

2

Mastering Resource Creation and Validation 33

3

Securing Your Web API 63

4

Creating Custom Middleware   95

5

Creating Comprehensive Logging Solutions   115

6

Real-Time Communication with SignalR   141

7

Building Robust API Tests: a Guide to Unit and Integration Testing   167

Preface

Since ASP.NET was completely redesigned and rebranded as the open source ASP.NET Core in 2016, ASP.NET Core has gone on to establish itself as the leading framework for building backend Web APIs. The framework consistently outranks other enterprise solutions in performance benchmarks while offering a robust feature set that includes built-in dependency injection, a lightweight modular HTTP request pipeline, and powerful model binding that automatically maps data from HTTP requests to action method parameters.

With the wealth of information available on ASP.NET Core, finding practical, implementation-focused guidance can be challenging. This cookbook cuts through the theory to provide you with clear, actionable recipes for solving common Web API development challenges.

We have endeavored to make every recipe practical and immediately useful for solving real problems we encounter on the job. The recipes in this cookbook cover authentication, performance optimization, data access, caching strategies, real-time communication, and cloud integration. Whether you're building a simple REST API or architecting complex distributed systems, you'll find relevant, practical solutions you can immediately apply to your projects.

Who this book is for

This book is for intermediate-level .NET developers looking for actionable solutions to common problems in Web API development. Those coming from another backend stack such as Java will find this book a quick crash course in building web APIs with .NET. The book assumes working knowledge of C# and ASP.NET Core fundamentals, focusing instead on practical solutions for performance optimization, security implementation, caching strategies, real-time communication, and distributed system architecture. You'll learn industry best practices and real-world techniques that can be immediately applied to your projects, whether you're designing new APIs or enhancing existing ones.

What this book covers

Chapter 1, *Practical Data Access in ASP.NET Core Web APIs*, focuses on efficient data retrieval with KeySet pagination using Entity Framework Core. This chapter covers creating mock databases with Bogus, enhancing error handling via ProblemDetails, and exploring a couple of the new LINQ methods for data aggregation. It also includes configuring CORS for metadata exposure and optimizing access to the first and last pages.

Chapter 2, Mastering Resource Creation and Validation, explores creating, validating, and updating resources in your web API. We cover model validation techniques using data annotations, custom validation attributes, and the FluentValidation library. We implement PUT and PATCH requests for updating resources, leveraging AutoMapper for efficient object mapping, and managing cascade deletes. Additionally, this chapter introduces Scalar as a user-friendly alternative to Swagger UI for interactive Open API documentation.

Chapter 3, Securing Your Web API, covers essential security strategies for ASP.NET Core APIs. The chapter focuses on enforcing HTTPS through custom middleware and certificates for various environments. It demonstrates implementing ASP.NET Core Identity, cookie-based authentication (still relevant for interfacing with legacy systems and browser-based clients), and JWT-based authentication for stateless authorization. Policy-based and role-based authorization are explored to create robust security boundaries to protect your API.

Chapter 4, Creating Custom Middleware, explains how to extend ASP.NET Core's request pipeline with specialized components that enhance your API. The chapter demonstrates implementing health checks to monitor API status, including a custom database performance health check that measures query execution times against configurable thresholds. It shows how to document these health endpoints in OpenAPI using the new Document Transformers feature. Additionally, we will create security-enhancing middleware for adding protective headers and factory-based middleware for on-the-fly response format transformations.

Chapter 5, Creating Comprehensive Logging Solutions, demonstrates how to capture and analyze API activity using Serilog and Seq, creating a centralized logging system that enhances debugging and monitoring. It covers logging all HTTP requests with custom diagnostic context properties, tracking controller and action method names, combining ASP.NET Core's HttpLogging with Serilog, crafting detailed structured log objects in controllers, and configuring secure access to logging services with API keys.

Chapter 6, Real-Time Communication with SignalR, demonstrates how to implement bidirectional, real-time functionality in your Web API applications. The chapter shows how to create interactive experiences such as live polls, real-time chat, and private messaging using Microsoft's SignalR technology. We cover integrating JWT authentication with SignalR connections, invoking hub methods from HTTP controllers, customizing user identification, implementing direct messaging between specific users, and creating admin-controlled group management.

Chapter 7, Building Robust API Tests: a Guide to Unit and Integration Testing, is all about unit and integration testing. We will set up xUnit unit tests and enhance them with AutoFixture, NSubstitute, and FluentAssertions. For integration testing, we use WebApplicationFactory with authentication to test the complete API pipeline.

Chapter 8, GraphQL: Designing Flexible and Efficient APIs, provides practical recipes for implementing GraphQL APIs, a powerful alternative to REST. We cover creating real-time updates with GraphQL subscriptions, implementing mutations for data modifications, and building efficient pagination, filtering, and sorting capabilities that work with IQueryable. Also, we use Hot Chocolate Fusion to combine multiple independent GraphQL APIs into a unified schema through a gateway pattern, a modern approach to distributed GraphQL valuable in microservice architectures.

Chapter 9, Deploying and Managing Your WebAPI in the Cloud, guides you through cloud deployment and management of ASP.NET Core web APIs. We cover integrating Azure core services, securing configurations with Key Vault, and crafting API gateways with YARP for efficient traffic management and geo-based load balancing. Additionally, we explore migrating to .NET Aspire for unified orchestration, monitoring, and integrating Dockerized services such as Prometheus for persistent telemetry data.

Chapter 10, The Craft of Caching, provides various caching strategies for ASP.NET Core web APIs, progressing from client-side to server-side solutions. It begins with manual HTTP header manipulation and the `ResponseCache` attribute for client-side caching. The chapter then transitions to server-side distributed caching using Redis via .NET Aspire, covering output caching, `IDistributedCache`, and the new `HybridCache`. `HybridCache` is highlighted as a powerful tool that combines in-memory and distributed caching for optimal performance and simplified cache management.

Chapter 11, Beyond the Core, is about inter-service communication patterns in distributed .NET applications. This chapter provides recipes for microservice communication through gRPC in .NET Aspire, implementing both unary calls and bidirectional streaming for real-time data exchange. Next, we use **Distributed Application Runtime (Dapr)** with .NET Aspire to implement service-to-service interactions, covering publish/subscribe messaging for real-time updates and state management for sharing data between services.

To get the most out of this book

The recipes in this book are built with .NET 9, which was released in November 2024 as a **standard-term support (STS)** release with 18 months of support from Microsoft. .NET follows a predictable release cycle with a new version every year – even-numbered versions (such as .NET 8) are **long-term support (LTS)** releases with 3 years of support, while odd-numbered versions (such as .NET 9) are STS releases. All code examples have been tested with .NET 9, but the patterns and approaches should remain applicable to future versions as well. Visit https://dotnet.microsoft.com/en-us/platform/support/policy/dotnet-core for more information.

Software/Hardware covered in the book	OS Requirements
.NET 9 SDK	Windows, Mac OS X, and Linux (Any)
PowerShell 7.5	
Docker Desktop	

If you are using the digital version of this book, we advise you to type the code yourself or access the code via the GitHub repository (link available in the next section). Doing so will help you avoid any potential errors related to the copying and pasting of code.

For Windows users, we recommend Windows Terminal for the PowerShell examples.

Download the example code files

You can download the example code files for this book from GitHub at `https://github.com/PacktPublishing/ASP.NET-9-Web-API-Cookbook`. In case there's an update to the code, it will be updated on the existing GitHub repository.

We also have other code bundles from our rich catalog of books and videos available at `https://github.com/PacktPublishing/`. Check them out!

Conventions used

There are a number of text conventions used throughout this book.

`Code in text`: Indicates code words in text, database table names, folder names, filenames, file extensions, pathnames, dummy URLs, user input, and Twitter handles. Here is an example: "Replace `throw new NotImplementedException();` with our registration name and a dictionary to store the results of testing our database."

A block of code is set as follows:

```
using System.Data;
using System.Diagnostics;
using Microsoft.Extensions.Diagnostics.HealthChecks;
using Microsoft.Extensions.Options;
```

When we wish to draw your attention to a particular part of a code block, the relevant lines or items are set in bold:

```
using System.Data;
using System.Diagnostics;
using Microsoft.Extensions.Diagnostics.HealthChecks;
using Microsoft.Extensions.Options;
```

Any command-line input or output is written as follows:

```
dotnet add package Grpc.Net.ClientFactory
dotnet add package Grpc.Tools
dotnet add package Google.Protobuf
```

Bold: Indicates a new term, an important word, or words that you see onscreen. For example, words in menus or dialog boxes appear in the text like this. Here is an example: "One way to confirm that CORS is allowing our response headers to be displayed is simply via the **Network** tab in our browser."

> **Tips or important notes**
> Appear like this.

Sections

In this book, you will find several headings that appear frequently (*Getting ready, How to do it..., How it works..., There's more...,* and *See also*).

To give clear instructions on how to complete a recipe, use these sections as follows:

Getting ready

This section tells you what to expect in the recipe and describes how to set up any software or any preliminary settings required for the recipe.

How to do it...

This section contains the steps required to follow the recipe.

How it works...

This section usually consists of a detailed explanation of what happened in the previous section.

There's more...

This section consists of additional information about the recipe in order to make you more knowledgeable about the recipe.

See also

This section provides helpful links to other useful information for the recipe.

Get in touch

Feedback from our readers is always welcome.

General feedback: If you have questions about any aspect of this book, mention the book title in the subject of your message and email us at customercare@packtpub.com.

Errata: Although we have taken every care to ensure the accuracy of our content, mistakes do happen. If you have found a mistake in this book, we would be grateful if you would report this to us. Please visit www.packtpub.com/support/errata, selecting your book, clicking on the Errata Submission Form link, and entering the details.

Piracy: If you come across any illegal copies of our works in any form on the Internet, we would be grateful if you would provide us with the location address or website name. Please contact us at copyright@packtpub.com with a link to the material.

If you are interested in becoming an author: If there is a topic that you have expertise in and you are interested in either writing or contributing to a book, please visit authors.packtpub.com.

Share Your Thoughts

Once you've read *ASP.NET Core 9 Web API Cookbook*, we'd love to hear your thoughts! Scan the QR code below to go straight to the Amazon review page for this book and share your feedback.

https://packt.link/r/1835880355

Your review is important to us and the tech community and will help us make sure we're delivering excellent quality content.

Free Benefits with Your Book

This book comes with free benefits to support your learning. Activate them now for instant access (see the "*How to Unlock*" section for instructions).

Here's a quick overview of what you can instantly unlock with your purchase:

PDF and ePub Copies

Next-Gen Web-Based Reader

Access a DRM-free PDF copy of this book to read anywhere, on any device.

Use a DRM-free ePub version with your favorite e-reader.

Multi-device progress sync: Pick up where you left off, on any device.

Highlighting and notetaking: Capture ideas and turn reading into lasting knowledge.

Bookmarking: Save and revisit key sections whenever you need them.

Dark mode: Reduce eye strain by switching to dark or sepia themes

How to Unlock

UNLOCK NOW

Scan the QR code (or go to packtpub.com/unlock). Search for this book by name, confirm the edition, and then follow the steps on the page.

Note: Keep your invoice handy. Purchases made directly from Packt don't require an invoice.

1

Practical Data Access in ASP.NET Core Web APIs

ASP.NET Core 9 Web API Cookbook aims to be your comprehensive toolbox for building web APIs with ASP.NET Core 9—Microsoft's latest version of ASP.NET Core. Our goal is to give you practical recipes you can use on the job. This cookbook provides step-by-step solutions to workaday problems such as implementing efficient data access patterns and secure authentication flows, to leveraging cutting-edge technologies such as .NET Aspire for cloud orchestration and distributed caching with **HybridCache**.

Throughout multiple chapters, we will cover the entire spectrum of RESTful APIs—from implementing robust testing strategies in *Chapter 7* to working with .NET Aspire in *Chapter 9* and tackling caching in *Chapter 10*. While RESTful APIs using JSON are the primary focus, the ASP.NET Core 9 web API offers additional powerful technologies for building APIs, such as **GraphQL** for efficient querying, **gRPC** for high-performance communication, and **SignalR** for real-time functionality. If you are transitioning from a legacy .NET Framework background, don't miss the chapter on middleware. Middleware is perhaps the most significant architectural change from the module and handler system in .NET Framework.

In this chapter, we will explore best practices for retrieving data from an ASP.NET Core web API, including techniques for communicating from the data access layer to the consumer of the API. We will focus on paging and retrieving data with **Entity Framework (EF) Core**. We will also cover two of the three new LINQ methods, `CountBy` and `AggregateBy`, to return additional grouping information on your data.

The following recipes will be covered in this chapter:

- Creating a mock database for EF Core with Bogus
- Using `ProblemDetails` to return more robust error information
- Creating a categories endpoint using the new LINQ `CountBy`
- Implementing `KeySet` pagination
- Configuring a CORS policy to expose pagination metadata
- Implementing efficient first- and last-page access with EF Core

- Testing the API in PowerShell
- Using the new `AggregateBy` LINQ method to return the average price per category

> **Free Benefits with Your Book**
>
> Your purchase includes a free PDF copy of this book along with other exclusive benefits. Check the *Free Benefits with Your Book* section in the Preface to unlock them instantly and maximize your learning experience.

Technical requirements

The only requirement for this chapter is that you have the .NET 9 SDK installed. The .NET SDK supports macOS, Linux, and Windows. You can download it from the official .NET website here: `https://dotnet.microsoft.com/en-us/download/dotnet/9.0`.

Once installed, you can confirm its availability by running the following commands in your terminal:

```
# List installed sdks
dotnet --list-sdks

# View general .NET info
dotnet -info
```

This book is designed to be as IDE-agnostic and OS-agnostic as possible. None of the recipes in this book is dependent on Visual Studio or any specific IDE. This is one of the reasons why we focus on terminal commands instead of relying on Visual Studio's GUI-based workflows. Feel free to use the IDE of your choice, such as VS Code JetBrains Rider, or even command-line editors such as Vim.

The starter code for this chapter is located at `https://github.com/PacktPublishing/ASP.NET-9-Web-API-Cookbook/tree/main/start/chapter01`.

Creating a mock database for EF Core with Bogus

Let's start by creating a basic web API that will serve as the foundation for the rest of the projects in this chapter. We will use SQLite's in-memory database provider with EF Core, eliminating the need for database files or server connections. The API's database will be populated with mock data generated by Bogus.

Getting ready

To begin, you will need the following:

- The .NET 9 SDK, which can be downloaded from `https://dotnet.microsoft.com/en-us/download/dotnet/9.0`

How to do it...

1. Open the terminal and create a new web API:

    ```
    dotnet new webapi -o mockAPI -f net9.0 --no-https --auth none
    ```

2. Navigate to the project directory and create a new .gitignore file:

    ```
    dotnet new gitignore
    ```

3. Install EF Core and its SQLite provider:

    ```
    dotnet add package Microsoft.EntityFrameworkCore
    dotnet add package Microsoft.EntityFrameworkCore.Sqlite
    ```

4. Install Bogus for creating mock data. New in .NET 9, we also have to manually add Swagger support:

    ```
    dotnet add package Bogus
    dotnet add package Swashbuckle.AspNetCore.SwaggerUI
    ```

5. Create a folder named Models. Create a file called Product.cs and fill in the following Product class:

    ```
    namespace mockAPI.Models;

    public class Product
    {
        public int Id { get; set; }
        public string Name { get; set; } = string.Empty;
        public decimal Price { get; set; }
        public int CategoryId { get; set; }
    }
    ```

6. Create a sibling folder called Data. In that folder, create your AppDbContext.cs file. Fill in a AppDbContext class, which will inherit from DbContext:

    ```
    using Microsoft.EntityFrameworkCore;
    using mockAPI.Models;
    namespace mockAPI.Data;

    public class AppDbContext : DbContext
    {
        public AppDbContext(DbContextOptions<AppDbContext> options):
            base(options) { }
    ```

7. Still inside the `AppDbContext` class, on the next line, define the `'DbSet'` property to use your new `Products` class:

```
public DbSet<Product> Products { get; set; }
```

8. On the next line, define the `OnModelCreating` method:

```
protected override void OnModelCreating(ModelBuilder
modelBuilder)
{
    base.OnModelCreating(modelBuilder);
    modelBuilder.Entity<Product>(entity =>
    {
        entity.HasKey(e => e.Id);
        entity.Property(e => e.Name).IsRequired();
        entity.Property(e => e.Price).HasColumnType(
            "decimal(18,2)");
    });
}
```

9. Open the `Program.cs` file. Delete all the boilerplate code that .NET generated; we are going to start from scratch.

10. At the top of `Program.cs`, import our new `Data` namespace, as well as the namespace for models and Bogus itself:

```
using mockAPI.Data;
using mockAPI.Models;
using Microsoft.EntityFrameworkCore;
using Microsoft.Data.Sqlite;
using Bogus;
```

11. Next, we will create the builder, register the OpenAPI service, and create a connection to our in-memory database that will persist for the application's lifetime:

```
var builder = WebApplication.CreateBuilder(args);

builder.Services.AddOpenApi();

var connection = new SqliteConnection("DataSource=:memory:");
connection.Open();
```

12. After creating the SQLite connection, we need to add the `DbContext` registration:

```
builder.Services.AddDbContext<AppDbContext>(options =>
    options.UseSqlite(connection));
```

13. On the next line, inject a scoped service that opens a connection to the in-memory database and then confirms that the connection has been created:

```
var app = builder.Build();

using (var scope = app.Services.CreateScope())
{
    var services = scope.ServiceProvider;
    var context = services.GetRequiredService<AppDbContext>();

    context.Database.EnsureCreated();
}
```

> **Service lifetime selection**
>
> We need to register a scoped service to interact with EF Core's DbContext. This is counterintuitive; it might seem like a singleton service would be a more appropriate lifetime for working with a database. However, EF Core's DbContext is designed to be short-lived and is not thread-safe for concurrent operations.

14. Expand the scoped service to seed your in-memory database with fake data, only if your database context is empty:

```
if (!context.Products.Any())
{
    var productFaker = new Faker<Product>()
        .RuleFor(p => p.Name, f => f.Commerce.ProductName())
        .RuleFor(p => p.Price, f => f.Finance.Amount(
            50,2000))
        .RuleFor(p => p.CategoryId, f => f.Random.Int(
            1,5));
    var products = productFaker.Generate(10000);
    context.Products.AddRange(products);
    context.SaveChanges();
}
```

15. Let's add a minimal API endpoint we can use for testing:

```
app.MapGet("/products", async (AppDbContext db) =>
    await db.Products.OrderBy(p =>
        p.Id).Take(10).ToListAsync());
```

16. Before we run the application, let's manually add SwaggerUI support:

```
app.MapOpenApi();
if (app.Environment.IsDevelopment())
{
    app.UseSwaggerUI(options =>
    {
        options.SwaggerEndpoint("/openapi/v1.json", "v1");
    });
}
app.Run();
```

17. Run the application. You can visit `http://localhost<yourport>/swagger/index.html` and click on the **Products** endpoint to see our fake data generated by Bogus:

```
dotnet run
```

How it works...

You registered your `AppDbContext` with the service provider at startup, which is the standard way to integrate EF Core into ASP.NET Core dependency injection. This allows the database context to be available for your controllers, services, and so on.

You also added a scoped service provider that checks whether your database is empty. The scoped lifetime ensures that a new `AppDbContext` is created for each request, preventing any data inconsistencies that can plague singleton instances of database connections. If the database is empty, it will be seeded using the `Faker<T>` class from Bogus.

We also used the SQLite in-memory database provider for EF Core. This allows us to create a database entirely in memory without requiring an external SQLite file. While EF Core also includes an `InMemory` database provider, it is considered a legacy option and is not recommended for testing. Unlike the `InMemory` provider, SQLite's in-memory database supports transactions and raw SQL, making it a closer approximation of a real-world database.

See also...

- The Bogus repository has plenty of useful information and links: `https://github.com/bchavez/Bogus`

- A complement to Bogus, which can help automatically generate mock data based on your model structure: `https://github.com/nickdodd79/AutoBogus`

Using ProblemDetails to return more robust error information

In this recipe, we will enhance our API's error handling by leveraging **ProblemDetails**, a standardized way to provide detailed error information as defined in the HTTP specification.

ProblemDetails allows ApiController to transform error status codes into structured and informative error responses. ProblemDetails is part of the HTTP specification and a great way to return additional error information if something goes wrong with an endpoint. We will explore how to create custom ProblemDetails objects and customize them to include meaningful details, such as including a traceId from HttpContext within the ProblemDetails object itself.

Getting ready

This recipe uses a starter project that includes a basic controller with endpoints already set up and configured. This recipe is not a direct continuation of the preceding recipe.

You can clone the starter project from here: https://github.com/PacktPublishing/ASP.NET-9-Web-API-Cookbook/tree/main/start/chapter01/problemDetails.

How to do it...

1. Open the Program.cs file. On the line right after AddControllers(), let's register customization options using AddProblemDetails():

```
builder.Services.AddProblemDetails(options =>
    options.CustomizeProblemDetails = (context) =>
    {
        var httpContext = context.HttpContext;
        context.ProblemDetails.Extensions["traceId"] = Activity.
            Current?.Id ?? httpContext.TraceIdentifier;
        context.ProblemDetails.Extensions["supportContact"] =
            "support@example.com";
```

2. Starting on the next line, let's enhance our ProblemDetails by adding custom messages for different status codes:

```
if (context.ProblemDetails.Status == StatusCodes.
    Status401Unauthorized)
{
    context.ProblemDetails.Title = "Unauthorized
                                    Access";
    context.ProblemDetails.Detail = "You are not
            authorized to access this resource.";
```

```
        }
        else if (context.ProblemDetails.Status == StatusCodes.
            Status404NotFound)
        {
            context.ProblemDetails.Title = "Resource Not Found";
            context.ProblemDetails.Detail = "The resource you
                            are looking for was not found.";
        }
        else
        {
            context.ProblemDetails.Title = "An unexpected error
                            occurred";
            context.ProblemDetails.Detail = "An unexpected error
                occurred. Please try again later.";
        }
    });
```

3. Navigate to `ProductsController.cs`, in the `Controllers` folder. Modify the endpoint that retrieves a product by its ID endpoint. We are going to specify the various responses we expect from the endpoint using the `ProducesResponseType` attribute and return appropriate `ProblemDetails` objects for error responses:

```
// GET: /products/{id}
[HttpGet("{id}")]
[ProducesResponseType(StatusCodes.Status200OK, Type =
typeof(ProductDTO))]
[ProducesResponseType(StatusCodes.Status404NotFound, Type =
typeof(ProblemDetails))]
[ProducesResponseType(StatusCodes.Status401Unauthorized, Type =
typeof(ProblemDetails))]
[ProducesResponseType(StatusCodes.Status500InternalServerError,
Type = typeof(ProblemDetails))]
public async Task<ActionResult<ProductDTO>> GetAProduct(int id)
{
    logger.LogInformation($"Retrieving product with id {id}");
```

4. Create a `try` block to attempt to retrieve our product:

```
try
    {
        var product = await productsService.GetAProductAsync(
            id);

        if (product == null)
```

```
    {
        return Problem(
            detail: $"Product with ID {id} was not found.",
            title: "Product not found",
            statusCode: StatusCodes.Status404NotFound,
            instance: HttpContext.TraceIdentifier
            );
    }

    return Ok(product);
}
```

5. Now add a catch for other errors. Let's catch `Unauthorized Access`, which will return its own `ProblemDetails`:

```
catch (UnauthorizedAccessException ex)
{
    logger.LogError(ex, "Unauthorized access");
    return Problem(
        detail: ex.Message,
        title: "Unauthorized Access",
        statusCode: StatusCodes.Status401Unauthorized,
        instance: HttpContext.TraceIdentifier
        );
}
```

6. Finally, let's also catch general exceptions:

```
catch (Exception ex)
{
    logger.LogError(ex, $"An error occurred while
        retrieving product with id {id}");
    return Problem(
        detail: "An unexpected error occurred while
            processing your request.",
        title: "Internal Server Error",
        statusCode: StatusCodes.
            Status500InternalServerError,
        instance: HttpContext.TraceIdentifier
        );
}
}
```

7. Start your app with the following code:

```
dotnet run
```

8. Direct your web browser to go to the `404` "Not Found" URL for a `ProductId` that cannot exist.

Figure 1.1 illustrates trying to get an invalid ID, directly via the web browser:

```
        ✕    Q        ⓘ    localhost:5148/Products/-150000

1  {
2      "type": "https://httpstatuses.io/404",
3      "title": "Not Found",
4      "status": 404,
5      "traceId": "00-2621fd242bcc79d16f8a116ca570a103-fa99731702fd2fab-00",
6      "supportContact": "support@example.com"
7  }
```

Figure 1.1 – ProblemDetails returned with traceId and supportContact

How it works...

In this recipe, we relied on the built-in `ProblemDetails` support in ASP.NET Core 9 to create custom problem messages when your endpoints return errors.

`ProblemDetails` objects are automatically generated for some errors. We simply injected `AddProblemDetails` with the `CustomizeProblemDetails` class to create custom messages.

In previous versions of ASP.NET Core, we had to rely on external NuGet packages for the meaningful customization of `ProblemDetails`. ASP.NET Core 9 allows us to have more advanced control over the `ProblemDetails` response.

By customizing `ProblemDetails`, we can provide more detailed and useful error information to the clients, including trace IDs and support contact information.

See also

`ProblemDetails` is not unique to ASP.NET Core—read all about the `ProblemDetails` HTTP spec here: `https://datatracker.ietf.org/doc/html/rfc9457`.

Creating a categories endpoint using the new LINQ CountBy() method

.NET 9 introduces CountBy(), a powerful new LINQ method that simplifies the common task of grouping and counting elements. This method replaces the traditional pattern of combining GroupBy with Count, making your code more concise and readable. In this recipe, we'll create an endpoint that uses CountBy() to efficiently report how many products exist in each category, demonstrating how this new method can simplify data aggregation tasks.

Getting ready

You can clone the starter project for this recipe here: https://github.com/PacktPublishing/ASP.NET-9-Web-API-Cookbook/tree/main/start/chapter01/countBy.

How to do it...

1. In the starter project, let's navigate to the Models folder and create a new file called CategoryDTO.cs. In this file, we will define a new DTO record:

    ```
    namespace CountBy.Models;

    public record CategoryDTO
    {
        public int CategoryId { get; init; }

        public int ProductCount { get; init; }
    }
    ```

2. In the Services folder, create a file named IProductsService.cs. In this file, we are going to define a contract for a GetCategoryInfoAsync service method:

    ```
    using CountBy.Models;
    namespace CountBy.Services;

    public interface IProductsService {
        Task<IEnumerable<ProductDTO>> GetAllProductsAsync();
        Task<IReadOnlyCollection<CategoryDTO>>
            GetCategoryInfoAsync();
    }
    ```

3. Implement the service method using `CountBy()` on your `DbContext`:

```
public async Task<IReadOnlyCollection<CategoryDTO>>
GetCategoryInfoAsync()
    {
        var products = await  context.Products.AsNoTracking().
                    ToListAsync();

        var productsByCategory = products.CountBy(p =>
            p.CategoryId).OrderBy(x => x.Key);
        return productsByCategory.Select(categoryGroup => new
        CategoryDTO
        {
            CategoryId = categoryGroup.Key,
            ProductCount = categoryGroup.Value
        }).ToList(

    }
```

4. Now let's navigate to our `ProductsController.cs` file in the `Controllers` folder. Add the attributes to the `CategoryInfo` endpoint:

```
// GET: /Products/CategoryInfo
[HttpGet("CategoryInfo")]
[ProducesResponseType(StatusCodes.Status200OK, Type =
typeof(IEnumerable<CategoryDTO>))]
[ProducesResponseType(StatusCodes.Status204NoContent)]
[ProducesResponseType(StatusCodes.Status500InternalServerError)]
```

5. Let's expand the `GetCategoryInfo` controller method:

```
public async Task<ActionResult<IEnumerable<CategoryDTO>>>
GetCategoryInfo()
{
    logger.LogInformation("Retrieving Category Info");
    try
    {
        var products = await productsService.
            GetCategoryInfoAsync();

        if (!products.Any())
            return NoContent();

        return Ok(products);
    }
    catch (Exception ex)
    {
```

```
        logger.LogError(ex, "An error occurred while
                        retrieving all products");
        return StatusCode(StatusCodes.
                        Status500InternalServerError);
    }
}
```

6. Build your new project:

    ```
    dotnet run
    ```

7. Test out your new endpoint at `Products/CategoryInfo` and see how many products you have in each category.

    Since this is a `GET` endpoint, we can test it with our web browser, as shown in the following screenshot:

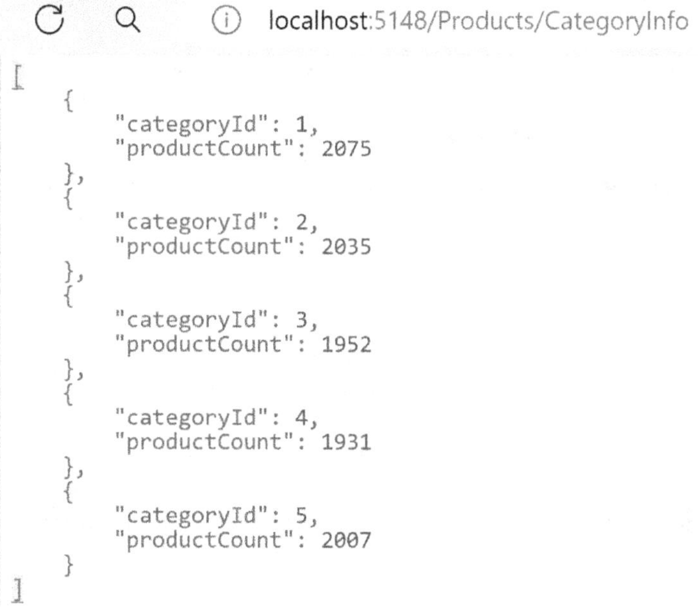

    ⟳ Q   ⓘ localhost:5148/Products/CategoryInfo

    ```
    [
        {
            "categoryId": 1,
            "productCount": 2075
        },
        {
            "categoryId": 2,
            "productCount": 2035
        },
        {
            "categoryId": 3,
            "productCount": 1952
        },
        {
            "categoryId": 4,
            "productCount": 1931
        },
        {
            "categoryId": 5,
            "productCount": 2007
        }
    ]
    ```

Figure 1.2 – Our data now with a categoryId

How it works...

We explored the use of the new LINQ CountBy() operator to create an endpoint that returns how many products you have by each category. CountBy() provides a new, more elegant way to categorize data, replacing the need to use both GroupBy() and Count() in aggregation operations. It's important to note that CountBy() is a LINQ-to-objects method, not a LINQ-to-entities method.

This means when used with EF Core, it will first materialize the query (loading all records into memory) before performing the counting operation. For large datasets in production scenarios, you might want to consider using `GroupBy()` directly on the `IQueryable` instead. In addition to database queries, `CountBy()` is particularly useful for in-memory operations such as analyzing API usage statistics by grouping and counting requests based on different criteria such as client IP, user agent, or endpoint path.

Implementing KeySet pagination

It is usually inadvisable to return all the available data from a `GET` endpoint. You may think you can get away without paging, but non-paged `GET` endpoints often have a surprisingly bad effect on network load and application performance. They can also prevent your API from scaling. Other resources on this topic often demonstrate `OFFSET FETCH` style pagination (*Skip and Take when using EF Core*). While this approach is easy to understand, it has a hidden cost: it forces the database engine to read through every single row leading up to the desired page.

A more efficient technique is to work only with indices and not full data rows. For ordered data, the principle is simple: if a higher ID than exists on your page can be found somewhere in the database, then you know more data is available. This is called **keyset pagination**.

In this recipe, we will implement keyset pagination in ASP.NET Core using EF Core, harnessing the power of indexes for optimal performance.

Getting ready

Clone the repository available here: `/start/chapter01/keyset`. You won't be using any new external dependencies for this endpoint. This project has one non-paged `GET` endpoint.

How to do it...

1. In your `Models` folder, create an abstract base class called `PagedResponse.cs`:

    ```
    namespace cookbook.Models;

    public abstract record PagedResponse<T>
    {
        public IReadOnlyCollection<T> Items { get; init; } = Array.
            Empty<T>();
        public int PageSize { get; init; }
        public bool HasPreviousPage { get; init; }
        public bool HasNextPage { get; init; }
    }
    ```

> **An important note on where to place paging logic**
>
> At this point, a lot of people would put business logic in HasPreviousPage and HasNextPage.
> I am not a fan of putting business logic in setters, as this tends to obfuscate the logic. It makes
> code harder to read as one often forgets that properties are being modified without explicit
> method calls. If you have to use a setter, it should handle data access and not logic. It's a personal
> choice, but it is generally better to place this logic in explicit methods.

2. Create a `PagedProductResponseDTO` instance in the `PagedProductResponseDTO.cs` file that simply inherits from `PagedResponseDTO<ProductDTO>`:

```
namespace cookbook.Models;


public record PagedProductResponseDTO :
PagedResponseDTO<ProductDTO>
{
}
```

3. Now navigate to the `Services` folder. Update the `IProductsService` interface:

```
using cookbook.Models;
namespace cookbook.Services;

public interface IProductsService {
    Task<IEnumerable<ProductDTO>> GetAllProductsAsync();
    Task<PagedProductResponseDTO> GetPagedProductsAsync(int
    pageSize, int? lastProductId = null);
}
```

4. In the `ProductsServices.cs` file. Implement the `GetPagedProductsAsync` method.
    For now, you will just create a queryable on your database context:

```
public async Task<PagedProductResponseDTO>
GetPagedProductsAsync(int pageSize, int? lastProductId = null)
    {
        var query = context.Products.AsQueryable();

    }
```

5. Before you query any data, check that an ID exists in the database that is higher than the ID
    of the last row you returned:

```
public async Task<PagedProductResponseDTO>
    GetPagedProductsAsync(int pageSize, int? lastProductId =
        null)
    {
        var query = context.Products.AsQueryable();
```

```
            if (lastProductId.HasValue)
            {
                query = query.Where(p => p.Id > lastProductId.
                                        Value);
            }
```

6. On the next line, query the remaining indexes in DbContext to get a page of products:

```
        var pagedProducts = await query
            .OrderBy(p => p.Id)
            .Take(pageSize)
            .Select(p => new ProductDTO
            {
                Id = p.Id,
                Name = p.Name,
                Price = p.Price,
                CategoryId = p.CategoryId
            })
            .ToListAsync();
```

7. Next, calculate the last ID from the page you just retrieved:

```
    var lastId = pagedProducts.LastOrDefault()?.Id;
```

8. Use AnyAsync to see whether any IDs exist higher than the last one you fetched:

```
    var hasNextPage = await context.Products.AnyAsync(
        p => p.Id > lastId);
```

9. Finish the method by returning your results along with the PageSize, HasNextPage, and HasPreviousPage metadata:

```
        var result = new PagedProductResponseDTO
        {
            Items = pagedProducts.Any() ? pagedProducts: Array.
                    Empty<ProductDTO>(),
            PageSize = pageSize,
            HasNextPage = hasNextPage,
            HasPreviousPage = lastProductId.HasValue
        };
        return result;
    }
}
```

> **Important note**
>
> It is somewhat expensive to return a `TotalCount` of results. So, unless there is a clear need for the client to have a `TotalCount`, it is better to leave it out. You will return more robust pagination data in the next recipe.

10. Back in your `Controller`, import the built-in `System.Text.Json`:

```
using System.Text.Json;
```

11. Finally, implement a simple controller that returns your paginated data with links to both the previous page and the next page of data. First, return a bad request if no page size is given:

```
// GET: /Products
[HttpGet]
[ProducesResponseType(StatusCodes.Status200OK, Type =
typeof(IEnumerable<ProductDTO>))]
[ProducesResponseType(StatusCodes.Status204NoContent)]
[ProducesResponseType(StatusCodes.Status500InternalServerError)]
    public async Task<ActionResult<IEnumerable<ProductDTO>>>
GetProducts(int pageSize, int? lastProductId = null)
    {
        if (pageSize <= 0)
        {
            return BadRequest("pageSize must be greater than
                              0");
        }
    }
```

12. Close the method by returning a paged result:

```
        var pagedResult = await _productsService.
            GetPagedProductsAsync(pageSize, lastProductId);

        var previousPageUrl = pagedResult.HasPreviousPage
            ? Url.Action("GetProducts", new { pageSize,
                lastProductId = pagedResult.Items.First().Id })
            : null;
        var nextPageUrl = pagedResult.HasNextPage
            ? Url.Action("GetProducts", new { pageSize,
                lastProductId = pagedResult.Items.Last().Id })
            : null;

        var paginationMetadata = new
        {
            PageSize = pagedResult.PageSize,
```

```
                        HasPreviousPage = pagedResult.HasPreviousPage,
                        HasNextPage = pagedResult.HasNextPage,
                        PreviousPageUrl = previousPageUrl,
                        NextPageUrl = nextPageUrl
                };
```

13. Finally, use `Headers.Append` so we don't get yelled at for adding a duplicate header key. This could easily confuse our consuming client. We will also make sure the JSON serializer doesn't convert our & to its Unicode character:

```
var options = new JsonSerializerOptions
        {
            Encoder = System.Text.Encodings.Web.
                JavaScriptEncoder.UnsafeRelaxedJsonEscaping
        };

        Response.Headers.Append("X-Pagination",
            JsonSerializer.Serialize(
                paginationMetadata, options));

        return Ok(pagedResult.Items);
```

14. Run the app, go to `http://localhost:5148/swagger/index.html`, and play with your new paginator. For example, try a `pageSize` value of `250` and a `lastProductId` value of `330`. Note that the metadata provides the client links to the previous and next page.

    In *Figure 1.3*, you can see our pagination metadata being returned, via the Swagger UI:

Response headers

```
cache-control: public,max-age=120
content-type: application/json; charset=utf-8
date: Tue,21 May 2024 00:19:23 GMT
server: Kestrel
transfer-encoding: chunked
x-pagination:
{"PageSize":250,"HasPreviousPage":true,"HasNextPage":true,"PreviousPageUrl":"/Product
s?pageSize=250&lastProductId=81","NextPageUrl":"/Products?
pageSize=250&lastProductId=330"}
```

Figure 1.3: Our pagination metadata in the x-pagination header

How it works...

We implemented a keyset paginator that works with a variable page size. Keyset pagination works with row IDs instead of offsets. When the client requests a page, the client provides both a requested page size and the ID of the last result they have consumed. This approach is more efficient than traditional skip/take pagination because it works directly with indexes rather than sorting and skipping through the entire dataset. The EF Core query behind our `GetProducts` endpoint avoids the more common *skip/take* pattern but does use the *take* method to retrieve the page of data. We leveraged EF Core's `AnyAsync` method to directly check whether any products exist after the one fetched for the current page. We then generated URLs for the previous and next pages using `Url.Action`. Finally, we returned this information in a pagination metadata object to help clients navigate through the data.

See also

- Here's a great overview of `KeySet` with members of the EF Core team: `https://www.youtube.com/watch?v=DIKH-q-gJNU`

- Here are two useful libraries for keyset pagination in EF Core:

  - `https://github.com/mrahhal/MR.EntityFrameworkCore.KeysetPagination`

  - `https://github.com/mrahhal/MR.AspNetCore.Pagination`

Configuring a CORS policy to expose pagination metadata

In this recipe, we will allow clients to access pagination metadata from the server response by configuring a special CORS policy that exposes pagination metadata.

Getting ready

This recipe picks up exactly where the preceding recipe ended. If you are jumping around in the book, you can begin this recipe following along at `https://github.com/PacktPublishing/ASP.NET-9-Web-API-Cookbook/tree/main/start/chapter01/CORS`.

How to do it...

1. Register a new CORS policy that allows clients to consume your X-Pagination data.

2. Navigate to the `Program.cs` file and place the following code right after where you register your `ProductService` but before `var app = builder.Build();`:

```
builder.Services.AddCors(options =>
{
    options.AddPolicy("CorsPolicy", builder =>
```

```
                builder.AllowAnyOrigin()
                    .AllowAnyMethod()
                    .AllowAnyHeader()
                    .WithExposedHeaders("X-Pagination"));
    });
```

3. Right before `app.MapControllers()`, enable the CORS policy, like so:

```
app.UseCors("CorsPolicy");
app.MapControllers();
app.Run();
```

4. Run your API with the new CORS policy:

    dotnet run

5. One way to confirm that CORS is allowing our response headers to be displayed is simply via the **Network** tab in our browser:

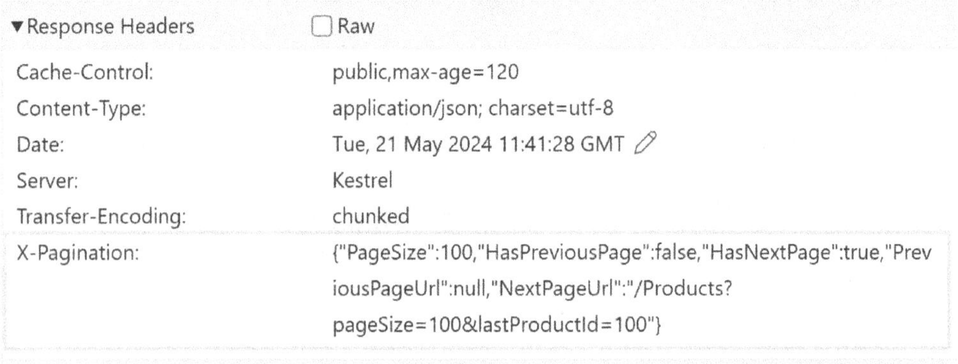

▼ Response Headers	☐ Raw
Cache-Control:	public,max-age=120
Content-Type:	application/json; charset=utf-8
Date:	Tue, 21 May 2024 11:41:28 GMT ✐
Server:	Kestrel
Transfer-Encoding:	chunked
X-Pagination:	{"PageSize":100,"HasPreviousPage":false,"HasNextPage":true,"PreviousPageUrl":null,"NextPageUrl":"/Products?pageSize=100&lastProductId=100"}

Figure 1.4: Note HasPreviousPage and HasNextPage in the X-Pagination header

Important note

Keep in mind that, when testing on localhost, a CORS policy is more lenient and you will probably see these headers regardless. You might not see the full impact of CORS during local development. This recipe is critical when deploying your web API and allowing a variety of clients to consume your API.

How it works...

We applied a CORS policy that allows requests from any origin, `AllowAnyOrigin`. When the client consuming our API is hosted on a different origin than the API, we have to start thinking about CORS policies. We added the `WithExposedHeaders("X-Pagination")` policy to ensure that the header that contains our pagination data is accessible to the client.

Implementing efficient first- and last-page access with EF Core

In this recipe, we'll expand our keyset pagination implementation to efficiently handle first and last page access by leveraging EF Core's entity tracking and `Find` method. Users often navigate directly to the first or last page of paginated results, so these pages should load as quickly as possible, while still remaining reasonably fresh.

Getting ready

This recipe builds on the two preceding recipes. You can clone the starter project here: `https://github.com/PacktPublishing/ASP.NET-9-Web-API-Cookbook/tree/main/start/chapter01/firstLastPage`.

How to do it...

1. Open the `Program.cs` file. Register an in-memory cache on the line after `AddControllers();`:

   ```
   builder.Services.AddMemoryCache();
   ```

2. Open the `PagedResponse.cs` file inside the `Models` folder. Update your `PagedResponse` model to include `TotalPages`:

   ```
   namespace cookbook.Models;

   public abstract record PagedResponse<T>
   {
       public IReadOnlyCollection<T> Items { get; init; } = Array.
         Empty<T>();
       public int PageSize { get; init; }
       public bool HasPreviousPage { get; init; }
       public bool HasNextPage { get; init; }
       public int TotalPages { get; init; }
   }
   ```

3. Open `ProductReadService.cs` in the `Services` folder. At the bottom of the class, create a new helper method for retrieving and caching total pages. When it is time to recalculate the total pages count, we are going to take that opportunity to clear EF Core's change tracker—forcing a fresh first and last page:

```
public async Task<int> GetTotalPagesAsync(int pageSize)
{
    if (!cache.TryGetValue(TotalPagesKey, out int totalPages))
    {
        context.ChangeTracker.Clear();
        var totalCount = await context.Products.CountAsync();
        totalPages = (int)Math.Ceiling(totalCount / (double)
            pageSize);
        cache.Set(TotalPagesKey, totalPages,
            TimeSpan.FromMinutes(2));
    }
    return totalPages;
}
```

> **Important note**
> We have used a basic `ResponseCache` in the controller previously, but this is the first time we are introducing caching to the service layer.

4. On the next line, create another very simple helper method for invalidating the cached total pages:

```
public void InvalidateCache()
{
    Cache.Remove(TotalPagesKey);
}
```

5. Still in the `ProductReadService.cs` file, scroll up to the top of the file, and add the constant for our cached `TotalPages` key at the top of the `ProductReadService` class, after the class definition:

```
using Microsoft.Extensions.Caching.Memory;
public class ProductReadService(AppDbContext context,
IMemoryCache cache) : IProductReadService
{
    private const string TotalPagesKey = "TotalPages";
```

6. Still in the `ProductReadService.cs` file, delete the entire `GetPagedProductsAsync` method implementation. We'll rebuild it to leverage EF Core's entity tracking and `Find` method.

7. Continuing in `ProductReadService.cs`, let's start rebuilding `GetPagedProductsAsyncMethod`. Start with the method signature and variables we will need:

```
public async Task<PagedProductResponseDTO>
GetPagedProductsAsync(int pageSize, int? lastProductId = null)
{
    var totalPages = await GetTotalPagesAsync(pageSize);
    List<Product> products;
    bool hasNextPage;
    bool hasPreviousPage;
```

8. On the next line, add the first-page handling logic using `Find`:

```
if (lastProductId == null)
{
    products = new List<Product>();
    for (var i = 1; i <= pageSize; i++)
    {
        var product = await context.Products.FindAsync(i);
        if (product != null)
        {
            products.Add(product);
        }
    }
    hasNextPage = products.Count == pageSize;
    hasPreviousPage = false;
}
```

9. On the next line, add the last-page handling logic:

```
else if (lastProductId == ((totalPages - 1) * pageSize))
{
    products = new List<Product>();
    for (var i = lastProductId.Value; i < lastProductId.Value +
        pageSize; i++)
    {
        var product = await context.Products.FindAsync(i);
        if (product != null)
        {
            products.Add(product);
        }
    }
    hasNextPage = false;
    hasPreviousPage = true;
}
```

10. Now, before we place our regular keyset pagination logic, let's take this opportunity to clear the `ChangeTracker` so a fresh first and last pages will be returned. On the next line, place this:

```
else
{
    context.ChangeTracker.Clear();
```

11. On the next line, let's implement our ordinary keyset pagination logic. Note: it is critical that we do not use `AsNoTracking()` in our query:

```
IQueryable<Product> query = context.Products;
query = query.Where(p => p.Id > lastProductId.Value);
products = await query
    .OrderBy(p => p.Id)
    .Take(pageSize)
    .ToListAsync();

var lastId = products.LastOrDefault()?.Id;
hasNextPage = lastId.HasValue &&
    await context.Products.AnyAsync(p => p.Id > lastId);
hasPreviousPage = true;
}
```

12. Add the `return` statement and close the `GetPagedProductsAsync` method:

```
return new PagedProductResponseDTO
{
    Items = products.Select(p => new ProductDTO
    {
        Id = p.Id,
        Name = p.Name,
        Price = p.Price,
        CategoryId = p.CategoryId
    }).ToList(),
    PageSize = pageSize,
    HasPreviousPage = hasPreviousPage,
    HasNextPage = hasNextPage,
    TotalPages = totalPages
};
}
```

13. Finally, open the `ProductsController.cs` file in the `Controller` folder. Let's modify the pagination in the `GetProducts` action method to include `FirstPageUrl` and `LastPageUrl` after `NextPageUrl`:

```
var paginationMetadata = new
{
    PageSize = pagedResult.PageSize,
    HasPreviousPage = pagedResult.HasPreviousPage,
    HasNextPage = pagedResult.HasNextPage,
    TotalPages = pagedResult.TotalPages,
    PreviousPageUrl = pagedResult.HasPreviousPage
        ? Url.Action("GetProducts", new { pageSize,
        lastProductId = pagedResult.Items.First().Id })
        : null,
    NextPageUrl = pagedResult.HasNextPage
        ? Url.Action("GetProducts", new { pageSize,
        lastProductId = pagedResult.Items.Last().Id })
        : null,
    FirstPageUrl = Url.Action("GetProducts", new { pageSize }),
    LastPageUrl = Url.Action("GetProducts", new { pageSize,
        lastProductId = (pagedResult.TotalPages - 1) * pageSize
    })
};
// method continues
```

14. Run the web API:

```
dotnet run
```

15. Open your web browser and navigate to the Swagger UI interface at `http://localhost:<yourport>/swagger/index.html`. Try the **Products** endpoint. Note the first- and last-page URLs in the X-Pagination header as shown in the following screenshot:

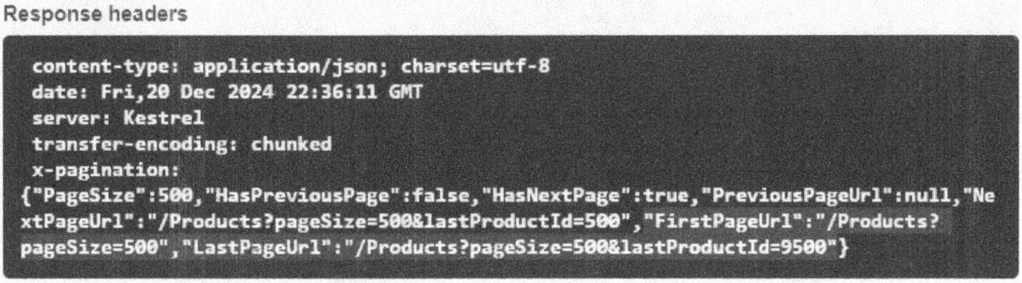

Figure 1.5 – FirstPageUrl and LastPageUrl

To navigate to the last page, try entering the page size and product ID into the Swagger boxes representing query parameters. If you are using a debugger, you'll see `Find` retrieving products from the change tracker without hitting the database.

How it works...

This recipe leverages EF Core's entity tracking system and `Find` method to efficiently serve the first and last page. We used `IMemoryCache` to cache only the total page calculation. We did not use `IMemoryCache` to cache the actual product data (which is the approach we would take with output caching). Instead, we let EF Core's change tracker handle entity caching through `Find`. Note that `Find` will not execute a database query if the entity is already loaded into the **change tracker**. To prevent stale data, we clear the change tracker at two strategic points: during regular pagination and when recalculating the total page count every two minutes. This dual invalidation strategy ensures that while the first and last pages can be served quickly from the tracker, no tracked entity can be stale for more than two minutes. Since the total count typically changes less frequently than individual records, the total count is a better candidate for formal caching in `IMemoryCache` compared to caching the entire result set.

See also

- Read more about all the features of the memory cache in .NET 9 at `https://learn. microsoft.com/en-us/dotnet/api/system.runtime.caching. memorycache?view=net-9.0`

- Commercial and community projects for creating a second-level cache for EF Core:

  - `https://www.alachisoft.com/ncache/ef-core-cache.html`

  - `https://github.com/VahidN/EFCoreSecondLevelCacheInterceptor`

Testing the API in PowerShell

When testing your API, relying solely on tools such as **cURL** or **Swagger** can limit your options. In this recipe, we will confirm that the API is correctly implemented via PowerShell. We will retrieve pagination metadata, navigate through pages, and ensure that the returned data is what we expect it to be. We will accomplish this using the built-in **Invoke-WebRequest** to inspect our custom **X-Pagination** header. We will type this recipe directly into the PowerShell terminal.

> **Important note**
> While we'll be using PowerShell in this recipe, rest assured that we'll also cover other popular tools such as Postman throughout this book—equipping you with a diverse set of testing techniques.

Getting ready

Clone the starting code from here: `https://github.com/PacktPublishing/ASP.NET-9-Web-API-Cookbook/tree/main/start/chapter01/psTesting`. It contains a web API similar to the other APIs we have built in this chapter.

You will need to open PowerShell or use something like Windows Terminal with PowerShell. PowerShell is cross-platform, so you don't have to be on Windows to follow along with this recipe. The end project folder for this recipe has these commands saved in a PowerShell script if you want to compare. Instead of writing a script file, we will be entering these commands directly into the terminal.

How to do it...

1. Run the application using the following command:

   ```
   dotnet run
   ```

2. Open your PowerShell terminal. Let's create some variables for your test URL. Save your `baseUrl` and the endpoint you want to test with `pageSize` in separate variables:

   ```
   $baseUrl = "http://localhost:5148"
   $testEndpoint = "/Products?pageSize=10"
   $fullUrl = $baseUrl + $testEndpoint;
   ```

> **Important note**
>
> Remember: your `baseUrl` has whatever port number `dotnet run` is serving your API on.

In the terminal, you should now see our API being served on the local host.

```
Microsoft.Hosting.Lifetime[14]
Now listening on: http://localhost:5148
```

Figure 1.6 – dotnet run starting the API on port 5148, your port may be different

3. Now call the endpoint and save the response in a variable:

   ```
   $response = Invoke-WebRequest -Uri $fullUrl -Headers @{"Accept"
   = "application/json"}
   ```

> **Important note**
>
> One alternative way of querying an endpoint in PowerShell is `Invoke-RestMethod`, which directly converts a JSON response to a PowerShell object. However, `Invoke-WebRequest` has advantages, as it provides access to more detailed information about the HTTP response, including headers, status codes, and cookies.

4. Save the pagination metadata in variables:

```
$xPaginationHeader = $response.Headers["X-Pagination"]
$xPagination = $xPaginationHeader | ConvertFrom-Json
```

5. Ensure that the correct pagination data is present.

Figure 1.7 shows the $xPagination variable in our PowerShell terminal:

```
C:\> $xPagination


PageSize          : 10
HasPreviousPage   : False
HasNextPage       : True
PreviousPageUrl   :
NextPageUrl       : /Products?pageSize=10&lastProductId=10
```

Figure 1.7 – Pagination metadata displayed in PowerShell

6. Save a URL for NextPage in a variable:

```
$nextPageUrl = $baseUrl + $xPagination.NextPageUrl
```

7. Call the next page and examine the results:

```
$response = Invoke-WebRequest -Uri $nextPageUrl
$jsonContent = $response.Content | ConvertFrom-Json
$jsonContent | Format-Table -AutoSize
```

Figure 1.8 shows the next page of data displayed in PowerShell:

```
C:\my-coding-projects\webapi-cookbook\end\chapter01\psTesting
!]> $jsonContent | Format-Table -AutoSize

id name                        price categoryId
-- ----                        ----- ----------
11 Unbranded Cotton Car       1265.37          3
12 Unbranded Granite Bacon     366.89          4
13 Refined Concrete Fish      1423.99          3
14 Refined Metal Chips         278.21          1
15 Sleek Frozen Gloves        1273.56          5
16 Intelligent Granite Towels  438.14          1
17 Small Soft Bacon            853.86          3
18 Incredible Plastic Tuna    1409.96          5
19 Unbranded Cotton Computer   546.52          3
20 Sleek Concrete Fish        1752.04          3
```

Figure 1.8 – The next page of data displayed in PowerShell

How it works...

We verified our pagination headers and played around with paged data directly in the terminal. We also formatted response content in PowerShell and learned about `Invoke-WebRequest`, which is one way we can manipulate our APIs from the terminal. The response from `Invoke-WebRequest` includes headers, which we accessed to get the `X-Pagination` custom header. This header contains our pagination metadata such as the total number of pages, the current page, and links to the next and previous page. `Invoke-WebRequest` lets you access all response headers directly, making it easy to parse a custom header like `X-Pagination`.

Another similar cmdlet is `Invoke-RestMethod`, which automatically parses your JSON and returns a smaller response object. The advantage of `Invoke-WebRequest` is that it can include more information. `Invoke-RestMethod` is fantastic for simple REST API interactions but `Invoke-WebRequest` can be better suited for complex interactions.

Using the new AggregateBy LINQ method to return the average price per category

In this recipe, we will demonstrate a practical example of using the new `AggregateBy` LINQ method. We are going to return the average price per product on each page our API returns using `AggregateBy`. Now, `AggregateBy` is one of the three new LINQ methods in .NET 9. It is another grouping method like `CountBy` but with a twist: you provide your own seed and aggregation function.

Getting ready

In this recipe, we will build on our previous paged `GET` endpoint that returns links to previous and next pages.

You can clone the starting project here: `https://github.com/PacktPublishing/ASP.NET-9-Web-API-Cookbook/tree/main/start/chapter01/aggregateBy`.

How to do it...

1. Add a dictionary to the existing `PagedResponse` abstract record in `Models/PagedResponse.cs`. This will hold your average price per category:

    ```
    public Dictionary<int, decimal> AveragePricePerCategory
    { get; init; } = new();
    }
    ```

Your record should now look like this:

```
namespace AggregateBy.Models;

public abstract record PagedResponse<T>
{
    public IReadOnlyCollection<T> Items { get; init; } = Array.
        Empty<T>();
    public int PageSize { get; init; }
    public bool HasPreviousPage { get; init; }
    public bool HasNextPage { get; init; }
    public int TotalPages { get; init; }
    public int LastPage { get; init; }

    public Dictionary<int, decimal> AveragePricePerCategory {
        get; init; } = new();

}
```

2. In your service, create a private helper method to calculate your average price per category using AggregateBy:

```
private async Task<Dictionary<int, decimal>>
GetAveragePricePerCategoryAsync(List<ProductDTO> products)
{
    if (products == null || !products.Any())
    {
        return new Dictionary<int, decimal>();
    }

    var aggregateByTask = Task.Run(() =>
    {
        var aggregateBy = products.AggregateBy(
            product => product.CategoryId,
            x => (Sum: 0m, Count: 0),
            (acc, product) => (acc.Sum + product.Price, acc.
                            Count + 1)
        );

        var averagePriceByCategory = aggregateBy.
        ToDictionary(
            kvp => kvp.Key,
            kvp => Math.Round(kvp.Value.Sum / kvp.Value.
                            Count, 2)
        );
```

```
            return averagePriceByCategory;
    });

        return await aggregateByTask;
    }
```

3. Await the helper method and add the aggregated data to the response:

```
        var averagePricePerCategory = await
    GetAveragePricePerCategoryAsync(pagedProducts);

        var result = new PagedProductResponseDTO
        {
            Items = pagedProducts,
            PageSize = pageSize,
            HasNextPage = hasNextPage,
            HasPreviousPage = lastProductId.HasValue,
            AveragePricePerCategory = averagePricePerCategory
        };

        return result;
```

4. In `ProductsController.cs`, update the returned metadata object to include `AveragePricePerCategory`:

```
        var paginationMetadata = new
        {
            PageSize = pagedResult.PageSize,
            HasPreviousPage = pagedResult.HasPreviousPage,
            HasNextPage = pagedResult.HasNextPage,
            PreviousPageUrl = previousPageUrl,
            NextPageUrl = nextPageUrl,
            AveragePricePerCategory = pagedResult.
                AveragePricePerCategory
        };
```

5. Run the new version of your web API and observe the new metadata (either by using CURL, by using your browser's network tab, by navigating to swagger UI `http:localhost:<yourport>/swagger/index.html`, or by using PowerShell's `Invoke-WebRequest`):

```
x-pagination: {"PageSize":400,"HasPreviousPage":true,
"HasNextPage":true,"PreviousPageUrl":"/Products?pageSize=400
&lastProductId=81","NextPageUrl":"/Products?pageSize=400
&lastProductId=480","AveragePricePerCategory":
{"3":1066.73,"1":937.33,"4":1038.46,"2":956.31,"5":1121.53}}
```

How it works...

In this recipe, we learned how to take our returned list of objects and calculate additional category grouping information using the new LINQ method AggregateBy. Now, AggregateBy can be a bit confusing, so let's break it down:

```
var aggregateBy = products.AggregateBy(
            product => product.CategoryId,
            x => (Sum: 0m, Count: 0),
            (acc, product) => (acc.Sum + product.Price, acc.Count
                                                            + 1)
```

We first pass the property we want to group by product => product.CategoryId. Then, we pass a tuple of seed values (Sum: 0m, Count: 0). Note that 0m makes sure that sum starts at 0 as a decimal.

AggregateBy goes to work on that tuple and returns a tuple of the newly aggregated products by category. The resulting tuple is then converted to a dictionary while calculating the average price.

This is all done inside Task.Run to ensure the aggregation runs asynchronously.

See also

- Here's the proposal for the new AggregateBy with a detailed explanation of how it works: https://github.com/dotnet/runtime/issues/91533?source=post_page-----c2df66d20e1b

- You can find a detailed article comparing the new LINQ methods to traditional grouping approaches here: https://medium.com/codenx/net9-alpha-linq-updates-c2df66d20e1b

Get This Book's PDF Version and Exclusive Extras

UNLOCK NOW

Scan the QR code (or go to packtpub.com/unlock). Search for this book by name, confirm the edition, and then follow the steps on the page.

Note: Keep your invoice handy. Purchases made directly from Packt don't require an invoice.

2

Mastering Resource Creation and Validation

In this chapter, we will explore creating, validating, and updating data in a web API. We will cover `POST`, `PUT`, and `PATCH` operations, uncovering the critical concepts of model validation and model binding – essential features of ASP.NET Core. Additionally, we will explore Scalar, a new and user-friendly option for an interactive OpenAPI UI. This will allow us to move beyond Swagger UI, which is no longer included as the default tool for generating OpenAPI documentation.

We will focus on the best practice of validating inputs added to our database. To do this, we will use model validation and model binding, which together form the model state – a dictionary containing both the state of the model and the validation results.

The following are the recipes we're going to cover in this chapter:

- Model validation with data annotations
- Creating a custom validation attribute
- Implementing complex validation logic using `IValidateObject`
- Creating complex validation rules with `FluentValidation`
- Updating resources with `PUT` and `AutoMapper`
- Managing cascade delete with `AutoMapper`
- Updating specific model fields with `PATCH` and `JsonPatchDocument`

Technical requirements

For the recipes in this chapter, you'll need the following:

- **Git**: Make sure you have Git installed.

- **.NET 9 SDK**: The .NET 9 SDK is available here: https://dotnet.microsoft.com/en-us/download/dotnet/9.0.

- **DB Browser for SQLite**: Unlike *Chapter 1*, where we used the in-memory SQLite provider for EF Core, this chapter will use a real SQLite database that persists to disk. SQLite works with a single file rather than connecting to a server with a connection string. SQLite, due to its simplicity, allows you to concentrate on understanding validation best practices without the extra layers of checks and guardrails seen in databases such as Microsoft SQL Server. It can be helpful to view the database we will be creating with DB Browser for SQLite, which is available here: https://sqlitebrowser.org/.

- **A note on mappers**: The projects in this chapter use both EF Core and Dapper. Please check the GitHub end projects folder to see the full Dapper versions alongside the EF Core versions of each recipe. There is nothing additional to install besides the Dapper NuGet package (available at https://www.nuget.org/packages/Dapper), which is listed in the .csproj project files of the online versions.

Model validation with data annotations

We will start by exploring the simplest form of model validation in ASP.NET Core – model validation using data annotations.

Data annotations allow you to decorate model properties with attributes that specify validation criteria. This ensures that the data received from the user adheres to defined rules and formats, preventing invalid data from causing errors or inconsistencies. By utilizing data annotations, we can also provide more specific feedback when a client POSTs data that does not conform to the model's properties. This technique is a lot better than returning a vague generic error message to the client. Instead of returning a generic error, this approach guides the client on what properties need to be modified to meet the required criteria.

In this recipe, we will use DataAnnotations to apply model validation. The starter project for this chapter is a Web API with two controllers. Both controllers have one endpoint that returns identical data from the same database. We will create validation rules using .NET DataAnnotations.

Getting ready

The starter project code for this recipe can be cloned here: https://github.com/PacktPublishing/ASP.NET-9-Web-API-Cookbook/tree/main/start/chapter02/DataAnnotations

How to do it...

1. Navigate to the root directory in the terminal and run `dotnet run`.

2. If you go to `http://localhost:5217/scalar/chapter2` in your web browser, you should see the following web page for interacting with our API:

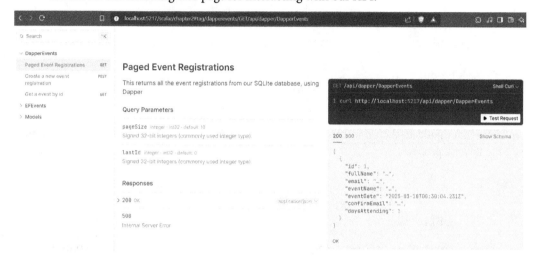

Figure 2.1 – Scalar API documentation generated from OpenAPI JSON

The starter project for this chapter already includes a DTO object we will use for our first validation recipe. You can find this DTO class in `start/chapter02/DataAnnotations/Models`.

So far, we have a Web API that only returns data. Let's add a POST request that accepts `EventRegistrationDTO` with validation via `DataAnnotations`.

`EventRegistrationDTO` already has a required email address property and a confirmation email address. This DTO already contains some barebones annotations – `[Required]` and `[Compare]`. The `DataAnnotations` attribute will require that the email addresses have to match, thanks to a `[Compare]` validation attribute alone. The required number of days to stay and name are also marked as required thanks to the `[Required]` attribute:

```
using System.ComponentModel.DataAnnotations;

namespace DataAnnotations.Models;

public class EventRegistrationDTO
{
    public int Id { get; set; }

    [Required]
```

```
public required string FullName { get; set; }

[Required]
[EmailAddress]
public required string Email { get; set; }

[Required]
public required string EventName { get; set; }

[Required]
[DataType(DataType.Date)]
public DateTime EventDate { get; set; }
```

Note that thanks to the `Compare` attribute, the `ConfirmEmail` property is compared to the `Email` property:

```
[Required]
[Compare("Email", ErrorMessage = "Email addresses do not
          match.")]
public string ConfirmEmail { get; set; } = string.Empty;
```

The final property in our `EventRegistrationDTO` class validates that it will only accept integers between 1 and 7:

```
[Required]
[Range(1, 7, ErrorMessage = "Number of days attending must
                            be between 1 and 7.")]
public int DaysAttending { get; set; }
}
```

3. Create a new `POST` endpoint in the `EFEventsController.cs` file. Validate our model based on the provided data annotations:

```
[HttpPost]
public async Task<IActionResult>
CreateEventRegistration([FromBody] EventRegistrationDTO
eventRegistrationDto)
    {
        if (!ModelState.IsValid)
        {
            return BadRequest(ModelState);
        }
        var createdEvent = await _service.
        CreateEventRegistrationAsync(eventRegistrationDto);
        return CreatedAtAction(nameof(GetEventRegistrationById),
        new { id = createdEvent.Id }, createdEvent);
    }
```

Here, we used `CreatedAtAction` to return where the client can retrieve the newly created resource.

> **Important note**
>
> By *created resource*, we mean data that was added to our database via a POST endpoint. After the creation of a hardcoded path, the client is given the location of your `GetEventRegistrationById` controller using nameof. This is a better practice than returning a hardcoded path, in case the controller routing is changed in the future.

4. Now you can implement the service method, update `EFCoreService`, and define the contract in `IEFCoreService.cs`:

```
using events.Models;
using Microsoft.AspNetCore.Mvc;

namespace events.Services;

public interface IEFCoreService
{
...

    Task<EventRegistrationDTO>
    CreateEventRegistrationAsync(EventRegistrationDTO
    eventRegistrationDTO);

}
```

5. In `EFCoreService.cs`, implement the `CreateEventRegistrationAsync` method:

```
public async Task<EventRegistrationDTO>
CreateEventRegistrationAsync(EventRegistrationDTO
eventRegistrationDTO)
    {
        var eventRegistration = new EventRegistration
        {
            FullName = eventRegistrationDTO.FullName,
            Email = eventRegistrationDTO.Email,
            EventName = eventRegistrationDTO.EventName,
            EventDate = eventRegistrationDTO.EventDate,
            DaysAttending = eventRegistrationDTO.DaysAttending
        };

        var result = await _repository.
        CreateEventRegistrationAsync(eventRegistration);
```

```
        return new EventRegistrationDTO
        {
            Id = result.Id,
            FullName = result.FullName,
            Email = result.Email,
            EventName = result.EventName,
            EventDate = result.EventDate,
            ConfirmEmail = result.Email,
            DaysAttending = result.DaysAttending
        };
    }
```

The `CreateEventRegistrationAsync` method we just implemented allows our DTO to interact with our repository method. Our repository method is the part of the data access layer that directly interacts with the database. It also returns a DTO version of the data we created, back to the client.

6. Now we will create the contract for the new `CreateEventRegistrationAsync` method, the method that directly interacts with our database: `IEFCoreRepository.cs`:

```
using events.Models;

namespace events.Repositories;

public interface IEFCoreRepository
{

    ...

    Task<EventRegistration>
        CreateEventRegistrationAsync(EventRegistration
        eventRegistration);

}
```

7. Implement `CreateEventRegistrationAsync` in `EFCoreRepository.cs`:

```
public async Task<EventRegistration>
CreateEventRegistrationAsync(EventRegistration
eventRegistration)
    {
        _context.EventRegistrations.Add(eventRegistration);
        await _context.SaveChangesAsync();
        return eventRegistration;
    }
```

> **Important note**
>
> You are returning a fully created DTO object from what was added to the database. In EF Core, if using `SaveChangesAsync()`, the object will be updated with any database-generated values; it is not the exact same object that was passed in.

8. Finally, let's decorate our `Controller` method with attributes. `EndpointSummary` and `EndpointDescription` will inform our OpenAPI spec generator what this method is used for. The `ProducesResponseType` attribute specifies the expected return types from this method:

```
[HttpPost]
[EndpointSummary("Create a new event registration")]
[EndpointDescription("POST to create a new event
registration.  Accepts a EventRegisrationDTO.")]
[ProducesResponseType(StatusCodes.Status201Created)]
[ProducesResponseType(StatusCodes.Status400BadRequest)]
public async Task<IActionResult>
PostEventRegistration([FromBody] EventRegistrationDTO
eventRegistrationDto)
```

9. In the Scalar UI, you can now test this endpoint. Here is an example of an object our validation rules will accept:

```
{
    "Email": "j.smith@fakeemail.com",
    "FullName": "Joe Smith",
    "EventName": "C# Convention",
    "ConfirmEmail": "j.smith@fakeemail.com",
    "DaysAttending": 5,
    "EventDate": "2025-12-01"
}
```

10. Try changing `ConfirmEmail` to another email address. If the confirmation email differs from the original email, we will get a bad request:

```
"title": "One or more validation errors occurred.",
"status": 400,
"errors": {
  "ConfirmEmail": [
    "Email addresses do not match."
  ]
```

How it works...

In this recipe, we implemented a POST method that validates our model with various DataAnnotations attributes, coupled with ModelState.IsValid() checks. ModelState.IsValid() is provided out of the box by ASP.NET Core. One thing to note with your Web API controllers, because our Controller class is decorated with [ApiController], we do not strictly have to use ModelState.IsValid – an automatic HTTP 400 response is returned on an invalid model. Keep in mind that this is only if the entire model is valid or invalid – it does not help us return specific information on what properties might be invalid. However, it is still a best practice to include ModelState.IsValid, as it allows for an easier extension to extend your controller method with additional validation logic in the future.

> **Using Dapper instead of EF Core**
>
> In the included GitHub repository – there are versions of the recipes in this chapter using micro-ORM Dapper. For the recipe we just implemented, the only difference is the implementation of the repository method. Notice how Dapper allows us to write our own SQL and directly interact with the database. Take a look here: https://github.com/PacktPublishing/ASP.NET-9-Web-API-Cookbook/blob/main/end/chapter02/DataAnnotations/Repositories/DapperRepository.cs

Creating a custom validation attribute

In this recipe, we will create our own custom validation attribute to validate incoming data to our API. We will also learn how to retry model binding with TryValidateModel.

Getting ready

This recipe picks up where the preceding recipe left off. You can find a starter project here: https://github.com/PacktPublishing/ASP.NET-9-Web-API-Cookbook/tree/main/start/chapter02/CustomAnnotations

How to do it...

1. Create a new custom validation attribute class in the Models folder, which inherits from ValidationAttribute:

    ```
    using System.ComponentModel.DataAnnotations;

    namespace CustomAnnotations.Models;

    public class AllowedValuesAttribute : ValidationAttribute
    {
    ```

```
        private readonly List<string> _allowedValues;

        public AllowedValuesAttribute(params string[] allowedValues)
        {
            _allowedValues = allowedValues?.ToList() ?? new
            List<string>();
        }

        protected override ValidationResult? IsValid(object? value,
            ValidationContext validationContext)
        {
            if (value == null || !_allowedValues.Contains(
                value.ToString()!))
            {
                return new ValidationResult(
                    $"The field{validationContext.DisplayName}
                    must be one of the following values:
                        {string.Join(", ", _allowedValues)}.");
            }
            return ValidationResult.Success ?? null;
        }
    }
```

2. Now we can use this attribute in our EventRegistrationDTO. Let's put it over the EventName property:

```
        [Required]
        [AllowedValues("C# Conference", "WebAPI Workshop",
                ".NET Hangout")]
        public string EventName { get; set; } = string.Empty;
```

3. Run dotnet run and test our endpoint again. You will find that the event name has to be one of the three values we specified: "C# Conference", "WebAPI Workshop", or ".NET Hangout":

```
{   "type": "https://tools.ietf.org/html/rfc9110#section-15.5.1",
    "title": "One or more validation errors occurred.",
    "status": 400,
    "errors": {
      "EventName": [
        "The field EventName must be one of the following values:
          C# Conference, WebAPI Workshop, .NET Hangout."
      ]
    },
```

```
    "traceId": "00-f873c0c420bdae412cb7151d63473adf-
19760900483172dc-00"
}
```

How it works...

We created `AllowedValuesAttribute`, a custom validation attribute that enforces specific allowed values for a property in our model. The attribute's constructor accepts a list of allowed values, and the `IsValid` method checks whether the provided value is within this list. If the value does not match any of the allowed values, a validation error is returned. We can use this property to enforce custom validation rules for other string properties. The best part is that we did not have to implement any new validation logic in the controller; we just decorated the properties in the DTO model with the attribute.

Implementing complex validation logic with IValidateObject

In this recipe, we will implement custom validation logic in our DTO class using `IValidateObject`. This will allow us to create validation logic for an entire model instead of only one property.

Getting ready

The starting code for this project resides here: `https://github.com/PacktPublishing/ASP.NET-9-Web-API-Cookbook/tree/main/start/chapter02/IValidateObject`.

How to do It...

1. Modify your existing `EventRegistrationDTO` to inherit from `IValidateObject`:

```
using System;
using System.Collections.Generic;
using System.ComponentModel.DataAnnotations;

namespace events.Models
{
    public class EventRegistrationDTO : IValidatableObject
    {
        ...
```

2. Create the `Validate` method, which yields a `ValidationResult` if the date is not in the future:

```
public IEnumerable<ValidationResult> Validate(ValidationContext
validationContext)
    {
        if (EventDate < DateTime.Now)
        {
            yield return new ValidationResult(
                "Event date must be in the future.",
                new[] { nameof(EventDate) });
        }
    }
```

3. Add a second validation conditional that compares two properties. The following example will validate that anyone named Garry or Luke is not to be registered for the conference:
```
public IEnumerable<ValidationResult> Validate(ValidationContext
validationContext):
```

```
    {
        ...
        if ((FullName.Contains("Garry") || FullName.
        Contains("Luke")) && EventName == "C# Conference")
        {
            yield return new ValidationResult(
                $"{FullName} is banned from {EventName}.",
                new[] { nameof(FullName), nameof(EventName)
});
        }
```

4. Test your new validation rules via PowerShell. You can open up the terminal in VS Code and try the following:

```
$body = @{
    FullName = "Garry Cabrera"
    Email = "garry@example.com"
    EventName = "C# Conference"
    EventDate = "2025-12-01"
    ConfirmEmail = "garry@example.com"
    DaysAttending = 5
}

$jsonBody = $body | ConvertTo-Json

Invoke-RestMethod -Uri 'http://localhost:5217/api/EFEvents'
-Method POST -Headers $headers -Body $jsonBody
```

The response shows your validation logic working. You will get validation errors both on the event being in the past, and having a banned person trying to register:

```
Invoke-RestMethod: {"type":"https://tools.ietf.org/html/
rfc9110#section-15.5.1","title":"One or more validation errors
occurred.","status":400,"errors":{"FullName":["Garry Cabrera is
banned from C# Conference."],"EventDate":["Event date must be
in the future."],"EventName":["Garry Cabrera is banned from C#
Conference."]},"traceId":"00-1e5030f86979eb422e3cc97e47e82d6d-
6071047522ccd0a8-00"}
```

How it works...

We used `IValidateObject` to implement validation logic that involves multiple model properties. You created robust validation without altering the controller logic. The `Validate` method is automatically called by ASP.NET Core during model validation, making sure all custom rules are always applied. `IValidateObject` validation rules are particularly helpful in scenarios where the validation logic needs to consider the state of the entire object rather than just individual properties.

Creating complex validation rules with FluentValidation

In this recipe, we will learn how to create complex validation rules using the `FluentValidation` library. `FluentValidation` offers a more fluent and flexible way to define validation logic.

Getting ready

We are going to continue working with the same DTO. However, all the validation rules have been removed – both the simple data annotations and the rules created via `IValidateObject`. The code for this project resides here: `chapter02/FluentValidation`.

How to do it...

1. Open the project in Visual Studio Code.

2. Open the terminal and type `dotnet run`.

3. Open the browser and go to `http://localhost:5217/scalar/chapter2`.

    You have a basic API with some `DataAnnotations` and a custom `DataAnnotations` attribute on the DTO.

4. Install the `FluentValidation` NuGet package:

    ```
    dotnet add package FluentValidation.AspNetCore
    ```

5. Note that our DTO currently has no validation rules. Add the following code to the
    EventRegistrationDTO.cs file:

```csharp
namespace FluentExample.Models;

public class EventRegistrationDTO
{
    public int Id { get; set; }

    public string FullName { get; set; } = string.Empty;

    public string Email { get; set; } = string.Empty;

    public string EventName { get; set; } = string.Empty;

    public DateTime EventDate { get; set; }

    public string ConfirmEmail { get; set; } = string.Empty;

    public int DaysAttending { get; set; }

}
```

6. Create a new file called EventRegistrationDTOValidator.cs in the Models folder.
    Let's define the EventRegistrationDTOValidator class in this file:

```csharp
using FluentValidation;
using FluentExample.Models;

public class EventRegistrationDTOValidator :
AbstractValidator<EventRegistrationDTO>
{
    public EventRegistrationDTOValidator()
    {

    }
}
```

7. Now we will add back the validation rule that makes properties `Required`:

```
using FluentValidation;

namespace FluentExample.Models;

public class EventRegistrationDTOValidator :
AbstractValidator<EventRegistrationDTO>
{
    public EventRegistrationDTOValidator()
    {
        RuleFor(x => x.FullName)
            .NotEmpty().WithMessage("Full name is required.");

        RuleFor(x => x.Email)
            .NotEmpty().WithMessage("Email is required.");

        RuleFor(x => x.EventName)
            .NotEmpty().WithMessage("Event name is required.");

        RuleFor(x => x.EventDate)
            .NotEmpty().WithMessage("Event date is required.");

        RuleFor(x => x.ConfirmEmail)
            .NotEmpty().WithMessage("Confirm email is
                                    required.");

        RuleFor(x => x.DaysAttending)
            .NotEmpty().WithMessage("Days attending is
                                    required.");
    }
}
```

8. At the top of the `Program.cs` file, we will need to import the required namespaces for the `FluentValidation` library:

```
using FluentValidation;
using FluentValidation.AspNetCore;
```

9. Still in `Program.cs`, we will need to register our validators for dependency injection right after `Services.AddControllers();`:

```
builder.Services.AddControllers();
builder.Services.AddFluentValidationAutoValidation();
```

```
builder.Services.AddValidatorsFromAssemblyContaining
<EventRegistrationDTOValidator>();
```

> **Important note**
>
> In Scalar UI, you can now test the required rule. Notice the other validation rules are not in effect. This endpoint will return 201 Created. Ahead is an example of successfully testing the endpoint with Scalar UI.

Here is an example of creating the Event Registration resource via the Scalar UI:

Response 50ms 201 Created

∨ Body

```
{
    "id": 10009,
    "fullName": "Luke Avedon",
    "email": "john.doe@example.com",
    "eventName": "C# Conference",
    "eventDate": "1901-12-01T00:00:00",
    "confirmEmail": "john.doe@example.com",
    "daysAttending": 3
}
```

Figure 2.2 – Our example JSON object – used to successfully create an event registration

10. Let's try using the following object. Note that this time, FullName is now null. This will cause our validation to kick in and throw an error:

```
{
    "FullName": null,
    "Email": "john.doe@example.com",
    "EventName": "C# Conference",
    "EventDate": "2025-12-01",
    "ConfirmEmail": "john.doe@example.com",
    "DaysAttending": 3
}
```

Figure 2.3 shows us trying to create an object with a null value in `FullName`. Because `FullName` is null, we receive a 400 error with a message informing us of the problem:

Figure 2.3 – Validation error due to a null value in FullName

11. Add a `.EmailAddress()` rule to our `FluentValidator`. This enforces that the email address must be a valid email address:

```
public class EventRegistrationDTOValidator :
AbstractValidator<EventRegistrationDTO>
{
    public EventRegistrationDTOValidator()
    {
        RuleFor(x => x.FullName)
            .NotEmpty().WithMessage("Full name is required.");

        RuleFor(x => x.Email)
            .Not Empty().WithMessage("Email is required.")
            .EmailAddress().WithMessage("A valid email is
                                        required.");

...
```

12. Add in the same advanced validation logic that you created with `IValidateObject` but now with `FluentValidation`:

```
public class EventRegistrationDTOValidator :
AbstractValidator<EventRegistrationDTO>
{
    public EventRegistrationDTOValidator()
```

```
{
    …
    RuleFor(x => x.FullName)
        .Must(name => !name.Contains("Garry") &&
            !name.Contains("Luke"))
        .WithMessage("{PropertyValue}
            is not allowed in the full name.");

    RuleFor(x => x.EventName)
        .Must(value =>
            new[] { "C# Conference", "WebAPI Workshop",
                ".NET Hangout" }.Contains(value))
        .WithMessage("Event name must be one of the
            specified values.");

    RuleFor(x => x.EventDate)
        .GreaterThan(DateTime.Now).WithMessage("Event date
                must be in the future.");

    RuleFor(x => x.ConfirmEmail)
        .Equal(x => x.Email).WithMessage("Email addresses do
            not match.");

    RuleFor(x => x.DaysAttending)
        .InclusiveBetween(1, 7).WithMessage("Number of days
        attending must be between 1 and 7.");
}
```

13. In the Scalar UI, you can see our old validation rules are back in effect. Paste the following JSON object into the Body section for our endpoint on Scala UI. You can use either the Dapper controller or the EF Core controller:

```
{
    "FullName": "Luke Avedon",
    "Email": "luke.avedon@example.com",
    "EventName": "C# Conference",
    "EventDate": "1925-12-01",
    "ConfirmEmail": "lukeNOTAnEmail",
    "DaysAttending": 3
}
```

If we test this endpoint, we can now see multiple validation rules in play:

Response 123ms 400 Bad Request

∨ Body

```json
{
  "type": "https://tools.ietf.org/html/rfc9110#section-15.5.1",
  "title": "One or more validation errors occurred.",
  "status": 400,
  "errors": {
    "FullName": [
      "Luke Avedon is not allowed in the full name."
    ],
    "EventDate": [
      "Event date must be in the future."
    ],
    "ConfirmEmail": [
      "Email addresses do not match."
    ]
  },
  "traceId": "00-9d6237ebcddbe46956e1201d15978c63-295b902e995a7d72-00"
}
```

Figure 2.4 – FullName, EventDate, and ConfirmEmail validation in action

How it works...

We created a validator class that inherits from `AbstractValidator<T>`, where `T` is the type of the model to be validated – in this case, `EventRegistrationDTO`. Inside the constructor of this validator class, we defined various rules using the `RuleFor` method. Each `RuleFor` method call specifies a property of the model and sets up a validation rule for it.

For example, with `RuleFor(x => x.FullName).NotEmpty().WithMessage("Full name is required.")` we can enforce custom validation logic. With `Must()` we can specify that a property must satisfy some condition, such as `FullName` must not contain a certain string.

One nice thing about `FluentValidation` is that its fluent API for defining rules feels natural if you are already used to working with the Fluent API in Entity Framework Core.

See also

- `https://github.com/FluentValidation/FluentValidation`
- `https://docs.fluentvalidation.net/en/latest/start.html`

Updating resources with PUT and AutoMapper

This recipe will demonstrate how to update an existing resource using PUT requests. Proper handling of resource updates is crucial for maintaining data integrity. For this task, you will learn how to use **AutoMapper**, a popular object-to-object mapping library. `AutoMapper` facilitates the mapping between **Data Transfer Objects (DTOs)** and entity models. `AutoMapper` also helps us reduce the boilerplate code needed for manual property mapping.

Getting ready

The repository is available here: `https://github.com/PacktPublishing/ASP.NET-9-Web-API-Cookbook/tree/main/end/chapter02/AutoMapper`. This starter project is different from the one we left off with, so it is crucial that you clone it if you want to follow along. The starter project includes an `AdditionalContactInfo` model for storing secondary contact details, which we'll be mapping alongside our main `EventRegistration` model.

How to do it...

1. Clone the repository using Git. The starter project for this recipe has many changes from the end of the preceding recipe, so please do download it.

2. Open the terminal. From within the `chapter02\start\AutoMapper` folder, type `dotnet build`.

3. In the terminal, install the `AutoMapper` NuGet package:

   ```
   dotnet add package AutoMapper
   ```

4. In the `Program.cs` file, import the `AutoMapper` namespace and register the AutoMapper service:

   ```
   using AutoMapper;
   using events.Models;

   …

   builder.Services.AddAutoMapper(typeof(EventProfile));
   var app = builder.Build();

   app.UseResponseCaching();
   app.MapOpenApi();
   ```

5.   Create a file called `EventProfile.cs` and fill in our `EventProfile` class:

```
using AutoMapper;
namespace events.Models
{
    public class EventProfile : Profile
    {
        public EventProfile()
        {
            CreateMap<EventRegistrationDTO, EventRegistration>()
                .ForMember(dest => dest.AdditionalContact,
                    opt => opt.MapFrom(
                        src => src.AdditionalContact));
            CreateMap<AdditionalContactInfoDTO,
                    AdditionalContactInfo>();
            CreateMap<EventRegistration, EventRegistrationDTO>()
                .ForMember(dest => dest.AdditionalContact,
                    opt => opt.MapFrom(
                        src => src.AdditionalContact));
            CreateMap<AdditionalContactInfo,
                    AdditionalContactInfoDTO>();
        }
    }
}
```

This profile defines relationships between various classes. We have a new `AdditionalContactInfo` model that is now mapped to our `EventRegistration` object:

```
using events.Repositories;
using events.Models;
using Microsoft.AspNetCore.Mvc;
using AutoMapper;

namespace events.Services;

public class EFCoreService : IEFCoreService
{
    private readonly IEFCoreRepository _repository;
    private readonly IMapper _mapper;

    public EFCoreService(IEFCoreRepository repository,
    IMapper mapper)
    {
        _repository = repository;
```

```
        _mapper = mapper;

    }
```

6. Create the contract for the service method in `IEFCoreSerivce.cs`:

```
public interface IEFCoreService
{
...

        Task UpdateEventRegistrationAsync(EventRegistrationDTO
eventRegistrationDto);
}
Implement the CreateEventRegistrationAsync method:
public async Task
UpdateEventRegistrationAsync(EventRegistrationDTO
eventRegistrationDto)
    {
        var eventRegistration = _mapper.
            Map<EventRegistration>(eventRegistrationDto);
        await _repository.UpdateEventRegistrationAsync(
            eventRegistration);

    }
```

7. Create a PUT endpoint to fully update an existing endpoint:

```
[HttpPut("{id}")]
[EndpointSummary("Update an existing event registration")]
[EndpointDescription("PUT to update an existing event
registration. Accepts an EventRegistrationDTO.")]
[ProducesResponseType(StatusCodes.Status200OK)]
[ProducesResponseType(StatusCodes.Status400BadRequest)]
[ProducesResponseType(StatusCodes.Status404NotFound)]
[ProducesResponseType(StatusCodes.Status500InternalServerError)]
public async Task<IActionResult> PutEventRegistration(int id,
[FromBody] EventRegistrationDTO eventRegistrationDto)
{
    if (id <= 0 || id != eventRegistrationDto.Id)
    {
        return BadRequest("Id is invalid or does not match the
                            event registration.");
    }

    try
    {
        var existingEvent = await _service.
            GetEventRegistrationByIdAsync(id);
```

```
        if (existingEvent == null)
        {
            return NotFound();
        }

        await _service.UpdateEventRegistrationAsync(
            eventRegistrationDto);
        return Ok(eventRegistrationDto);
    }
    catch (Exception ex)
    {
        _logger.LogError(ex, "An error occurred while updating
            event registration with Id: {Id}", id);
        return StatusCode(500, "An error occurred while updating
            event registration.");
    }
}
```

8. Run `dotnet run` in your terminal. Open your browser and go to `http://localhost:5217/scalar/chapter2#tag/efevents/put/api/EFEvents/{id}` to interact with the new endpoint.

How it works...

We defined `EventProfile`, which establishes the relationships between `EventRegistration` and `AdditionalContactInfo` (as well as the relationship between their DTOs). When a `PUT` request is received, `AutoMapper` maps the incoming DTO to the corresponding domain model, ensuring all related properties are correctly set. The starter project already had defined this additional contact info class and defined it as an owned entity in EF Core's `AppDbContext`.

The only difference between the EF Core and the Dapper implementation is the repository methods. You can also see the Dapper implementation in the final GitHub project, `https://github.com/PacktPublishing/ASP.NET-9-Web-API-Cookbook/tree/main/end/chapter02/AutoMapper`.

Managing cascade delete with AutoMapper

In this recipe, we will leverage our **AutoMapper** setup to implement the deletion of `EventRegistration` and its dependent entity, `AdditionalContact`. This ensures that when `EventRegistration` is deleted, its related `AdditionalContact` information is also handled.

Getting ready

The starting code for this project is found here: `https://github.com/PacktPublishing/ASP.NET-9-Web-API-Cookbook/tree/main/start/chapter02/CascadeDelete`. This recipe picks up where the preceding recipe ended.

How to do it...

1. Add the `DELETE` endpoint to your controller. In your `EFEventsController`, let's get started by adding the following attributes for a new `DELETE` endpoint:

    ```
    [HttpDelete("{id}")]
    [EndpointSummary("Delete an existing event registration")]
    [EndpointDescription("DELETE to remove an existing event
    registration.")]
    [ProducesResponseType(StatusCodes.Status200OK)]
    [ProducesResponseType(StatusCodes.Status404NotFound)]
    [ProducesResponseType(StatusCodes.Status500InternalServerError)]
    ```

2. Under these attributes, fill in the rest of the `DeleteEventRegistration` method:

    ```
    public async Task<IActionResult> DeleteEventRegistration(int id)
    {
        if (id <= 0)
        {
            return BadRequest("Id must be greater than 0");
        }

        try
        {
            var existingEvent = await _service.
                                GetEventRegistrationByIdAsync(id);
            if (existingEvent == null)
            {
                return NotFound();
            }

            await _service.DeleteEventRegistrationAsync(id);
            return Ok();
        }
        catch (Exception ex)
        {
            _logger.LogError(ex, "An error occurred while deleting
                event registration with Id: {Id}", id);
    ```

```
              return StatusCode(500, "An error occurred while deleting
    event registration.");
        }
    }
```

3. In your `IEFCoreService`, add the method signature for deleting an event registration:

```
public interface IEFCoreService
{
    Task DeleteEventRegistrationAsync(int id);
}
```

4. Implement the `DeleteEventRegistrationAsync` method in `EFCoreService.cs`:

```
public async Task DeleteEventRegistrationAsync(int id)
{
    await _repository.DeleteEventRegistrationAsync(id);
}
```

5. Navigate to `EFCoreRepository.cs` and implement the `DeleteEventRegistrationAsync` repository method:

```
{
    Task DeleteEventRegistrationAsync(int id);
}
public async Task DeleteEventRegistrationAsync(int id)
{
    if (_context.EventRegistrations == null)
    {
        throw new InvalidOperationException(
            "EventRegistrations DbSet is null");
    }
    var eventRegistration = await _context.
        EventRegistrations.FindAsync(id);
    if (eventRegistration != null)
    {
        _context.EventRegistrations.Remove(
            eventRegistration);
        await _context.SaveChangesAsync();
    }
}
```

How it works...

We created a DELETE endpoint that can remove an existing registration. AutoMapper helps manage the mapping and ensures that dependent entities, such as the AdditionalContact DTO are handled correctly. This effectively performs a cascade delete where the main EventRegistration entity also appropriately handles its related AdditionalContact information.

Updating specific model fields with PATCH and JsonPatchDocument

Using a PATCH request, we can update specific fields of a data entity (resource) without sending the entire object to the endpoint. In this recipe, we will leverage the JsonPatchDocument library to target and modify only the fields you need to change. This approach ensures minimal data transfer and precise updates to your resources.

Getting ready

The code for the starter project resides here: chapter02\start\JsonPatchDocument. This recipe picks up where the previous one left off.

How to do it...

1. First, install the required packages:

    ```
    dotnet add package Microsoft.AspNetCore.JsonPatch

    dotnet add package Microsoft.AspNetCore.Mvc.NewtonSoftJson
    ```

    We are not going to use System.Text.Json as our JSON provider in this example. Although it is possible to set up JsonPatch with System.Text.Json, it is more work. Import the Mvc.Formatters namespace and register that you would like to use Newtonsoft for Json on our controllers:

    ```
    builder.Services.AddControllers()
        .AddNewtonsoftJson();
    ```

2. Import the JsonPatch namespace at the top of FEventsController.cs:

    ```
    using Microsoft.AspNetCore.JsonPatch;
    ```

3. Still in `EFEventsController.cs`, add the attributes that will be used by our PATCH endpoint:

```
[HttpPatch("{id}")]
[Consumes("application/json-patch+json")]
[EndpointSummary("Partially update an existing event
registration")]
[EndpointDescription("PATCH to update specific fields of an
existing event registration.")]
[ProducesResponseType(StatusCodes.Status200OK)]
[ProducesResponseType(StatusCodes.Status400BadRequest)]
[ProducesResponseType(StatusCodes.Status404NotFound)]
[ProducesResponseType(StatusCodes.Status500InternalServerError)]
```

4. Start filling in the `PatchEventRegistration` method, which takes an `EventRegistrationDTO` from the request body, and if this body is empty, returns `Invalid request`:

```
public async Task<IActionResult> PatchEventRegistration(int id,
[FromBody] JsonPatchDocument<EventRegistrationDTO> patchDoc)
{
    if (patchDoc == null || id <= 0)
    {
        return BadRequest("Invalid request");
    }
    ...
```

5. Continue the method and try to create the event while making sure it does not already exist via `TryValidateModel`:

```
try
{
    var existingEvent = await _service.
        GetEventRegistrationByIdAsync(id);
    if (existingEvent == null)
    {
        return NotFound();
    }

    patchDoc.ApplyTo(existingEvent, ModelState);

    if (!TryValidateModel(existingEvent))
    {
        return BadRequest(ModelState);
    }

    await _service.UpdateEventRegistrationAsync(
```

```
        existingEvent);
    return Ok(existingEvent);
}
```

6.   Finally, log any errors. For any other errors not yet handled, let's return a 500 HTTP status code:

```
catch (Exception ex)
{
    logger.LogError(ex, "An error occurred while patching
        event registration with Id: {Id}", id);
    return StatusCode(500, "An error occurred while patching
        event registration.");
}
}
```

7.   You will need to update our EF Core repository method so it will detach the existing entity if needed, to avoid tracking conflicts.

Change `UpdateEventRegistrationAsync` in `EFCoreRepository` to detach if EF Core is already tracking the requested entity:

```
public async Task UpdateEventRegistrationAsync(EventRegistration
eventRegistration)
{
    var existingEntity = await _context.EventRegistrations!.
        FindAsync(eventRegistration.Id);
    if (existingEntity == null)
    {
        throw new InvalidOperationException("Entity not
            found.");
    }

    _context.Entry(existingEntity).State = EntityState.
        Detached;

    _context.EventRegistrations.Update(eventRegistration);
    await _context.SaveChangesAsync();
}
```

8.   Open the terminal, run `dotnet run` and visit the endpoint.

You can now use our PATCH endpoint to update our model of data one property at a time. The magic of PATCH is we avoid having to pass a full model, by only targeting a couple of fields:

```
[
    { "op": "replace", "path": "/FullName", "value": "Updated
        Name" },
```

```
    { "op": "replace", "Path": "/EventName", "value": "WebAPI
        Workshop"}
]
```

Update both `FullName` and `EventName`. Our previous validation rules are still in effect. For example, our validation results will prevent the client from updating a `FullName` field without updating the event name.

Make sure that you remember to specify an ID as a query string parameter, so our PATCH endpoint knows which event registration resource in our database to update. Also, be sure that you are sending the `require` with a `Content-Type` of `application/json-patch+json`. The default value may be application/json so be sure to change it. This is the standard `Content-Type` for JSON Patch documents.

Figure 2.5 shows a successful update of the resource via the Scalar UI:

Figure 2.5 – A successful update via PATCH

How it works...

We implemented a PATCH endpoint that allows updating specific fields of an existing resource using the JSON Patch standard. We used the `JsonPatchDocument` class, which allows for easily creating single field updates with minimal changes to any code outside of the controller.

When a PATCH request is received, `JsonPatchDocument` reads the included patch operations and applies them to the targeted fields of the existing model. The `patchDoc.ApplyTo(existingEvent, ModelState)` method handles mapping our patch operation and is smart enough to only update the specified fields.

We added a `[Consumes("application/json-patch+json")]` attribute to the PATCH controller, enforcing the correct media type for patch operations. By using AutoMapper in our service layer, we can seamlessly map the updated DTO to the entity model, ensuring clean and maintainable code.

While our example demonstrates the `replace` operation, JSON Patch also supports other operations such as `add` for adding new values, `remove` for deleting values, `copy` for duplicating values between paths, `move` for relocating values, and `test` for verifying values before making changes.

See also

- `https://learn.microsoft.com/en-us/aspnet/core/web-api/jsonpatch?view=aspnetcore-9.0`

- `https://jsonpatch.com/`

3

Securing Your Web API

This chapter is about **security**. The collection of recipes in this chapter covers the two fundamental aspects of API security: ensuring secure communication through HTTPS and implementing authentication and authorization mechanisms.

The first two recipes in this chapter focus on HTTPS implementation, guiding you through enforcing HTTPS and setting up custom development domains with self-signed certificates. Then, we will shift to focus on ASP.NET Core's authentication and authorization capabilities. We will implement both cookie-based and **JSON Web Token** (**JWT**)-based authentication, along with role-based and policy-based access control.

We are going to cover the following recipes in this chapter:

- Rejecting HTTP requests with custom `ProblemDetails` middleware
- Setting up HTTPS on a custom domain – creating a self-signed certificate with PowerShell
- Setting up ASP.NET Core Identity
- Using cookie authentication in ASP.NET Core Web API
- JWT authentication with Identity
- Implementing policy-based and role-based authentication

Technical requirements

For the recipes in this chapter, you'll need the following:

- **.NET 9 SDK**: For the recipes in this chapter, make sure you have `Git` and the **.NET 9 SDK** installed on your machine. The .NET 9 SDK is available here: `https://dotnet.microsoft.com/en-us/download/dotnet/9.0`.

- **SQLite**: We will still be using a SQLite database in this chapter. If you haven't already, it would be a good idea to download the free DB Browser (SQLite), which is available here: `https://sqlitebrowser.org/`.

Rejecting HTTP requests with custom ProblemDetails middleware

In this recipe, we'll create middleware that enforces HTTPS for all incoming requests to your ASP.NET Core Web API. While it's ideal to configure your web server or load balancer (e.g., IIS, NGINX) to exclusively handle HTTPS traffic, implementing HTTPS-enforcing middleware provides an additional layer of security. This ensures HTTPS enforcement regardless of deployment configuration.

While ASP.NET Core provides **HTTP Strict Transport Security (HSTS)** to enforce HTTPS connections in web browsers (assuming the web browser respects HSTS), this HSTS implementation has some limitations: For example, it does not affect API clients such as mobile apps or desktop applications. Further, the first request is still vulnerable (until the HSTS header is received). To address these limitations, we'll create middleware that enforces HTTPS for all incoming requests, regardless of client type.

Our custom HTTPS middleware will ensure that any HTTP requests are rejected with a clear and standardized response. This response will include a unique trace ID for easy troubleshooting and logging. Notably, when using a reverse proxy such as NGINX, our middleware will still return the correct headers, ensuring consistent behavior across different deployment scenarios.

Getting ready

The starter code for this recipe can be found here: `https://github.com/PacktPublishing/ASP.NET-9-Web-API-Cookbook/tree/main/start/chapter03/BlockHTTP`

> **Important note**
> To test this recipe locally, you will need a developer certificate. Thanks to the dotnet CLI, you can create one easily. Just type the following into your terminal:
>
> ```
> dotnet dev-certs https --trust
> ```

How to do it...

1. Create a folder called `Errors`. In this folder, create a new file called `CustomHttpProblemDetails.cs`. In this file, let's create `CustomHttpProblemDetails` that inherits from `ValidationProblemDetails`, as follows:

    ```
    using Microsoft.AspNetCore.Mvc;

    namespace Chapter03.Errors;
    ```

```
public class CustomHttpProblemDetails : ValidationProblemDetails
{
    public CustomHttpProblemDetails(HttpContext context)
    {
        Title = "Bad Request";
        Status = StatusCodes.Status400BadRequest;
        Detail = "HTTP requests are not allowed. Please use
            HTTPS.";
        Instance = $"{context.Request.Path} ({context.
            TraceIdentifier})";
    }
}
```

> **Why** `ValidationProblemDetails`?
>
> `ValidationProblemDetails` is the default response type for HTTP 400 responses. This class is more often used with `InvalidModelStateResponseFactory` to convert invalid `ModelStateDIctionary` objects into `IActionResult`. However, `ValidationProblemDetails` is also used for other types of validation errors, including rejecting HTTP requests. We are simply inheriting from `ValidationProblemDetails` to maintain consistency with the default response type for HTTP 400 responses.

2. Add a `Dictionary` for the request headers, after which we add both the request path and generate a unique trace identifier. Then, add in a `Dictionary` that contains the request headers:

```
public class CustomHttpProblemDetails : ValidationProblemDetails
{
    ...

        Instance = $"{context.Request.Path} ({context.
            TraceIdentifier})";

        Dictionary<string, string?> relevantHeaders = new
            Dictionary<string, string?>
        {
            {"Host", context.Request.Headers["Host"]},
            {"User-Agent", context.Request.Headers[
                "UserAgent"]},
            {"X-Forwarded-Proto", context.Request.Headers[
                "XForwarded-Proto"]},
            {"X-Forwarded-For", context.Request.Headers[
                "XForwarded-For"]}
        };
```

```
                    Extensions["headers"] = relevantHeaders;


    }
```

3. Create a new folder called Middleware. In this folder, create a file called HttpOnlyMiddleware.cs and add the following code skeleton using Chapter03.Errors;:

```
namespace Chapter03.Middleware;

public class HttpOnlyMiddleware
{
 private readonly RequestDelegate _next;
    public HttpOnlyMiddleware(RequestDelegate next)
    {
        _next = next;
    }
}
```

Notice how our middleware will store a reference to the next piece of middleware in the pipeline via RequestDelegate.

4. Create the main InvokeAsync method to check for Http. If the request is HTTP and not HTTPS, return our custom ProblemDetails and bad request status code:

```
public async Task InvokeAsync(HttpContext context)
    {
        if (!context.Request.IsHttps)
        {
            var problemDetails = new
            CustomHttpProblemDetails(context);

            context.Response.StatusCode = StatusCodes.
                Status400BadRequest;
            context.Response.ContentType = «application/
                problem+json»;

        await context.Response.WriteAsJsonAsync(problemDetails);

    return;

    }
```

Note the return statement at the end of the preceding conditional. If the request is not HTTPs, by returning here, we actually terminate the entire middleware request pipeline, because the next piece of middleware is never called.

5. If the conditional check fails, let's await the next piece of middleware:

```
        return ;
    }


        await _next(context);

    }

}
```

This now allows the next piece of middleware to be called, if the HTTPS check passes.

6. Register the middleware and configure forwarded headers.

In `Program.cs`, import the built-in `HttpOverrides;` namespace and the namespace of our custom middleware:

```
using Microsoft.AspNetCore.HttpOverrides;
using Chapter03.Middleware;
```

7. Configure the forwarded headers options:

```
builder.Services.Configure<ForwardedHeadersOptions>(options =>
{
    options.ForwardedHeaders = ForwardedHeaders.XForwardedFor |
        ForwardedHeaders.XForwardedProto;
    options.KnownNetworks.Clear();
    options.KnownProxies.Clear();
});
```

8. Register `UseForwardedHeaders` and our custom middleware as the first two middleware pipelines, right after `var app = builder.Build();`:

```
var app = builder.Build();

app.UseForwardedHeaders();
app.UseMiddleware<HttpOnlyMiddleware>();
```

Run the application with `dotnet run`. Here is an example of trying to access the Scalar OpenAPI documentation for our API: notice the custom `ProblemDetails` returned:

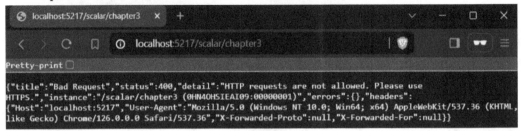

Figure 3.1 – Our custom problem details blocking HTTP requests

How it works...

We created an additional security measure: middleware that blocks incoming HTTP requests early in the middleware pipeline, even if Kestrel, or whatever deployment server you use, is set up to still listen to HTTP. In a properly configured production environment, your server should be set up to only accept HTTPS connections. This middleware acts as a safeguard in case of misconfigurations or in development scenarios where HTTP might still be enabled. Ideally, no HTTP request should be able to be sent in the first place.

Setting up HTTPS on a custom domain – creating a self-signed certificate with PowerShell

The **dotnet dev-certs tool** is designed primarily for development using localhost. However, there are times when using localhost is not sufficient. While developing our API locally, it is often necessary to run the API on a custom domain name. This guide will show you how to create a self-signed certificate for a custom domain using PowerShell.

Getting ready

There is no starter project for this recipe. For reference, you can see the self-signed certificate I created with this recipe here: `https://github.com/PacktPublishing/ASP.NET-9-Web-API-Cookbook/tree/main/end/chapter03/SelfSignedCertificate`

This recipe is targeted at Windows users. If you are using a different operating system, the steps may slightly differ.

This recipe requires PowerShell in your terminal.

How to do it...

1. Choose a domain name. We are going to use `"dev.webapi-book.com"`:

    ```
    $domainName = "dev.webapi-book.com"
    ```

2. Create the self-signed certificate:

    ```
    $cert = New-SelfSignedCertificate -DnsName $domainName
    -CertStoreLocation "cert:\LocalMachine\My" -NotAfter (Get-Date).
    AddYears(1)
    ```

3. Choose a password, and convert it to a secure string:

    ```
    $pwd = ConvertTo-SecureString -String "ExamplePassword" -Force
    -AsPlainText
    ```

4. Save the path for the certificate:

    ```
    $certPath = ".\Certificates"
    ```

5. Test the path for the certificate, and if needed create the path:

    ```
    if (!(Test-Path $certPath)) {
    New-Item -ItemType Directory -Force -Path $certPath
    }
    ```

6. Export the certificate to the path we just defined, with our password:

    ```
    $path = Join-Path $certPath "dev-webapi-book-cert.pfx"
    Export-PfxCertificate -Cert $cert -FilePath $path -Password $pwd
    ```

7. Add the certificate to the trusted root store:

    ```
    $rootStore = New-Object System.Security.Cryptography.
    X509Certificates.X509Store "Root","LocalMachine"
    $rootStore.Open("ReadWrite")
    $rootStore.Add($cert)
    $rootStore.Close()
    ```

We successfully created the certificate and installed it in both `LocalMachine` and `TrustedRoot` – to act as our development-only certificate authority.

Figure 3.2 shows verifying the installation with **Microsoft Management Console (MMC)**:

Figure 3.2 – The LocalMachine installation of our self-signed certificate

And here is our certificate in the `TrustedRoot` store:

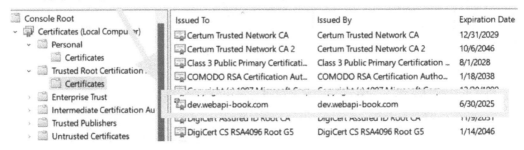

Figure 3.3 – Certificate installed in Trusted Root

You can also verify the installation with PowerShell, by using the following commands:

```
Get-ChildItem -Path Cert:\LocalMachine\My | Where-Object {$_.
Subject -like "CN=dev.webapi-book.com"} | Format-List *
Get-ChildItem -Path Cert:\LocalMachine\Root | Where-Object {$_.
Subject -like "CN=dev.webapi-book.com"} | Format-List *
```

How it works...

We created a self-signed certificate using PowerShell's built-in tools. We installed this certificate not only in `LocalMachine` but also `TrustedRoot`. `TrustedRoot` can act as our own certificate authority, which can enable a custom domain to be used for our local development. By adding our certificate to the `TrustedRoot` store, we're essentially telling our system to trust this certificate as if it were issued by a legitimate **Certificate Authority (CA)**. This setup allows us to simulate a production-like environment while developing locally.

See also...

- **DigiCert** is a leading provider of professional TLS certificates: `https://docs.digicert.com/?lang=en`

- **Let's Encrypt**, a provider of free TLS certificates: `https://letsencrypt.org/`

- Create a self-signed certificate using the OpenSSL CLI instead of PowerShell: `https://devopscube.com/create-self-signed-certificates-openssl/`

Setting up ASP.NET Core Identity

In this recipe, we will set up **ASP.NET Core Identity**. Identity provides a comprehensive solution for authentication, authorization, and user management, protecting your data and resources. Identity is a powerful tool that makes handling user accounts and permissions much easier for developers.

Getting ready...

The starter project for this recipe can be found here: `https://github.com/PacktPublishing/ASP.NET-9-Web-API-Cookbook/tree/main/start/chapter03/IdentitySetup`

You can also continue from the preceding recipe. The starter project does not have the custom domain self-signed certificate we used in the preceding recipe. For now, we will go back to running the examples on localhost. So If you did not install the self-signed certificate before, no problem. In this recipe, we are still following the best practice of not listening on HTTP at all so you will have to create a dev cert:

```
dotnet dev-certs https --clean
dotnet dev-certs https --trust
```

Accept any pop-up alerts that appear when you clean and add a new developer certificate.

DB Browser for SQLite is also recommended as we will be taking a look at our database. It is available here: `https://sqlitebrowser.org/`.

How to do it...

1. Add the package for `Microsoft.AspNetCore.Identity.EntityFrameworkCore`.

   In the terminal, type the following:

   ```
   dotnet add package Microsoft.AspNetCore.Identity.
   EntityFrameworkCore
   ```

2. Add the package for `EntityFrameworkCore.Design`:

   ```
   dotnet add package Microsoft.EntityFrameworkCore.Design
   ```

3. In `Program.cs`, add the namespace for Identity:

    ```
    Using Microsoft.AspNetCore.Identity;
    ```

4. Configure the Identity services. Add it right after `builder.Services.AddDbContext<AppDbContext>` as Identity depends on DbContext:

    ```
    // Add Identity services
    builder.Services.AddIdentity<IdentityUser, IdentityRole>()        .
    AddEntityFrameworkStores<AppDbContext>()
    .AddDefaultTokenProviders();
    ```

5. Enable authentication middleware right after our current `app.UseCors()` middleware:

    ```
    app.UseCors();
    app.UseAuthentication();
    ```

6. In our `Models` folder, create a new file called `RegisterDTO.cs` and add a `RegisterDTO` class to model the user:

    ```
    public class RegisterDTO
    {
        public string Email { get; set; }

        public string Password { get; set; }
    }
    ```

    Because this DTO is only for registering the user with email and password, it only has two properties. This class in no way represents the full user model, which for now is provided by Identity.

7. Now we add `DataAnnotations` to our DTO class for basic model validation. In `RegisterDTO.cs`, import the `DataAnnotations` namespace:

    ```
    using System.ComponentModel.DataAnnotations;
    ```

8. Now fill out the attributes for the `RegisterDTO` class:

    ```
    namespace events.Models;

    public class RegisterDTO
        {
            [Required]
            [EmailAddress]
            public required string Email { get; set; }

            [Required]
            [StringLength(100, MinimumLength = 6)]
    ```

```
       public required string Password { get; set; }
    }
```

9. In our `Controller` folder, create a new file called `AccountController.cs`.

    Add the following using statements:

    ```
    using Microsoft.AspNetCore.Identity;
    using Microsoft.AspNetCore.Mvc;
    using events.Models;
    ```

10. Now create our controller class. Note the constructor takes in the `UserManager` class from Identity:

    ```
    namespace events.Controllers;

    [ApiController]
    [Route("api/[controller]")]
    public class AccountController(UserManager<IdentityUser>
    userManager) : ControllerBase
    {
    ```

11. Add in a `POST` endpoint, which creates a new user given an email and password:

    ```
    [HttpPost("register")]
    [ProducesResponseType(StatusCodes.Status200OK)]
    [ProducesResponseType(StatusCodes.Status400BadRequest)]
    public async Task<IActionResult> Register(RegisterDTO model)
    {
        if (!ModelState.IsValid)
        {
            return BadRequest(ModelState);
        }
        var user = new IdentityUser { UserName = model.Email,
            Email = model.Email };
        var result = await _userManager.CreateAsync(user,
            model.Password);

        if (result.Succeeded)
        {
            return Ok(new { message = "User registered successfully"
            });
        }
        return BadRequest(new { errors = result.Errors.Select(e
                => e.Description) });
    }
    ```

12. Now create an endpoint to delete a user:

```
[HttpDelete("delete/{email}")]
[ProducesResponseType(StatusCodes.Status200OK)]
[ProducesResponseType(StatusCodes.Status404NotFound)]
[ProducesResponseType(StatusCodes.Status400BadRequest)]
        public async Task<IActionResult> Delete(string email)
        {
            var user = await _userManager.
FindByEmailAsync(email);
            if (user == null)
            {
                return NotFound(new { message = "User not found"
});
            }

            var result = await _userManager.DeleteAsync(user);
            if (result.Succeeded)
            {
                return Ok(new { message = "User deleted
                        successfully" });
            }
            return BadRequest(new { errors = result.Errors.
                            Select(e => e.Description) });
        }
    }
}
```

13. Update AppDbContext to inherit from Identity:

```
using Microsoft.AspNetCore.Identity.EntityFrameworkCore;
using Microsoft.EntityFrameworkCore;
using events.Models;
namespace events.Data;

public class AppDbContext : IdentityDbContext
{
    public AppDbContext(DbContextOptions<AppDbContext>options) :
        base(options) {}

    public DbSet<EventRegistration> EventRegistrations { get;
        set; } = null!;
}
```

> **Warning on EF migrations**
>
> If you are performing a migration on a database that was not initially created with an EF Core migration, you have to handle the migration script extremely carefully. Here, we are starting fresh with the same schema we have used before but no existing SQLite database.

14. In your terminal, make sure the `EF Core CLI` tools are installed globally:

    ```
    dotnet tool install --global dotnet-ef
    ```

    Visual Studio users might prefer to decline installing this global CLI tool and use the included tools in the Package Manager Console to run the migration with `Add-Migration IdentitySchema` and `Update-Database`.

15. Apply the migrations and set up the database.

    Generate and apply the necessary migrations to set up the Identity schema:

    ```
    dotnet ef migrations add IdentitySchema
    ```

16. Create a new migration that includes both the existing `EventRegistrations` table and the new Identity table. Update `DbSet` to include `EventRegistrations`:

    ```
    dotnet ef database update
    ```

17. Now, run the API and test the new endpoint:

    ```
    dotnet run
    ```

18. Create a new user at our `POST` endpoint.

    We can register a user by posting to `https://localhost:5001/api/Account/register`.

Figure 3.4 presents an example of creating a user via the Scalar interactive documentation at `https://localhost:5001/Scalar/chapter3`:

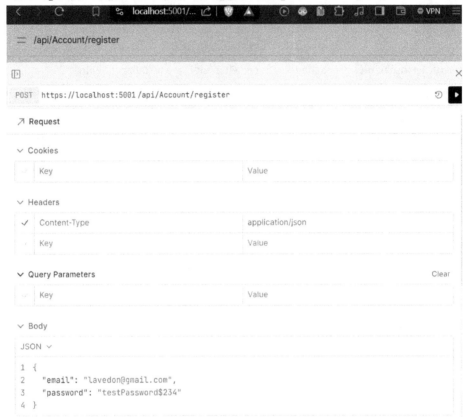

Figure 3.4 – Creating a new user

19. Using DB Browser, we can now view the user in our SQLite database file. This file can be found in the `Data` folder.

    Note the single user in our users table:

Figure 3.5 – A single user added to our users table

20. We can delete this user using the `delete` endpoint we created.

21. This time, let's try calling the endpoint from PowerShell. Let's delete our sole user using `Invoke-RestMethod`:

```
Invoke-RestMethod -Uri "https://localhost:5001/api/Account/
delete/lavedon@gmail.com" -Method DELETE
```

If you are using DB Browser, hit refresh and you will see that the user is now gone.

How it works...

ASP.NET Core Identity integrates seamlessly with your application by leveraging Entity Framework Core and your existing database context. When you add Identity services to your application, it extends `DbContext` with additional tables for managing users, roles, and claims. The `UserManager<IdentityUser>` service provides a high-level API for user operations, abstracting away the complexities of password hashing and database interactions. By creating `AccountController`, you expose endpoints for user registration and deletion, demonstrating basic Identity functionality. The use of **Data Transfer Objects (DTOs)** and data annotations ensures proper data validation before processing requests.

This recipe lays the groundwork for implementing more advanced security features such as **role-based access control (RBAC)** and **claims-based authorization**.

Using cookie authentication in ASP.NET Core Web API

In this recipe, we'll implement cookie-based authentication in our ASP.NET Core Web API. While **JSON Web Token (JWT)** authentication is often preferred for many API scenarios, cookie authentication remains relevant and valuable in ASP.NET Core development. It's worth noting that ASP.NET Core always works with an `asp.net_sessionid` cookie, making cookies an integral part of the framework regardless of the chosen authentication method. For Web APIs, cookie authentication can be particularly useful when dealing with **browser-based clients** or **single-page applications (SPAs)**. It offers benefits such as automatic renewal of authentication, simpler CSRF protection implementation, and easier management of token expiration on the server side.

By the end of this recipe, you'll have set up a cookie-based authentication system integrated with ASP.NET Core Identity, enabling secure user login, access control to protected endpoints, and logout functionality in your Web API.

Getting ready...

This project will pick up where the preceding recipe left off. The starter project can be found here: `https://github.com/PacktPublishing/ASP.NET-9-Web-API-Cookbook/tree/main/start/chapter03/CookieAuth`.

We are using the ASP.NET Core Identity setup from the preceding recipe. There are no new NuGet packages to install as Identity is built in.

To follow along with the testing portion, you will need a terminal with PowerShell.

How to do it...

1. Open `Program.cs` and import the namespace required to use cookie-based authentication:

    ```
    using Microsoft.AspNetCore.Authentication.Cookies;
    ```

2. Change `AddIdentity` to `AddIdentityCore`:

    ```
    builder.Services.AddIdentityCore<IdentityUser>()
    .AddEntityFrameworkStores<AppDbContext>()
        .AddDefaultTokenProviders();
    ```

3. After `builder.Services.AddIdentity`, register `CookieAuthentication`:

    ```
    builder.Services.AddAuthentication(CookieAuthenticationDefaults.
    AuthenticationScheme).AddCookie();
    ```

4. Modify the authentication scheme:

    ```
    builder.Services.AddAuthentication(options => { options.
    DefaultAuthenticateScheme = CookieAuthenticationDefaults.
    AuthenticationScheme; options.DefaultChallengeScheme
    = CookieAuthenticationDefaults.AuthenticationScheme;
    options.DefaultScheme = CookieAuthenticationDefaults.
    AuthenticationScheme; })
    ```

5. We will add the `AddCookie()` method to `AddAuthentication()`. Start by setting a name for our cookie:

    ```
    builder.Services.AddAuthentication(options =>
    {
        .AddCookie(options => { options.Cookie.Name =
                "WebAPICookbook";
    }
    ```

6. Restrict client-side scripts from accessing the cookie and set the `SameSite` security policy to `Strict`:

    ```
    options.Cookie.Name = "WebAPICookbook";
    options.Cookie.HttpOnly = true;
    options.Cookie.SameSite = SameSiteMode.Strict;
    options.Cookie.SecurePolicy = CookieSecurePolicy.Always;
    options.ExpireTimeSpan = TimeSpan.FromMinutes(60);
    options.SlidingExpiration = true;
    ```

In the preceding code, we also set the time limit for the cookie. In addition, we set the cookie to refresh if the user is active via `SlidingExpiration`.

7. Finally, we'll be returned a 401 status code if the user is unauthorized and a 403 status code if the user is forbidden:

```
options.Events = new CookieAuthenticationEvents
{
    OnRedirectToLogin = context =>
    {
        context.Response.StatusCode = StatusCodes.
            Status401Unauthorized;
        return Task.CompletedTask;
    },
    OnRedirectToAccessDenied = context =>
    {
        context.Response.StatusCode = StatusCodes.
            Status403Forbidden;
        return Task.CompletedTask;
    }
};
```

Events properties instead of redirection endpoints

Since we are not working with frontend views or a frontend application, we do not set redirection endpoints when authentication fails. For a Web API, we customize `options.Events` to customize behavior when authentication is required or access is denied.

8. Make sure the `app.UseAuthentication` middleware is registered in `Program.cs`. Add it after we register `app.UseCors()`:

```
app.UseCors();
app.UseAuthentication();
app.UseAuthorization();

app.MapControllers();
```

The order of middleware is crucial

Ensure that `app.UseAuthentication()` is called before `app.UseAuthorization()` and that both are before `app.MapControllers()`.

9. Create `LoginDTO`, which will be quite similar to the `RegisterDTO` we created earlier in this chapter:

```
using System.ComponentModel.DataAnnotations;

namespace events.Models;

public class LoginDTO
{
    [Required]
    [EmailAddress]
    public required string Email { get; set; }

    [Required]
    public required string Password { get; set; }
}
```

10. Open `AccountController.cs` and import the namespaces we will need:

```
using System.Security.Claims;
using Microsoft.AspNetCore.Authentication.Cookies;
using Microsoft.AspNetCore.Authentication;
using Microsoft.AspNetCore.Authorization;
```

11. Now add a login endpoint to `AccountController`:

```
[HttpPost("login")]
public async Task<IActionResult> Login(LoginDTO model)
{
    var user = await _userManager.FindByEmailAsync(model.Email);
    if (user != null && await _userManager.
        CheckPasswordAsync(user, model.Password))
    {
        await SignInAsync(user);
        return Ok(new { message = "User logged in successfully"
            });
    }
    return Unauthorized(new { message = "Invalid login attempt"
        });
}
```

12. We will create the `SignInAsync` method in a moment. Let's first create an endpoint for logging out:

```
[HttpPost("logout")]
public async Task<IActionResult> Logout()
{
    await HttpContext.SignOutAsync(CookieAuthenticationDefaults.
        AuthenticationScheme);
    return Ok(new { message = "User logged out successfully" });
}
```

13. Let's create a helper method that signs the user in and returns an authentication cookie:

```
private async Task SignInAsync(IdentityUser user)
{
    var claims = new List<Claim>
    {
        new Claim(ClaimTypes.Name, user.UserName!),
        new Claim(ClaimTypes.NameIdentifier, user.Id!),
    };

    var claimsIdentity = new ClaimsIdentity(claims,
        CookieAuthenticationDefaults.AuthenticationScheme);
    await HttpContext.SignInAsync(CookieAuthenticationDefaults.
        AuthenticationScheme, new ClaimsPrincipal(
            claimsIdentity));
}
```

This method creates `ClaimsPrincipal` for the user, which includes claims for the user's name and a unique identifier. These claims are then used to create `ClaimsIdentity` associated with the cookie authentication scheme.

SignInAsync and SignOutAsync

These methods are actually built into ASP.NET Core authentication. They are extension methods on `HttpContext`, defined in `AuthenticationHttpContextExtensions` and added in `Microsoft.AspNetCore.Authentication;`.

---

14. Finally, let's create a test GET endpoint that is secured by `[Authorize]`. Because this endpoint is secured, we should only be able to access it when we are signed in. Let's put this in the `EventsController` class.

15. Open `EventsController.cs` and import the `Authorization` namespace using `Microsoft.AspNetCore.Authorization;`.

16. Still in `EventsController.cs`, create our test `Authorization` action method:

```
[Authorize]
[HttpGet("authtest")]
public IActionResult AuthTest()
{
    return Ok("This endpoint is secured");
}
```

17. Now, run the API:

```
dotnet run
```

18. If you have not previously created a user, please do so. One easy way is via the Scalar OpenAPI documentation here: `https://localhost:5001/Scalar/chapter3`.

19. Now let's test the cookie-based authentication we just built via PowerShell:

   I.   Enter the following commands into your terminal. Replace the email and password with the one you used to create your user:

```
$baseUrl = "https://localhost:5001/api"
$loginBody = @{ email = "luke.avedon@gmail.com"; password =
"muffinCat123!" } | ConvertTo-Json
$session = New-Object Microsoft.PowerShell.Commands.
WebRequestSession
$loginResponse = Invoke-WebRequest -Uri "$baseUrl/
Account/login" -Method Post -Body $loginBody -ContentType
"application/json" -SessionVariable session
```

   II.   We can log in to the API and save our session. We can view our cookie like so:

```
$loginResponse.Headers["Set-Cookie"]
```

20. Now let's test our endpoint decorated with the [`Authorize`] attribute:

```
Invoke-RestMethod -Uri "$baseUrl/Events/authtest"
```

21. The request will return unauthorized. Now test it again with the saved session variable:

```
$authTestResponse = Invoke-WebRequest -Uri "$baseUrl/Events/
authtest" -Method Get -WebSession $session
$authTestResponse.Content
```

We should now have passed security and be able to see the following message returned:

```
This endpoint is secured.
```

How it works...

This recipe implements cookie-based authentication in ASP.NET Core Web API using Identity. The process begins by configuring authentication services in `Program.cs`, specifying `CookieAuthenticationDefaults` as the default scheme. The `AddCookie` method sets up crucial cookie options, including name, HTTP-only flag, `SameSite` policy, and expiration. During login, `SignInAsync` creates `ClaimsPrincipal` with user claims, which is then used to generate an authentication cookie. This cookie is sent to the client and used in subsequent requests to maintain the user's authenticated state. The `[Authorize]` attribute on endpoints such as `AuthTest` ensures that only authenticated users can access them.

JWT authentication with Identity

In this recipe, we'll implement JWT authentication. While cookie-based authentication is suitable for many scenarios, JWT offers a stateless alternative. One nice thing about working with JWT is we only have to concern ourselves with the token itself and not a cookie tied to a session. Also, cookies present many security challenges if we have an API that eventually has to work across multiple domain names. JWT allows the API to authenticate users without having to maintain the session state on the server. JWT is becoming generally preferred over authentication cookies.

Getting ready...

The starter project for this recipe can be found here: `https://github.com/PacktPublishing/ASP.NET-9-Web-API-Cookbook/tree/main/start/chapter03/JWTAuth`

The starter project is similar to the preceding recipe but with the cookie authentication removed.

A terminal with PowerShell is recommended for following along.

How to do it...

1. Install the **JWT Bearer** package: Open your terminal in the project directory and run the following command:

   ```
   dotnet add package Microsoft.AspNetCore.Authentication.JwtBearer
   ```

2. We will create a model for our JWT settings, in order to enforce defaults and better handle any issues. In the `Models` folder, create a file named `JwtSettings.cs` and fill in our JWTSettings class:

   ```
   namespace events.Models;

   public class JwtSettings
   {
       public string Key { get; set; } = string.Empty;
   ```

```
       public string Issuer { get; set; } = string.Empty;
       public string Audience { get; set; } = string.Empty;
       public int ExpirationInMinutes { get; set; } = 60;
// Default to 1 hour
}
```

3. Open `Program.cs` and import the necessary using import statements at the top of the file:

```
using Microsoft.AspNetCore.Authentication.JwtBearer;
using Microsoft.IdentityModel.Tokens;
using System.Text;
```

4. After where we registered `IdentityCore`, register our new `JwtSettings` class:

```
builder.Services.Configure<JwtSettings>(builder.Configuration.
GetSection("Jwt"));
```

5. The key we use to sign our token will be stored in an external file, not hardcoded in our C# code. For this recipe, we will use an external text file. Let's read that key in with the following code:

```
string keyPath = Path.Combine(builder.Environment.
ContentRootPath, "jwt-key.txt");
string jwtKey = File.ReadAllText(keyPath).Trim();
Console.WriteLine($"jwtKey is {jwtKey}");
```

6. Now create and populate our `JwtSettings` class:

```
var jwtSettings = new JwtSettings
{
    Key = jwtKey,
    Issuer = builder.Configuration["Jwt:Issuer"],
    Audience = builder.Configuration["Jwt:Audience"],
    ExpirationInMinutes = int.Parse(builder.
        Configuration["Jwt:ExpirationInMinutes"] ?? "60")
};
```

7. For extra safety, validate our `JwtSettings` class:

```
if (string.IsNullOrEmpty(jwtSettings.Key) ||
    string.IsNullOrEmpty(jwtSettings.Issuer) ||
    string.IsNullOrEmpty(jwtSettings.Audience))
{
    throw new InvalidOperationException("JWT settings are
        incomplete. Please check your configuration and jwt-key.
        txt file.");
}
```

```
Console.WriteLine($"JwtSettings created. Key length:
{jwtSettings.Key.Length}, Issuer: {jwtSettings.Issuer},
Audience: {jwtSettings.Audience}");
```

8. After the existing Identity setup, add our JWT authentication as a Singleton:

```
builder.Services.AddSingleton(jwtSettings);
```

9. Configure the JWT so we can use the IOptions pattern for login:

```
builder.Services.Configure<JwtSettings>(options =>
{
    options.Key = jwtSettings.Key;
    options.Issuer = jwtSettings.Issuer;
    options.Audience = jwtSettings.Audience;
    options.ExpirationInMinutes = jwtSettings.
        ExpirationInMinutes;
});
```

10. Configure AddAuthentication to use our JwtToken:

```
builder.Services.AddAuthentication(JwtBearerDefaults.
AuthenticationScheme)
    .AddJwtBearer(options =>
    {
        options.TokenValidationParameters = new
        TokenValidationParameters
        {
            ValidateIssuer = true,
            ValidateAudience = true,
            ValidateLifetime = true,
            ValidateIssuerSigningKey = true,
            ValidIssuer = builder.Configuration["Jwt:Issuer"],
            ValidAudience = builder.
            Configuration["Jwt:Audience"],
            IssuerSigningKey = new SymmetricSecurityKey(
                Encoding.UTF8.GetBytes(
                    builder.Configuration["Jwt:Key"]!))
        };
    });
```

Even though we generated our own JwtToken, we will still be using ASP.NET Core Identity
for user management. However, we are not going to be using Identity's built-in sign-in manager.

11. The final thing we will do in `Program.cs` is confirm that we still have both `app.UseAuthentication()` and `app.UseAuthorization();` placed after `app.UseCors();`.

   Now open `appsettings.json` and add the following JWT object:

   ```
   "Jwt": {
   "Issuer": "https://localhost:5001",
   "Audience": "https://localhost:5001",
   "ExpirationInMinutes": 60
   }
   ```

   Make sure this `"JWT"` setting is added after the `"Kestrel"` property and not as a child of `"Kestrel"`.

   In production, the `Issuer` and `Audience` would obviously be different, but when developing locally, localhost is fine.

12. Open `AccountController.cs` and import the needed namespaces:

   ```
   using Microsoft.AspNetCore.Identity;
   using Microsoft.AspNetCore.Mvc;
   using System.IdentityModel.Tokens.Jwt;
   using System.Security.Claims;
   using System.Text;
   using Microsoft.IdentityModel.Tokens;
   using Microsoft.Extensions.Options;
   using events.Models;
   ```

13. Adjust our constructor to take in the `JwtSettings` object:

   ```
   private readonly UserManager<IdentityUser> _userManager;
   private readonly JwtSettings _jwtSettings;

   public AccountController(UserManager<IdentityUser> userManager,
   IOptions<JwtSettings> jwtSettings)
   {
       _userManager = userManager;
       _jwtSettings = jwtSettings.Value;
   }
   ```

14. Modify our `Login` endpoint to generate the JWT token:

   ```
   [HttpPost("login")]
   public async Task<IActionResult> Login(LoginDTO model)
   {
       var user = await _userManager.FindByEmailAsync(model.Email);
       if (user != null && await _userManager.
   ```

```
         CheckPasswordAsync(user, model.Password))
      {
          var token = GenerateJwtToken(user);
          return Ok(new { token = token });
      }

      return Unauthorized(new { message = "Invalid login
                                    attempt" });
}
```

15. Let's create a helper method that generates the actual token. We will start off by throwing an exception if the key is null or empty:

```
private string GenerateJwtToken(IdentityUser user)
{
    if (string.IsNullOrEmpty(_jwtSettings.Key))
    {
        throw new InvalidOperationException("JWT key is null or
                                    empty");
    }
}
```

16. On the next line, fill in the rest of the method to generate the relevant claims:

```
var claims = new[]
{
    new Claim(JwtRegisteredClaimNames.Sub, user.Email),
    new Claim(JwtRegisteredClaimNames.Jti,
        Guid.NewGuid().ToString()),
    new Claim(ClaimTypes.NameIdentifier, user.Id)
};

var key = new SymmetricSecurityKey(Encoding.UTF8.GetBytes(
    _jwtSettings.Key));
var creds = new SigningCredentials(key,
    SecurityAlgorithms.HmacSha256);
var expires = DateTime.Now.AddMinutes(
    _jwtSettings.ExpirationInMinutes);

var token = new JwtSecurityToken(
    issuer: _jwtSettings.Issuer,
    audience: _jwtSettings.Audience,
    claims: claims,
    expires: expires,
    signingCredentials: creds
);
```

```
                      return new JwtSecurityTokenHandler().WriteToken(token);
        }
```

17. Finally, let's create the text file, which will hold our key. Call the file jwt-key.txt and place our key there:

```
ThisIsMySecretKey123!@#ThisShouldBeALongAndComplexString
```

Now, let's test our JWT token with PowerShell.

18. In the terminal, start our API:

```
dotnet run
```

19. Now let's test the API with PowerShell. Save the base URL in a variable:

```
$baseUrl = "https://localhost:5001/api"
```

20. Save the login credentials:

```
$loginBody = @{
    email = "luke@luke.com"
    password = "Muffin#1"
} | ConvertTo-Json
```

21. Log in to the app and save the token:

```
$loginResponse = Invoke-RestMethod -Uri "$baseUrl/Account/login"
-Method Post -Body $loginBody -ContentType "application/json"
$token = $loginResponse.token
```

Now let's copy our token and paste it into a JWT validator.

22. We can use the free online one at **jot.io**. This is an easy way to see what is stored in our token.

Open a web browser. Go to jwt.io and paste in our token.

In *Figure 3.6*, you can see the JWT website with our JWT token pasted in. On the right, you can see information on the header and payload:

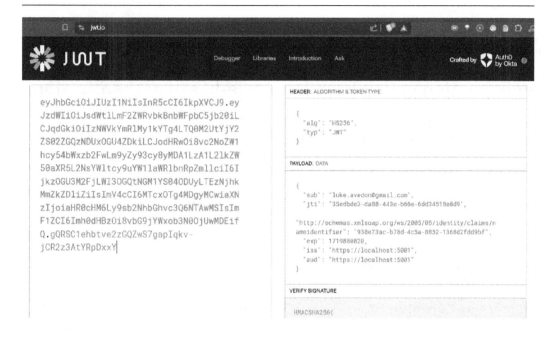

Figure 3.6 – Our token entered into the jwt.io website

23. Back in our PowerShell terminal, save the token to a `headers` variable:

```
$headers = @{
    Authorization = "Bearer $token"
}
```

24. Try accessing our protected endpoint:

```
Invoke-RestMethod -Uri "$baseUrl/Events/authtest" -Method Get
-Headers $headers
```

You should see the magic message `"This endpoint is secured"`.

How it works...

We implemented a stateless authentication mechanism, where all necessary information is contained within the token itself. We eliminated the need for the server-side session storage we have to rely on cookie-based authentication. We created a `JwtSettings` class that encapsulates all JWT configurations, including the secret key, issuer, audience, and token expiration time. When the user logs in, the `GenerateJwtToken` method creates the JWT token. The `AddAuthentication` and `AddJwtBearer` methods in `Program.cs` set up the JWT authentication middleware.

While we are using custom JWT generation, we still rely on ASP.NET Core Identity to take care of user management. Identity handles creating users, storing passwords securely, and validating credentials.

Implementing policy-based and role-based authentication

In this recipe, we will explore securing endpoints using both policies and roles. We will secure one endpoint only for use by admins. Then we will touch on the wild freedom given by policy-based authentication.

Getting ready...

This recipe starts off where the preceding one ended. We have already cleaned up the users in our database and created an admin role. We will build upon the JWT authentication we implemented in the previous recipe.

The starter code for this project can be found here: `https://github.com/PacktPublishing/ASP.NET-9-Web-API-Cookbook/tree/main/start/chapter03/RolesAndPolicies`

It might be a good idea to have DB Browser for SQLite so you can see how we set up an admin role.

How to do it...

1. Open the starter project. Look at the SQLite database in `\Data\SqliteDB.db`.

   You will notice that we have one single user. The normal ASP.NET Core Identity tables are set up (from previous recipes).

   Figure 3.7 shows that the `AspNetUserRoles` table has a single entry: a user ID linked to a role:

Figure 3.7 – The AspNetUserRoles table in DB Browser for SQLite

In the `AspNetRoles` table, we can see what roles we have defined. We currently have one role of `Admin`, as shown in *Figure 3.8*:

Figure 3.8 – The AspNetRoles table

2. Open our `AccountController.cs` file. We will modify the `GenerateJwtToken` method to add roles to our JWT token. We are going to make three small changes:

    I.   Change `GenerateJwtToken` to an async method.

    II. Call the `.GetRolesAsync` method on our instance of `UserManager`.

    III. Change the type of `Claims` from an array to `List<T>`:

    ```
    private async Task<string> GenerateJwtToken(IdentityUser user)
    {
        var claims = new List<Claim>
        {
            new Claim(JwtRegisteredClaimNames.Sub, user.Email),
            new Claim(JwtRegisteredClaimNames.Jti, Guid.NewGuid().
                ToString()),
            new Claim(ClaimTypes.NameIdentifier, user.Id)
        };

        // Add roles to claims
        var userRoles = await _userManager.GetRolesAsync(user);
        foreach (var role in userRoles)
        {
            claims.Add(new Claim(ClaimTypes.Role, role));
        }
    }
    ```

3. At the top of the `GenerateJwtToken` method, throw an `InvalidOperationException` method if the username is not given:

    ```
    if (string.IsNullOrEmpty(user.UserName))
    {
        throw new InvalidOperationException("User does not have a
            valid username");
    }
    ```

    Note that `string.IsNullOrEmpty` handles both null and empty string cases, so a separate null check on `user.UserName` is not necessary.

4. After we add our roles, we can add a single line of code to create our custom claim. This claim just takes our username and adds it as a claim:

    ```
    claims.Add(new Claim(ClaimTypes.Name, user.UserName));
    ```

5. Open `EventsController.cs` and secure the `authtest` GET endpoint to make sure only users with the `Admin` role can access the endpoint:

    ```
    [Authorize(Roles = "Admin")]
    [HttpGet("authtest")]
    ```

```
public IActionResult AuthTest()
{
    return Ok("This endpoint is secured for Admins only");
}
```

6. To enable roles, we have to update how we are adding Identity services – we will expand our `IdentityCore` registration:

```
builder.Services.AddIdentityCore<IdentityUser>(options =>
options.SignIn.RequireConfirmedAccount = false)
    .AddRoles<IdentityRole>()
    .AddEntityFrameworkStores<AppDbContext>()
    .AddDefaultTokenProviders();
```

7. Open `Program.cs`. Add a custom authorization policy. This policy will enforce that the user's name has to start with the letter L. Only users whose username starts with the letter L will be able to access any endpoint decorated with this policy:

```
builder.Services.AddAuthorization(options =>
{
    options.AddPolicy("UsernameStartsWithL", policy =>
        policy.RequireAssertion(context =>
            context.User.Identity?.Name != null &&
            context.User.Identity.Name.StartsWith("L",
                StringComparison.OrdinalIgnoreCase)));
});
```

8. Add a new endpoint in `EventsController.cs` to test this policy:

```
[Authorize(Policy = "UsernameStartsWithL")]
[HttpGet("l-users-only")]
public IActionResult LUsersOnly()
{
    return Ok("Your username starts with 'L'!");
}
```

9. Start the API via the terminal with the following:

```
Dotnet run
```

10. Log in via PowerShell just like in the previous recipe:

```
$baseUrl = "https://localhost:5001/api"
$loginBody = @{
    email = "luke@luke.com"
    password = "Muffin#1"
```

```
} | ConvertTo-Json
$loginResponse = Invoke-RestMethod -Uri "$baseUrl/Account/login"
-Method Post -Body $loginBody -ContentType "application/json"
$token = $loginResponse.token
```

11. Set up the `Authorization` header:

```
$headers = @{ Authorization = "Bearer $token" }
```

12. Test the Admin-only endpoint:

```
Invoke-RestMethod -Uri "$baseUrl/Events/authtest" -Method Get
-Headers $headers
```

13. Test the custom policy endpoint:

```
Invoke-RestMethod -Uri "$baseUrl/Events/l-users-only" -Method
Get -Headers $headers
```

If you like, you can create another user with a different name via the Register endpoint. If it has a name that does not start with L, the authorization policy will prevent that user from using this endpoint.

How it works...

This recipe demonstrates the implementation of both role-based and policy-based authorization using JWT tokens in ASP.NET Core. The `GenerateJwtToken` method in `AccountController` now includes both user roles and a way of adding our username as a custom claim to the token. The `[Authorize(Roles = "Admin")]` attribute on our endpoint works thanks to these roles added to the token. Our `[Authorize(Policy = "UsernameStartsWithL")]` attribute works thanks to the custom claims added to the JWT token.

See also...

- The **jwt.io** website is a great resource for learning about JWT tokens. This introductory overview is one of the best explanations out there on how JWT tokens work: `https://jwt.io/introduction`

- Microsoft's documentation on role-based authorization: `https://learn.microsoft.com/en-us/aspnet/core/security/authorization/roles?view=aspnetcore-8.0`

- An excellent article by Andrew Lock on custom authorization policies in ASP.NET Core: `https://andrewlock.net/custom-authorisation-policies-and-requirements-in-asp-net-core/`

Learn more on Discord

To join the Discord community for this book – where you can share feedback, ask questions to the authors, and provide solutions to other readers – scan the QR code or visit the link:

`https://packt.link/aspdotnet9WebAPI`

4

Creating Custom Middleware

In ASP.NET Core, middleware isn't just the backbone – it's the very nervous system of your application. Each piece of middleware is a neuron, connected in a chain of request delegates, firing in sequence to process incoming stimuli. At the heart of this intricate network flows the HTTP context, a pulsating lifeforce that carries vital information through every synapse of your application. In this chapter, we will manipulate the request pipeline to implement practical features that enhance daily API development.

We will start off by creating a custom database performance health check, showcasing how to extend the health check middleware to monitor specific, critical aspects of your application. This custom implementation illustrates the flexibility and extensibility of ASP.NET Core's middleware ecosystem.

Moving beyond health checks, we will explore custom middleware creation with a practical example of adding security headers. This recipe demonstrates how middleware can be used to enhance the security posture of your API without modifying existing endpoints.

Finally, we will culminate with an advanced topic: factory-based middleware for on-the-fly API response transformations.

We are going to cover the following recipes in this chapter:

- Building a health report for your API
- Adding health checks to OpenAPI using the new document transformers
- Creating a custom database performance health check
- Creating custom middleware for adding security headers
- Creating factory middleware for centralized data transformation

Technical requirements

For the recipes in this chapter, you'll need the following:

- **.NET 9 SDK**: Make sure you have `Git` and the **.NET 9 SDK** installed on your machine. The .NET 9 SDK is available here: `https://dotnet.microsoft.com/en-us/download/dotnet/9.0`.

- **SQLite**: We will still be using a SQLite database in this chapter. If you haven't already, it is a good idea to download the free DB Browser (SQLite), which is available here: `https://sqlitebrowser.org/`.

Building a health report for your API

Let's leverage the powerful ASP.NET Core Health Check middleware to monitor and report on the health of our API. In this recipe, we will utilize the Health Check middleware, enhanced with a custom JSON report to provide detailed insights into our API's critical components and dependencies, such as database connectivity. Additionally, we will override HTTP status codes to alert us to potential issues, such as degraded performance, ensuring our API remains robust and reliable.

Getting ready

Clone the starter project we are going to work with here: `https://github.com/PacktPublishing/ASP.NET-9-Web-API-Cookbook/tree/main/start/chapter04/HealthCheck`

How to do it...

1. In your terminal, install the required NuGet packages:

   ```
   dotnet add package Microsoft.Extensions.Diagnostics.HealthChecks
   ```

2. Open the `Program.cs` file and import the `HealthChecks` diagnostics library we are going to work with:

   ```
   using Microsoft.Extensions.Diagnostics.HealthChecks;
   ```

3. At the end of the `ConfigureServices` method, register a `health check` with `AddCheck()`:

   ```
   public void ConfigureServices(IServiceCollection services)
   {
       ...
       services.AddHealthChecks()
           .AddCheck("Database", () =>
           {
   ```

```
            using var connection = new SqliteConnection(
                Configuration.GetConnectionString(
                    "DefaultConnection"));
            try
            {
                connection.Open();
                return HealthCheckResult.Healthy();
            }
            catch (SqliteException)
            {
                return HealthCheckResult.Unhealthy();
            }
        }, tags: new[] { "database" });
```

4. Still in the `Program.cs` file, import the `AspNetCore HealthChecks` namespace:

    ```
    using Microsoft.AspNetCore.Diagnostics.HealthChecks;
    ```

5. Now map a health check endpoint inside our existing `app.UseEndpoints()`. Specify the HTTP status codes returned based on the health check status:

    ```
    app.UseEndpoints(endpoints =>
    {
        endpoints.MapControllers();
        endpoints.MapOpenApi();
        endpoints.MapScalarApiReference();

        endpoints.MapHealthChecks("/api/health",
                                  new HealthCheckOptions
        {
            ResultStatusCodes =
            {
                [HealthStatus.Healthy] =
                    StatusCodes.Status200OK,
                [HealthStatus.Degraded] =
                    StatusCodes.Status200OK,
                [HealthStatus.Unhealthy] =
                    StatusCodes.Status503ServiceUnavailable
            },
    ```

6. On the next line, configure a custom `HealthCheck` report that will be returned as JSON:

```
ResponseWriter = async (context, report) =>
{
    context.Response.ContentType = "application/
                                   json";
    var response = new
    {
        status = report.Status.ToString(),
        checks = report.Entries.Select(entry => new
        {
            name = entry.Key,
            status = entry.Value.Status.ToString(),
            description = entry.Value.Description,
            duration = entry.Value.Duration
        }),
        totalDuration = report.TotalDuration
    };
    await context.Response.
    WriteAsJsonAsync(response);
}
});
```

7. In your terminal, run our API project:

```
dotnet run
```

8. Test the HealthCheck endpoint. If you are using PowerShell, you can check your HealthCheck endpoint with `Invoke-RestMethod`:

```
Invoke-RestMethod -Uri 'https://localhost:5001/api/health'
```

9. You can also test the HealthCheck endpoint with a web browser. *Figure 4.1* shows the HealthCheck result in a web browser:

```
{"status":"Healthy","checks":[{"name":"Database","status":"Healthy","description":null,"duration":"00:00:00.0015948"}],"totalDuration":"00:00:00.0157660"}
```

Figure 4.1 – Viewing our health check in a web browser

How it works...

We began by adding middleware to handle health check requests in our ASP.NET Core application. A health check was registered to verify database connectivity, returning appropriate HTTP status codes (200 OK, 503 Service Unavailable) to signal the API's health. We further customized the health check by generating a detailed JSON report. Finally, we used MapHealthChecks to add a health check endpoint to our API, making it easy to monitor the health of our application.

Adding health checks to OpenAPI using the new document transformers

In all previous versions of ASP.NET Core (before .NET 9), integrating health checks into your OpenAPI documentation (such as Swagger) was surprisingly challenging – especially when using the MapHealthChecks method. The normal workaround was to create an entire health checks controller just so the Healthchecks endpoint would be mapped to OpenAPI.

With the introduction of the Microsoft.AspNetCore.OpenApi namespace in .NET 9, we now have a more elegant solution. This built-in functionality provides **Transformers** – powerful new tools that allow us to modify the OpenAPI document directly via the Program.cs file, integrating our HealthCheck without additional controllers.

Getting ready

You can pick up where we left off in the preceding recipe, or clone the starter project here:

```
https://github.com/PacktPublishing/ASP.NET-9-Web-API-Cookbook/tree/
main/start/chapter04/HealthCheckOpenAPI
```

How to do it...

1. At the top of Program.cs, import the Microsoft.OpenApi.Models namespace:

    ```
    using Microsoft.OpenApi.Models;
    ```

2. In the AddCheck() method in Program.cs, let's modify our HealthCheck to return a description:

    ```
    builder.Services.AddHealthChecks()
        .AddCheck("Database", () =>
        {
            using var connection = new SqliteConnection(
                Configuration.GetConnectionString(
                    "DefaultConnection"));
    ```

```
    try
    {
        connection.Open();
        return HealthCheckResult.Healthy(
            "Database connection is successful");
    }
    catch (SqliteException)
    {
    return HealthCheckResult.Unhealthy(
    "Unable to connect to the database");
            }
        }, tags: new[] { "database" });
    }
```

3. Now let's modify the `AddOpenApi()` method to use a transformer to set general OpenAPI information:

```
    builder.Services.AddOpenApi("chapter4", options =>
        {
            options.AddDocument((document, context,
                cancellationToken) =>
            {
                document.Info = new OpenApiInfo
                {
                    Title = "Chapter 4 API",
                    Version = "v1",
                    Description = "API for demonstrating health
                                    checks"
                };
```

4. Now continue to fill in the `UseTransformer` method. Let's add the path to our `HealthCheck` endpoint:

```
        document.Paths["api/health"] = new OpenApiPathItem
        {
          Operations = new Dictionary<OperationType,
                                        OpenApiOperation>
          {
            [OperationType.Get] = new OpenApiOperation
            {
            Summary = "Health Check",
            Description = "Performs a health check on the
                            application",
              Tags = new List<OpenApiTag> { new OpenApiTag {
```

```
                Name = "Health" } },
            Responses = new OpenApiResponses
            {
            ["200"] = new OpenApiResponse { Description = "OK"
        },

            ["503"] = new OpenApiResponse { Description =
                "Service Unavailable" }
            }
        }
    }
    };
```

5. Finally, close the `UseTransformer` method to return `Task.CompletedTask`:

```
            return Task.CompletedTask;
        });
    });
```

6. Run the API from your terminal:

```
dotnet run
```

7. In a web browser, navigate to `https://localhost:5001/scalar/chapter4#tag/health` to visit the Scalar OpenAPI explorer and check the result.

Figure 4.2 shows us testing out our now documented `HealthCheck`. You can see the description we just added displayed:

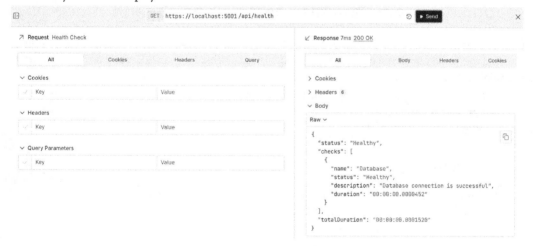

Figure 4.2 – Result of testing the health check we just documented

How it works...

We leveraged the new OpenAPI document transformers feature in ASP.NET Core to seamlessly integrate health checks into the API documentation. ASP.NET Core 9 provides three types of transformers: document transformers for global modifications, operation transformers for endpoint-specific changes, and schema transformers for data model modifications. We used the `AddDocumentTransformer` method to modify the entire OpenAPI document. We first set general API information using `document.Info`. Then, we manually added a new path for our health check endpoint using `document.Paths["api/health"]`. This creates `OpenApiPathItem` with a `GET` operation, complete with a summary, description, tags, and possible response codes. Transformers are similar to filters, but instead of modifying API endpoints, they allow us to transform our OpenAPI documentation – *Transformers! Filters in disguise.*

See also...

- All the amazing things you can do with Transformers in ASP.NET Core 9: `https://learn.microsoft.com/en-us/aspnet/core/fundamentals/minimal-apis/aspnetcore-openapi?view=aspnetcore-9.0#openapi-document-transformers`

- Here is the method for creating an entire controller, for the purposes of registering your `HealthCheck` endpoint with OpenAPI. Note the use of `[FromServices]`: `https://stackoverflow.com/questions/63066572/how-to-add-healthcheck-endpoint-to-apiexplorer-so-that-swashbuck-includes-it-in`

Creating a custom database performance health check

Database performance is a critical factor in system health. A basic connection health check may not offer a thorough assessment of database performance. In this recipe, we'll create a sophisticated, customizable database performance health check that goes beyond simple connectivity tests. We will measure query execution times, configure thresholds, and provide rich diagnostic information. This recipe can provide a template and jumping-off point to create your own custom `HealthChecks` perfectly suited to your Web API.

Getting ready

1. The starter project for this recipe can be found here: `https://github.com/PacktPublishing/ASP.NET-9-Web-API-Cookbook/tree/main/start/chapter04/CustomHealthCheck`

2. Clone the starter project or continue from the previous recipe.

How to do it...

1. In the `Middleware` folder, create a new file called `DatabasePerformanceOptions.cs` and fill in the code for the `DatabasePerformanceOptions` class:

```
namespace Books.Middleware;

public class DatabasePerformanceOptions
{
    public int QueryTimeoutThreshold { get; set; } = 1000;
    public int DegradedThreshold { get; set; } = 500;
    public string TestQuery { get; set; } = "SELECT COUNT(*)
        FROM Books";
}
```

The integer values represent milliseconds. Here, we specify the delay in database communication beyond which communication is considered faulty. We are going to set the default `QueryTimeoutThreshold` to 1 second (1,000 milliseconds) and `DegradedThreshold` to half a second (500 milliseconds).

2. In the same `Middleware` folder, create another file called `DatabasePerformanceHealthCheck.cs`. In this file, fill in the basic class structure for our new `DatabasePerformanceHealthCheck` class:

```
using Microsoft.Extensions.Diagnostics.HealthChecks;

namespace Books.Middleware;

public class DatabasePerformanceHealthCheck : IHealthCheck
{
    public Task<HealthCheckResult> CheckHealthAsync(
        HealthCheckContext context,
        CancellationToken cancellationToken = default)
    {
        throw new NotImplementedException();
    }
}
```

3. Add the required import `using` statements:

```
using System.Data;
using System.Diagnostics;
using Microsoft.Extensions.Diagnostics.HealthChecks;
using Microsoft.Extensions.Options;
```

4. Set up our constructor to pass in the `options` class we recently created. Also, set up the logger and database connection. We will use primary constructor syntax and eschew declaring explicit fields:

```
public class DatabasePerformanceHealthCheck(
    IDbConnection dbConnection,
    ILogger<DatabasePerformanceHealthCheck> logger,
    IOptionsMonitor<DatabasePerformanceOptions> options) :
    IHealthCheck
```

5. Replace `throw new NotImplementedException();` with our registration name and a dictionary to store the results of testing our database:

```
public Task<HealthCheckResult> CheckHealthAsync(
        HealthCheckContext context,
        CancellationToken cancellationToken = default)
{
    var optionsSnapshot = options.Get(
        context.Registration.Name);
    var data = new Dictionary<string, object>();
```

6. Start a `try` block, which will set up the test of our database:

```
try
{
    var stopwatch = Stopwatch.StartNew();
    dbConnection.Open();

    using var command = dbConnection.CreateCommand();
    command.CommandText = optionsSnapshot.TestQuery;
    command.CommandTimeout = optionsSnapshot.
        QueryTimeoutThreshold / 1000;

    using var reader = command.ExecuteReader();
    if (reader.Read())
    {
        var recordCount = reader.GetInt32(0);
        data.Add("RecordCount", recordCount);
    }

    stopwatch.Stop();
    var elapsed = stopwatch.ElapsedMilliseconds;
```

7. Now finish the `try` block by performing our actual threshold checks:

```
data.Add("QueryExecutionTime", elapsed);
data.Add("TestQuery", optionsSnapshot.TestQuery);

if (elapsed < optionsSnapshot.DegradedThreshold)
{
    return Task.FromResult(HealthCheckResult.Healthy(
        $"Database query completed in {elapsed}ms",
        data));
}
else if (elapsed < optionsSnapshot.QueryTimeoutThreshold)
{
    return Task.FromResult(HealthCheckResult.Degraded(
    $"Database query took {elapsed}ms, which is slower than
    expected",
    null));
}
else
{
    Return Task.FromResult(HealthCheckResult.Unhealthy(
    $"Database query took {elapsed}ms, indicating severe
    performance issues",
    null));
}
}
```

8. Add a `catch`. If we run into any problems performing the health check, return an unhealthy result. We need to wrap the synchronous result in a `Task` since the interface requires an `async` return type:

```
catch (Exception ex)
    {
    logger.LogError(ex, "Database health check failed");
    data.Add("ExceptionMessage", ex.Message);
    data.Add("ExceptionStackTrace", ex.StackTrace);
    return Task.FromResult(HealthCheckResult.Unhealthy(
        $"Database query failed: {ex.Message}",
        exception: ex,
        data: data);
    }
```

9. If the database connection is still open, close it:

```
finally
{
    if (dbConnection.State == ConnectionState.Open)
    {
        dbConnection.Close();
    }
}
```

10. In `Program.cs`, import our middleware namespace:

```
using Books.Middleware;
```

11. On the line after where we register our services, configure the connection to our database. For this recipe, we are using SQLite:

```
builder.Services.AddTransient<IDbConnection>(sp =>
    new SqliteConnection(Configuration.
GetConnectionString("DefaultConnection")));
```

12. On the next line, configure the options for our health check, using the `options` class we built:

```
builder.Services.
Configure<DatabasePerformanceOptions>(Configuration.
GetSection("DatabasePerformanceOptions"));
```

13. On the next line, replace the existing `AddHealthChecks()` with our new `DatabasePerformanceHealthCheck`:

```
services.AddHealthChecks()
    .AddCheck<DatabasePerformanceHealthCheck>("database_
performance", tags: ["database"]);
```

14. Now we can just set the values we want to use for our `HealthCheck` in `appsettings.json`:

```
{
  "ConnectionStrings": {
    "DefaultConnection": "Data Source=books.db"
  },
  "DatabasePerformanceOptions": {
    "QueryTimeoutThreshold": 1000,
    "DegradedThreshold": 500,
    "TestQuery": "SELECT COUNT(*) FROM Books"
  }
}
```

15. Now let's test this new `HealthCheck`. Run the API with `dotnet run` in PowerShell:

```
$result = Invoke-RestMethod -Uri https://localhost:5001/api/
health
$result.checks
```

Figure 4.3 shows a healthy result:

```
C:\my-coding-projects> $result.checks

name                   status   description                                 duration
----                   ------   -----------                                 --------
database_performance Healthy Database query completed in 0ms 00:00:00.0001871
```

Figure 4.3 – PowerShell output displaying a successful health check result

How it works...

We created our own custom `HealthCheck` by implementing the `IHealthCheck` interface. Because we used `IHealthCheck`, we can seamlessly integrate with ASP.NET Core's health check system. We used `IDbConnection` to make our custom class as reusable as possible. If reusability is not a priority, you can replace `IDbConnection` with a database-specific connection class that supports asynchronous methods such as `OpenAsync` and `ExecuteAsync`.

Here is what happens when the health check is invoked. It executes a configurable test query against the database, measuring the execution time. This time is then compared against the configurable thresholds (`DegradedThreshold` and `QueryTimeoutThreshold`) to determine the health status. The use of `IOptionsMonitor<DatabasePerformanceOptions>` allows for runtime configuration changes without requiring an application restart. Also, we can modify our threshold options by simply modifying the `appsettings.json` file.

Creating custom middleware for adding security headers

In this recipe, we will create custom middleware to add specific security headers to our API responses. These security headers protect against common web vulnerabilities such as clickjacking, MIME-type confusion attacks, **cross-site scripting** (**XSS**), and unauthorized content injection, thereby enhancing the overall security posture of the application.

Getting ready

The starter project for this recipe can be found here: `https://github.com/PacktPublishing/ASP.NET-9-Web-API-Cookbook/tree/main/start/chapter04/SecurityHeaders`

This recipe picks up where the preceding one left off.

How to do it...

1. In the `Middleware` folder, create the `AddHeadersMiddleware.cs` file in a class called `AddHeadersMiddleware`. Create the skeleton for the class:

```
public class AddHeadersMiddleware
{
    private readonly RequestDelegate _next;

    public AddHeadersMiddleware(RequestDelegate next)
    {
        _next = next;
    }

    public async Task InvokeAsync(HttpContext context)
    {
        await _next(context);

    }
}
```

2. Next, we invoke `RequestDelegate` to invoke the next piece of middleware in the pipeline.

Inside the `InvokeAsync` method, add our security headers.

Place `context.Response.Headers` and add statements inside an `OnStarting()` event handler. We make sure to append the headers here, before returning `Task.Completed`, so that all of our custom headers are added before the HTTP response continues to form:

```
public async Task InvokeAsync(HttpContext context)
    {
        context.Response.OnStarting(() =>
        {
            context.Response.Headers.Append("X-Frame-Options",
                "DENY");
            context.Response.Headers.Append("X-Content-Type-
                Options", "nosniff");
            context.Response.Headers.Append(
                "Content-SecurityPolicy", "default-src 'self';
                script-src 'self'; object-src'none';
                frame-ancestors 'none'; base-uri 'self';");

            return Task.CompletedTask;
        });
```

```
            await _next(context);
    }
```

3. In `Program.cs`, register the middleware early in the pipeline. We typically place security header middleware near the start, after `UseForwardedHeaders()` but before other middleware that might interact with headers or the response:

```
app.UseForwardedHeaders(); app.
UseMiddleware<AddHeadersMiddleware>(); app.UseResponseCaching();
```

4. Run our API with `dotnet run`. Let's test that the headers are correctly being added. Open a PowerShell terminal and type the following:

```
$result = Invoke-WebRequest -Uri "https://localhost:5001/api/
books"
$result.Headers
```

> **Important note**
>
> Our caching and pagination headers are still present in addition to our new security headers.

How it works...

We created a custom piece of middleware to enhance security by adding specific security headers to the HTTP responses. When a request is processed, the middleware first calls the next middleware in the pipeline using `_next(context)`. Before the response is sent, it adds headers such as `X-Frame-Options`, `X-Content-Type-Options`, and `Content-Security-Policy` to the response. We place our middleware early in the pipeline but after `app.UseForwardedHeaders()`, which allows load balancers and reverse proxies to add their necessary headers for routing and forwarding, but early enough that enhanced security before other middleware might interact with headers (such as response caching).

Creating factory middleware for centralized data transformation

Let's build some custom factory middleware that transforms our data. In this example, we will focus on transforming our JSON response into XML. Centralizing data transformation in middleware can allow for easier updates and optimizations. This approach enables your API to seamlessly support multiple data formats without cluttering your controllers with format-specific logic.

If the client requests XML in the header, we can implement middleware that will reformat the response accordingly. This can be an easy way to modify a vast API and support new client data format demands.

Getting ready

Clone the starter project here: `https://github.com/PacktPublishing/ASP.NET-9-Web-API-Cookbook/tree/main/start/chapter04/DataTransformation`.

The starter project is similar to the other recipes in this chapter, so feel free to continue from any previous recipe:

1. Open the project in your favorite code editor.

2. Keep your terminal ready with PowerShell so we can test our data transformations.

How to do it...

1. Create the `IResponseFormatter.cs` file:

```
namespace Books.Middleware;

public interface IResponseFormatterMiddleware : IMiddleware
{
    string GetContentType();
}
```

2. Now create a new file called `XmlFormatterMiddleware.cs`. In this file, let's start filling in the code for our `XmlFormatterMiddleware` class. The first thing we will do is inherit from the interface we just created. Let's also set up some very basic logging:

```
using System.Xml;
using System.Text.Json;

namespace books.Middleware;

public class
XmlFormatterMiddleware(ILogger<XmlFormatterMiddleware> logger) :
IMiddleware
{
```

3. Let's implement the `InvokeAsync` method. When our middleware is invoked, we will check the headers to see what media type is being asked for:

```
public async Task InvokeAsync(HttpContext context,
    RequestDelegate next)
{
    var originalBodyStream = context.Response.Body;

    using (var responseBody = new MemoryStream())
```

```
{
    context.Response.Body = responseBody;

    await next(context);

    if (context.Response.StatusCode == 200 &&
        context.Request.Headers["Accept"]
        .FirstOrDefault()?.Contains(
            "application/xml") == true)
    {
        context.Response.ContentType = "
            application/xml";
        responseBody.Seek(0, SeekOrigin.Begin);
        var responseContent = await new StreamReader(
            responseBody).ReadToEndAsync();
        logger.LogInformation(
            "Original response content:{Content}",
            responseContent);
        var jsonDocument = JsonDocument.Parse(
            responseContent);

        responseBody.SetLength(0);
```

4. On the next line, create an `XmlWriter` object to handle the actual transformations:

```
using (var xmlWriter = XmlWriter.Create(responseBody, new
XmlWriterSettings { Indent = true }))
    {
    xmlWriter.WriteStartDocument();
    xmlWriter.WriteStartElement("root");

    WriteElement(xmlWriter, jsonDocument.RootElement);

     xmlWriter.WriteEndElement();
     xmlWriter.WriteEndDocument();
```

5. Close out the `InvokeAsync` method by resetting the response's content length to match our new output:

```
        responseBody.Seek(0, SeekOrigin.Begin);
        context.Response.ContentLength = responseBody.
                                            Length;
        await responseBody.CopyToAsync(originalBodyStream);
    }
```

```
        context.Response.Body = originalBodyStream;
    }
```

6. In the same class and file, create a method that handles the actual writing to XML:

```
private void WriteElement(XmlWriter writer, JsonElement element)
    {
        switch (element.ValueKind)
        {
            case JsonValueKind.Object:
                foreach (var property in element.
                        EnumerateObject())
                {
                    writer.WriteStartElement(property.Name);
                    WriteElement(writer, property.Value);
                    writer.WriteEndElement();
                }
                break;

            case JsonValueKind.Array:
                foreach (var item in element.EnumerateArray())
                {
                    writer.WriteStartElement("item");
                    WriteElement(writer, item);
                    writer.WriteEndElement();
                }
                break;
```

7. Finally, let's handle the other states a JSON element can be in when parsed:

```
case JsonValueKind.String:
    writer.WriteString(element.GetString());
    break;

case JsonValueKind.Number:
    writer.WriteString(element.GetRawText());
    break;

case JsonValueKind.True:
    writer.WriteString("true");
    break;

case JsonValueKind.False:
    writer.WriteString("false");
    break;
```

```
case JsonValueKind.Null:
    writer.WriteAttributeString("xsi", "nil", "http://www.
w3.org/2001/XMLSchema-instance", "true");
    break;
```

8. Open `Program.cs`, and add the following line right before `AddControllers()`:

    ```
    builder.Services.AddTransient<XmlFormatterMiddleware>();
    ```

    We are using factory-based middleware (implementing `IMiddleware`), which must be registered in the dependency injection container.

9. Now add our middleware to the request pipeline. Add the following line on the line after `app.UseForwardedHeaders()`:

    ```
    app.UseMiddleware<XmlFormatterMiddleware>();
    ```

10. Let's run our Web API. Run it in your IDE or, in the terminal, type the following:

    ```
    dotnet run
    ```

11. Let's test our middleware in PowerShell. Open a terminal and try the following:

    ```
    Invoke-RestMethod -Uri "https://localhost:5001/api/books"
    -Headers @{"Accept" = "application/json"}
    ```

    Notice JSON is returned.

    If we change nothing else but replace `json` with `xml` in the header value, `xml` will be returned to us:

    ```
    Invoke-RestMethod -Uri "https://localhost:5001/api/books"
    -Headers @{"Accept" = "application/xml"}
    ```

How it works...

We built a factory-based middleware that intercepts a JSON response and converts it to XML. `XmlFormatterMiddleware` intercepts the response pipeline after the controller has processed the request. When an incoming request specifies `"application/xml"` in its `Accept` header, the middleware captures the original JSON response, deserializes it into `JsonDocument`, and then transforms it into XML format.

Unlike convention-based middleware, factory-based middleware in ASP.NET Core inherits from `IMiddleware` and is registered in the dependency injection container. This approach allows for greater flexibility and testability, as the middleware can be easily injected with dependencies and unit tested in isolation, making it more maintainable and adaptable to changing requirements.

Get This Book's PDF Version and Exclusive Extras

UNLOCK NOW

Scan the QR code (or go to `packtpub.com/unlock`). Search for this book by name, confirm the edition, and then follow the steps on the page.

Note: Keep your invoice handy. Purchases made directly from Packt don't require an invoice.

5

Creating Comprehensive Logging Solutions

Effective logging is not just a nice-to-have—it's a critical component of building robust, maintainable Web APIs. As our systems grow more complex, we need the ability to track, analyze, and understand everything that happens and has happened to our system. Trying to diagnose a critical issue in production without a comprehensive log trail can be a developer's worst nightmare.

In this chapter, we focus on the most practical and up-to-date techniques for effective logging. We will build structured, centralized logging solutions with a focus on Seq and Serilog. Serilog offers powerful structured logging features while working seamlessly with ASP.NET Core's built-in logging system. Seq, a powerful log management platform, saves us from the tedium of digging through database logs, offering a user-friendly interface for real-time log ingestion, searching, and analysis.

In this chapter, we're going to cover the following recipes:

- Logging all requests with Serilog and Seq
- Improving request logs with custom `DiagnosticContext` properties
- Logging controller and action method names
- Unified request logging – combining ASP.NET Core's `HttpLogging` with Serilog and Seq
- Crafting Serilog log objects in ASP.Net Core controllers
- Configuring Seq and Serilog with an API key

Technical requirements

For the recipes in this chapter, you'll need the following:

- **Docker**: We will be using Docker for the first time. Many of the recipes in this chapter require Docker. Although we will focus on running Docker from the terminal, we recommend first installing the full Docker Desktop:

  - *Download*: You can download Docker Desktop directly from here: `https://www.docker.com/products/docker-desktop/`

  - *Chocolatey*: For Windows users, if you have **Chocolatey** installed, you can install Docker Desktop with this command:

    ```
    choco install docker-desktop
    ```

- **.NET 9 SDK**: All recipes require the .NET 9 SDK: `https://dotnet.microsoft.com/en-us/download/dotnet/9.0`.

- **Code editor and PowerShell**: Feel free to use the code editor of your choice. While we demonstrate HTTP requests using PowerShell's `Invoke-RestMethod` cmdlet, you can easily adapt these examples to use `curl`, `wget`, or your preferred HTTP client.

Logging all requests with Serilog and Seq

There are many community projects for logging ASP.NET Core Web APIs. We are going to focus on **Serilog** for one simple reason. Serilog specializes in working with structured objects and not just text. This is called **structured logging**.

It is typically a bad idea to save logs in your main database. Logging generates a vast amount of information, which can place a significant strain on your main database. Furthermore, your database is optimized to query and return application data, not for the high-volume, write-heavy nature of logging. We will instead use **Seq** as our log sink. Seq is free for local use. In this recipe, we will set up Seq in a Docker container and use the Serilog middleware to log every request.

Getting ready

The starter project for this recipe can be found here: `https://github.com/PacktPublishing/ASP.NET-9-Web-API-Cookbook/tree/main/start/chapter05/SeqWithSerilog`.

How to do it...

1. Confirm that Docker is running.

    We will be using Docker to run our instance of Seq in a container. Let's make sure the Docker daemon is running. Open your terminal and type the following:

    ```
    docker info
    ```

    Look for any error messages that the daemon is not running. You do not want to see anything like this:

    ```
    Server:
    ERROR: error during connect: this error may
    indicate that the docker daemon is not running: Get
    "http://%2F%2F.%2Fpipe%2Fdocker_engine/v1.46/info": open //./
    pipe/docker_engine: The system cannot find the file specified.
    errors pretty printing info
    ```

2. In your code editor, create a new YAML file called docker-compose.yml. Make sure this is in the same folder as our project.

3. Enter the following code into docker-compose.yml:

    ```
    services:
      seq:
        image: datalust/seq:latest
        container_name: seq
        ports:
          - '5341:80'
        environment:
          - ACCEPT_EULA=Y
        volumes:
          - seq_data:/data
    volumes:
      seq_data:
    ```

4. Open your terminal. Make sure you are in the same folder as your project and run the following:

    ```
    docker compose up -d
    ```

5. Install the NuGet packages for Serilog and Seq:

    ```
    dotnet add package Serilog.AspNetCore
    dotnet add package Serilog.Sinks.Seq
    ```

    Now, let's configure our Logger in Program.cs.

6. First, create a new file called `ProgramExtensions.cs` and add the required namespaces:

```
using Serilog;
using Serilog.Events;
```

> **Note**
>
> Even though we are adding extension methods to the `WebApplicationBuilder` class, we do not have to include a `using` statement for `Microsoft.AspNetCore.Builder`, as it's automatically available through implicit global `using` statements in ASP.NET Core 9. These global `using` statements are enabled in your project file via the `<ImplicitUsings>enable</ImplicitUsings>` tag. After building your project, you can see all automatically included namespaces in the `obj/Debug/net9.0/[ProjectName].GlobalUsings.g.cs` file.

7. Still in the `ProgramExtensions.cs` file, let's fill in our `ProgramExtensions` class:

```
public static class ProgramExtensions
{
    public static WebApplicationBuilder ConfigureLogging(this
        WebApplicationBuilder builder)
    {
        Log.Logger = new LoggerConfiguration()
            .MinimumLevel.Debug()
            .MinimumLevel.Override("Microsoft", LogEventLevel.
                                    Information)
            .Enrich.FromLogContext()
            .WriteTo.Console()
            .WriteTo.Seq("http://localhost:5341")
            .CreateLogger();

        builder.Host.UseSerilog();

        return builder;
    }
}
```

> **Note**
>
> The URL `http://localhost:5341` in `WriteTo.Seq()` refers to the Seq server address defined in your `docker-compose.yml` file.

8. Now, let's update `Program.cs` to use our logging configuration. Let's add the two Serilog namespaces we need to the top of the file:

```
using Serilog;
```

9. Now, let's wrap our `Program.cs` startup in a `try-catch` block to properly log application startup and any errors:

```
try
{
    var builder = WebApplication.CreateBuilder(args);

    Log.Information("Starting Web API");
    builder.ConfigureLogging();
```

We log `"Starting Web API"` before we register any services. We then register our configuration logging before any other services.

10. Now, in the same file, skip down to our middleware pipeline. Add Serilog's middleware before anything else in the pipeline:

```
var app = builder.Build();

app.UseSerilogRequestLogging();
app.UseResponseCaching();
```

After `app.Run()`, we will end the `try` block we started in the previous step:

```
app.Run();
}
```

11. On the next line, define a `catch` block. This `catch` block writes a log to Serilog that our API did not start correctly:

```
catch (Exception ex)
{
    Log.Fatal(ex, "Application start-up failed");
    throw;
}
```

12. Add a `finally` clause to flush our log file:

```
finally
{
    Log.CloseAndFlush();
}
```

13. Test our main get endpoint:

```
Invoke-RestMethod "http://localhost:5217/api/books?pageSize=300"
```

The GET request we just made is automatically logged to Seq thanks to the Seq middleware. If we visit `http://localhost:5341` with our web browser, we can see our recent requests in the Seq UI. *Figure 5.1* shows the result of browsing the Seq log in our web browser:

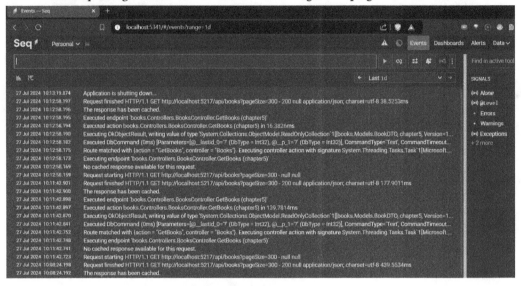

Figure 5.1 – Browsing logs with Seq

How it works...

We set up Seq in a local Docker container. Docker helps us more closely resemble a production environment on our local machine. We specified the image, port, and other configurations in the `docker-compose.yml` file. We then matched the port specified in `docker-compose.yml` with the port in our `Program.cs` file to ensure that Serilog can send logs to Seq correctly. Finally, we used the `UseSerilogRequestLogging` middleware to automatically log each HTTP request and its response. This middleware intercepts every HTTP request and logs details such as the request path, response status code, and the time taken to process the request. `MinimumLevel.Debug()` sets the base logging level, while `MinimumLevel.Override("Microsoft", LogEventLevel.Information)` reduces noise from Microsoft's framework logs. We did not even have to import **ILogger** into our controllers, and we were still able to log every HTTP request.

Improving request logs with custom DiagnosticContext properties

In this recipe, we'll enhance Serilog's request logging middleware to include additional useful information in a single, consolidated log entry for each request. We'll use `IDiagnosticContext` and `EnrichDiagnosticContext` to add custom properties that aren't logged by default.

Getting ready

The starter project can be found here: `https://github.com/PacktPublishing/ASP.NET-9-Web-API-Cookbook/tree/main/start/chapter05/EnrichDiagnosticContext`. Clone the project or continue from the preceding recipe.

Make sure Docker Desktop or your Docker daemon is running with the Seq container. The `docker compose` file is included in the starter project:

```
docker info
docker compose up -d
```

The starter project already has the required Serilog NuGet packages installed.

How to do it...

1. Create a new `Middleware` folder. In this folder, let's create a new file called `DiagnosticContextEnricher.cs`.

2. Add the following class skeleton to `DiagnosticContextEnricher.cs`:

    ```
    using Serilog;
    using Microsoft.AspNetCore.Http;

    namespace Books.Middleware;

    public class DiagnosticContextEnricher
    {
        public void EnrichFromRequest(IDiagnosticContext
            diagnosticContext, HttpContext httpContext)
        {
            ArgumentNullException.ThrowIfNull(diagnosticContext);
            ArgumentNullException.ThrowIfNull(httpContext);
            var request = httpContext.Request;
    ```

3. Let's start adding the custom properties that we want to log.

    First, we will log any query parameters. On the next line, log the query parameters that are sent along with each request:

    ```
    diagnosticContext.Set("QueryParameters", request.QueryString.
    Value ?? "");
    ```

4. On the next line, add the client IP address from `httpContext` and log it:

    ```
    diagnosticContext.Set("ClientIP",httpContext.Connection.
    RemoteIpAddress?.ToString() ?? "unknown");
    ```

5. Let's log the name of the called endpoint. We will use C# pattern matching to elegantly handle both the null check and endpoint declaration in a single line:

```
if (httpContext.GetEndpoint() is {} endpoint)
{
    diagnosticContext.Set("EndpointName", endpoint.DisplayName
        ?? "");
}
```

6. Now, let's log the content type of the response (i.e., whether the response is sending 'application/json', etc.):

```
diagnosticContext.Set("ContentType", httpContext.Response.
ContentType ?? "none");
```

7. Finally, let's track a custom header. Say our API uses X-Cache when a response is returned from the distributed cache. In that scenario, we could log whether or not the X-Cache header is present:

```
var isCached = httpContext.Response.Headers.ContainsKey("X-
Cache");
diagnosticContext.Set("IsCached", isCached);
    }
}
```

If the X-Cache header is present, our custom IsCached property will log true.

8. Open Program.cs and import the namespace for our custom middleware:

```
using Books.Middleware;
```

9. Register DiagnosticContextEnricher as a service:

```
builder.Services.AddSingleton<DiagnosticContextEnricher>();
```

10. Modify the registration of the Serilog middleware. For each HTTP request, we will grab the custom DiagnosticContextEnricher class we created from the dependency injection container and use it to enrich the diagnostic context:

```
app.UseSerilogRequestLogging(options =>
{
    options.EnrichDiagnosticContext = (diagnosticContext,
httpContext) => {
    var enricher = httpContext.RequestServices.
GetRequiredService<DiagnosticContextEnricher>();
    enricher.EnrichFromRequest(diagnosticContext, httpContext);
```

> **Setting the diagnostic context inline**
>
> Instead of creating our own separate class, we always have the option to set custom `diagnosticProperties` when we register the Serilog middleware. This can work well if you are only interested in logging standard HTTP request information that Serilog already provides by default.

11. Let's customize the actual log message. On the next line, modify the `MessageTemplate` property to make a custom log message that features our custom properties:

```
options.MessageTemplate = "HTTP {RequestMethod} {RequestPath}
responded {StatusCode} in {Elapsed:0.0000} ms. IP: {ClientIP},
Endpoint: {EndpointName}, Cached: {IsCached}, Query:
{QueryParameters}";
```

12. Let's continue customizing Serilog's output by enriching `diagnosticContext` with core information about incoming requests:

```
diagnosticContext.Set("RequestHost", httpContext.Request.Host.
Value ?? "");
diagnosticContext.Set("RequestScheme", httpContext.Request.
Scheme);
diagnosticContext.Set("QueryString", httpContext.Request.
QueryString.Value ?? "");
}
});
```

13. Finally, navigate to `ProgramExtensions.cs`, where our basic logger configuration resides. Let's reduce the noise of the default logger by overriding the default ASP.NET Core log level. We will change the overall minimum log level from `Debug` to `Information`. Here is our complete `LoggerConfiguration()`:

```
Log.Logger = new LoggerConfiguration()
    .MinimumLevel.Information()
    .MinimumLevel.Override("Microsoft", LogEventLevel.
                    Information)
    .MinimumLevel.Override("Microsoft.AspNetCore",
                    LogEventLevel.Warning)
    .Enrich.FromLogContext()
    .WriteTo.Console()
    .WriteTo.Seq("http://localhost:5341")
    .CreateLogger();
```

We set the minimum level to `Information` to capture standard operational events, while raising the `Microsoft.AspNetCore` level to `Warning` to avoid cluttering our logs with routine framework messages.

14. Open the terminal and run your application with the following:

    ```
    dotnet run
    ```

    Now, let's test our endpoints.

15. Open your terminal and try the following:

    ```
    Invoke-RestMethod "http://localhost:5217/api/books?pageSize=100"
    ```

16. If you don't have PowerShell, the same request will work with cURL, of course. Open a web browser and navigate to `http://localhost:5341`.

    You should see our recent request logged.

    Figure 5.2 shows our custom properties in a structured Seq log entry:

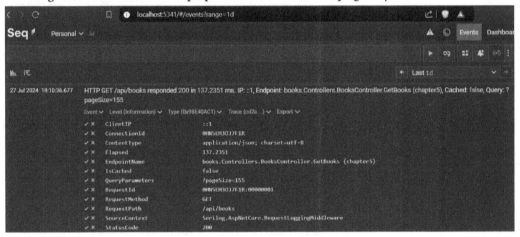

Figure 5.2 – Seq log with custom properties and a custom message template

How it works...

In this recipe, we modified the `EnrichDiagnosticContext` option of `UserSerilogRequestLogging`. This will only enrich HTTP request logs, not all event logs. We added custom data using `DiagnosticContext`'s `Set()` method. Since we have access to `HttpContext`, the life force of our ASP.Net Core Web API, we can retrieve any values that `HttpContext` has available and set them as properties on `IDiagnosticContext`. We encapsulated this enrichment logic in our `DiagnosticContextEnricher` middleware class and used dependency injection to make it available to the request logging pipeline. For each request, we resolved an instance of our enricher and used it to add custom properties to the diagnostic context.

We further customized the displayed logging output with `options.MessageTemplate` to show our custom made properties: `{ClientIP}`, `Endpoint: {EndpointName}`, `Cached: {IsCached}`, and `Query: {QueryParameters}`. If we had not set these properties in our custom EnrichDiagnosticContext class, our message template would simply display null values.

Logging controller and action method names

We can often make debugging a large API easier by logging the exact name of the action method called and what controller class the endpoint is a part of. Often, the action method name and `Controller` class should be obvious from the request path, but in a large API, especially one that has drifted from disciplined naming conventions, including the method and class name of the endpoint can make our life significantly easier. Luckily, ASP.NET Core has a built-in `ControllerActionDescriptor` class in the `Microsoft.AspNetCore.Mvc.Controllers` namespace that we can use with the `GetMetadata<T>()` method to easily display this information.

Getting ready

The starter project can be found here: `https://github.com/PacktPublishing/ASP.NET-9-Web-API-Cookbook/tree/main/start/chapter05/LogControllerAndAction`.

Make sure you have Seq and Docker set up, as described in the *Technical requirements* section at the beginning of this chapter.

How to do it...

1. Open `Program.cs` and add the necessary using statements:

    ```
    using Microsoft.AspNetCore.Mvc.Controllers;
    ```

2. Navigate to where the `UseSerilogRequestLogging` middleware is added to our middleware pipeline. Let's pass additional options to `EnrichDiagnosticContext`:

    ```
    app.UseSerilogRequestLogging(options =>
    {
        options.EnrichDiagnosticContext = (diagnosticContext,
            httpContext) =>
        {
            var actionDescriptor = httpContext.GetEndpoint()?.
                Metadata
                .GetMetadata<ControllerActionDescriptor>();

            if (actionDescriptor is not null)
            {
                diagnosticContext.Set("ActionName",
    ```

```
                                        actionDescriptor.ActionName);
            diagnosticContext.Set("ControllerName",
                actionDescriptor.ControllerName);
        }
    };
```

3. On the next line, still inside of the `UseSerilogRequestLogging` options, let's create a custom message template that prominently shows the controller name and action method name directly in the log statement:

```
options.MessageTemplate = "HTTP {RequestMethod} {RequestPath}
responded {StatusCode} in {Elapsed:0.0000} ms. Controller:
{ControllerName}, Action: {ActionName}";
});
```

4. In your terminal or code editor, start the API:

```
dotnet run
```

5. Open the terminal and test an endpoint:

```
Invoke-RestMethod "http://localhost:5217/api/books?pageSize=50"
```

6. Now, if we navigate to our Seq dashboard, our log message will clearly indicate the method name that was called:

```
HTTP GET  api/books responded 200 in 159.0570 ms. Controller:
  Books, Action: GetBooks
```

The action method and controller class name of the endpoint that was hit are clearly recorded. You can confirm this by navigating to the `BooksController.cs` file and examining the `GetBooks` method on *line 19*.

How it works...

We used the built-in ASP.NET Core `ControllerActionDescriptor` class to configure Serilog to record the name of the method and class used when an endpoint is hit. We also configured our log message to display this information prominently, without having to look in the structured log event properties. This setup can help us more easily debug a large API so we can easily know which classes and methods were involved in each request.

See also

There is a lot more we can do with the simple `ControllerActionDescriptor` class, such as logging endpoint metadata and information on any filters used by the action method. Check out the docs here: https://learn.microsoft.com/en-us/dotnet/api/microsoft.aspnetcore.mvc.controllers.controlleractiondescriptor.

Unified request logging – combining ASP.NET Core's HttpLogging with Serilog and Seq

ASP.NET Core's `HttpLogging` is a middleware provided by Microsoft that automatically logs information about HTTP requests and responses. Introduced with .NET 8, `HttpLogging` tends to be quite verbose by default. In this recipe, we will customize `HttpLogging` and combine it effectively with the Serilog logging middleware.

To achieve this, we will utilize `HttpLogging`'s `CombineLogs` property, which consolidates all enabled logs for a request and response into a single log entry at the end of the request. We will also use the `LoggingFields` property to precisely control what information is logged. Additionally, we'll demonstrate how to adjust logging verbosity based on the environment (development versus production) to manage log volume effectively.

By combining `HttpLogging` with Serilog, we can leverage the detailed HTTP information capture of `HttpLogging` with the powerful structured logging and sink capabilities of Serilog. This approach provides comprehensive yet manageable logging for our ASP.NET Core application.

Getting ready

The starter project for this recipe can be found here: `https://github.com/PacktPublishing/ASP.NET-9-Web-API-Cookbook/tree/main/start/chapter05/HttpLoggingAndSerilog`.

Make sure you have Seq installed and running with Docker, as described in the *Technical requirements* section at the beginning of this chapter.

If you are not starting from the starter project, make sure you have the NuGet package for Serilog installed.

How to do it...

1. Open the `Program.cs` file and add the necessary using statements:

    ```
    using Microsoft.AspNetCore.HttpLogging;
    ```

2. Add and configure the `HttpLogging` service after the existing service configurations:

    ```
    builder.Services.AddHttpLogging(logging =>
    {
        logging.LoggingFields = HttpLoggingFields.RequestMethod
            | HttpLoggingFields.RequestPath
            | HttpLoggingFields.RequestQuery
            | HttpLoggingFields.RequestHeaders
            | HttpLoggingFields.RequestBody
            | HttpLoggingFields.ResponseStatusCode
    ```

```
    | HttpLoggingFields.ResponseHeaders
    | HttpLoggingFields.ResponseBody;

logging.RequestHeaders.Add("Accept");
logging.ResponseHeaders.Add("WWW-Authenticate");
logging.MediaTypeOptions.AddText("application/javascript");
```

> **Important note**
>
> We are logging the `Accept` header instead of logging the sensitive `Authorization` header, which can be a security risk. The `Accept` header is generally safe to log.

3. Still within the `AddHttpLogging` configuration, let's set some environmental settings. Set our configuration to log fewer requests when we are deployed in production versus when our API is running in development:

```
if (builder.Environment.IsDevelopment())
{
    logging.RequestBodyLogLimit = 4096;
    logging.ResponseBodyLogLimit = 4096;
}
else
{
    logging.RequestBodyLogLimit = 1024;
    logging.ResponseBodyLogLimit = 1024;
}
```

4. On the next line, let's set the `CombinesLog` property to `true` and close the `AddHttpLogging` method:

```
logging.CombineLogs = true;
});
```

5. Now, let's register the `ASP.NET Core HttpLogging` middleware in place of the Serilog middleware (already implemented in the starter project).

    Replace the existing `UseSerilogRequestLogging()` with the following:

```
app.UseHttpLogging();
```

    Ensure that this middleware is added before other middleware so that logging captures the entire request pipeline. Our `ProgramExtensions.cs` file already includes `LoggerConfiguration`.

6. Run our application via the terminal:

```
dotnet run
```

7. Open your terminal and test the request with PowerShell or cURL:

```
Invoke-RestMethod "http://localhost:5217/api/books?pageSize=100"
```

8. Open Seq by opening a web browser and navigating to http://localhost:5341.

    In *Figure 5.3*, we can see a very robust HttpLogging log. It is also saved in a structured format thanks to Serilog.

    Note that, in this example, we are even logging the full response body:

Figure 5.3 – The HttpLogging log in Seq

How it works...

HttpLogging is built-in logging middleware that implements ILogger. We can set up HostBuilder to route HttpLogging through Serilog. Because we configured Serilog as the logging provider, logs generated by HttpLogging will go through Serilog. We also used Seq as a sink so we could easily store, work with, and manipulate our log data. We used the powerful CombineLogs property in HttpLogging to combine all of the logs it would generate on a request into one. It's important to keep in mind that CombineLogs only works directly with HttpLogging and not Serilog. However, the combined logs will be processed by Serilog.

Notice how we produced a structured version of a very comprehensive `HttpLogging` log, but we nowhere registered the `UseSerilogRequestLogger` middleware. Instead, `builder.Host.UseSerilog()` added in the `ProgramExtensions.cs` file ensures that Serilog serves as the logging provider and processes our event logs.

One significant improvement in ASP.NET Core's minimal hosting model is how we access environment information. In the older `Startup.cs` pattern, we needed to explicitly inject `IWebHostEnvironment`, store it in a field, and then reference that field. Now, `WebApplicationBuilder` includes the built-in `Environment` property, allowing us to directly check the environment with the `builder.Environment.IsDevelopment` method.

Crafting Serilog log objects in ASP.NET Core controllers

In this recipe, we'll enhance `BooksController` with advanced structured logging techniques using Serilog. We will start with a standard `ILogger` interface, and leverage Serilog's powerful structured logging capabilities to craft detailed, easily queryable log objects. This allows us to capture, query, and analyze complex log data that would be very difficult to manage with traditional string-based logging. We will use `LogContext` to add a consistent scope-wide property to our log. We will also query our log in Seq, using the properties of our structured log objects.

Getting ready

The starting project for this recipe can be found here: `https://github.com/PacktPublishing/ASP.NET-9-Web-API-Cookbook/tree/main/start/chapter05/CraftingDetailedLogObjects`.

We will be using Seq to query our log. Please make sure Seq is set up in a Docker container as per the *Technical requirements* section at the beginning of this chapter.

How to do it...

1. Open the `BooksController.cs` file inside the `Controllers` folder.

2. Import the required namespace for `LogContext`:

    ```
    using Serilog.Context;
    ```

3. Let's import `ILogger<T>` into our controller's constructor. We are using primary constructors in our controller so we only have to pass it as a parameter. Behind the scenes, .NET stores a reference to it in a private field:

    ```
    public class BooksController(IBooksService service,
    ILogger<BooksController> logger) : ControllerBase
    ```

4. We are now going to add logging to the `GetBooks` action method on *line 20*. The first thing we are going to do is wrap the entire method in a `using` statement. This `using` statement will allow `LogContext` to add a property to each structured log object in this method:

```
using (LogContext.PushProperty("EndpointName",
nameof(GetBooks)))
{
    try
    {
```

5. Next, in the `GetBooks` method, let's log both the book count and all of the pagination metadata in a structured Serilog object we will call `@PaginationMetadata`:

```
Response.Headers.Append("X-Pagination", JsonSerializer.
Serialize(paginationMetadata, options));

    logger.LogInformation("Retrieved {BookCount} books.
        Pagination: {@paginationMetadata}",
        pagedResult.Items!.Count, paginationMetadata);
```

6. On the next line, log the HTTP `StatusCode`:

```
    logger.LogInformation("Returning status code {StatusCode}",
        StatusCodes.Status200OK);
```

7. Now, let's create a custom log object, full of information on our endpoint, including query parameters and pagination data. This object will constitute a separate log entry, so we will want the pagination data here also:

```
var logObject = new {
    QueryParameters = new { PageSize = pageSize, LastId = lastId
},
    PaginationMetadata = paginationMetadata,
    BookCount = pagedResult.Items!.Count,
    FirstBookId = pagedResult.Items.FirstOrDefault()?.Id,
    LastBookId = pagedResult.Items.LastOrDefault()?.Id,
    GenreCounts = pagedResult.Items.GroupBy(b => b.Genre)
    .Select(g => new { Genre = g.Key, Count = g.Count() })
};
```

8. Let's assign `logObject` to a structured Serilog object, a `@BookOperationDetails` object:

```
logger.LogInformation("Books retrieved successfully. Details: {@
BookOperationDetails}", logObject);

return Ok(pagedResult.Items);
```

9.   Finally, log the unhappy path. Make sure to pass `Exception` ex into `catch`:

```
catch (Exception ex)
{
    logger.LogError(ex, "Error occurred while fetching
        books. QueryParams: {@QueryParameters}",
    new { pageSize, lastId });
    logger.LogInformation(
        "Returning status code {StatusCode}",
        StatusCodes.Status500InternalServerError);
    return StatusCode(500, "An error occurred while fetching
        books.");
}
```

10.   Open your terminal and run the API:

```
dotnet run
```

11.   Make some requests to our API endpoints to generate logs:

```
Invoke-RestMethod "http://localhost:5217/api/books?pageSize=300"
```

12.   Open a web browser and visit the Seq UI at `http://localhost:5314`.

13.   Let's query our logs for any occurrences of `GetBooks` returning books with `Fiction` in the genre title (case-insensitive):

```
EndpointName = "GetBooks" and BookOperationDetails.
GenreCounts[?].Genre like "%Fiction%"
```

14.   We can also search specifically for the `Science Fiction` genre:

```
EndpointName = "GetBooks" and BookOperationDetails.
GenreCounts[?].Genre like = "Science Fiction"
```

The following screen shows the results of searching for a specific genre (your database may generate different genres):

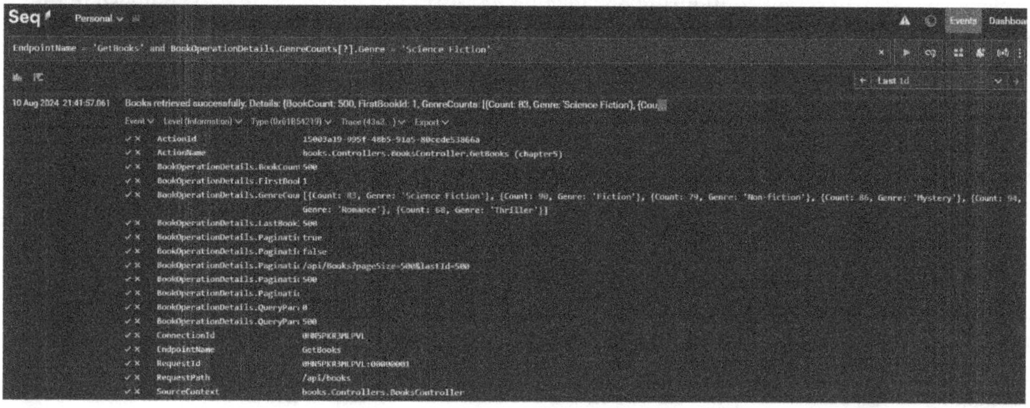

Figure 5.4 – Searching for the Science Fiction genre in GetBooks

How it works...

We used `LogContext.PushProperty` to add the `EndpointName` property to all log statements within this method. This is one way to add standard information to all log statements for a single endpoint.

We then created a custom structured log object for our entire `PaginationMetadata`. We also made a much more complex log object and stored that in `BookOperationDetails`. When logging errors, we also made sure to log what query parameters were used when the error occurred.

Finally, we learned how to query our structured log objects in Seq. Thanks to `LogContext`, we can easily use the endpoint name in our queries. We can also create statements to filter structured log objects based on their properties.

See also

- There are other modern approaches (such as `LoggerMessage.Define`) that do not require `LogContext`. This article gives an excellent overview: `https://andrewlock.net/defining-custom-logging-messages-with-loggermessage-define-in-asp-net-core/`.

- A great overview of how to search and query logs in Seq can be found here: `https://docs.datalust.co/docs/the-seq-query-language`.

Configuring Seq and Serilog with an API Key

In this recipe, we will set up configuring our logging not just in the application code but also in our `appsettings.json` file. We will set up login information for the Seq browser, generate an API key, and reference it securely in our configuration. This will allow multiple applications and APIs to use the same centralized logging sink. This way, you can monitor, analyze, and troubleshoot across your entire system. Additionally, we'll explore how to manage different configuration settings for various deployment environments.

Getting ready

The starter project code can be found here: `https://github.com/PacktPublishing/ASP.NET-9-Web-API-Cookbook/tree/main/start/chapter05/ConfigureSettings`.

Make sure you have the ability to run Seq in a Docker container as per the *Technical requirements* section at the beginning of this chapter.

How to do it...

1. First, let's open Seq in our web browser at `http://localhost:5341/`.

    If Seq is not running, open your terminal and start Seq via the `docker compose` file in the project:

    ```
    docker compose up -d
    ```

2. In the Seq user interface, click on **Settings** and click **ADD API KEY** to create an API key. This will register our API distinctly from other applications writing logs to our Seq server. The following screenshot shows the correct **Settings** menu in Seq:

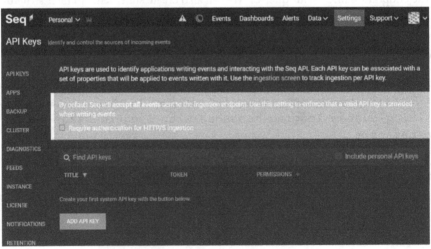

Figure 5.5 – Adding an API key in Seq

3. Let's fill in the **TITLE** value as `WebAPICookbook`. We will leave **PERMISSIONS** as **ingest**. We will leave the other defaults. Click **Save Changes**.

4. Copy the generated API token. Here is the token Seq generated for me: `6bjJzX1QAwtzck7lslZ0`.

5. Open the terminal. Make sure you are in the same root directory as your project.

6. Let's use `dotnet` secrets to add this API key as a secret. First, initialize user secrets for the project if you haven't already:

```
dotnet user-secrets init
```

7. Now, add the Seq API key as a secret:

```
dotnet user-secrets set "Seq:ApiKey" "6bjJzX1QAwtzck7lslZ0"
```

> **Note**
> Replace `"6bjJzX1QAwtzck7lslZ0"` with the API key you generated in *step 4*.

8. Install the NuGet packages for the Serilog sink:

```
dotnet add package Serilog.Sinks.Console
dotnet add package Serilog.Sinks.File
dotnet add package Serilog.Sinks.Seq
```

9. Open `appsettings.json`. Let's add a Serilog configuration object right after our `"Logging"` configuration, which explicitly specifies what Serilog sinks we would like to use:

```
"Logging": {
    "LogLevel": {
        "Default": "Information",
        "Microsoft.AspNetCore": "Warning"
    }
},
"Serilog": {
    "Using": ["Serilog.Sinks.Console", "Serilog.Sinks.File",
    "Serilog.Sinks.Seq"],
    "MinimumLevel": {
        "Default": "Information",
        "Override": {
            "Microsoft": "Warning",
            "System": "Warning"
        }
    },
```

10. On the next line, add the `WriteTo` configuration object to specify the sinks. This will configure logging to the console, a file, and Seq. Add the opening array bracket and first two sink configurations, but do not add the closing bracket yet as we'll add one more sink in the next step:

```
"WriteTo": [
  { "Name": "Console" },
  {
    "Name": "File",
    "Args": {
      "path": "./logs/log-.txt",
      "rollingInterval": "Day",
      "retainedFileCountLimit": 7,
      "outputTemplate": "{Timestamp:yyyy-MM-dd HH:mm:ss.fff zzz}
        [{Level:u3}] {Message:lj}{NewLine}{Exception}"
    }
  }
```

The preceding configuration also states that we will write logs to a file. To keep this file from getting out of hand, we will only write one day's logs to a file, before creating a new file for the next day's log. The – character in `log-.txt` will fill in the current day's date into our file path.

11. We will add one more property to our `WriteTo` array – an object for configuring Seq:

```
  {
    "Name": "Seq",
    "Args": {
      "serverUrl": "http://localhost:5341",
      "apiKey": ""
    }
  }
],
```

We specified a default `serverUrl`, which will be the fallback default for local development. We left `apiKey` empty as we will get it from secrets when our API starts up.

12. On the next line, let's specify what enrichers we want to add. Enrichers add additional logging details to all logs globally:

```
"Enrich": [
    "FromLogContext",
    "WithMachineName",
    "WithThreadId",
    "WithExceptionDetails"
  ],
  "Properties": { "Application": "ASP.NET-9-Web-API-Cookbook" },
```

13. Close appsettings.json and modify or create appsettings.Development.json in our project root. Add the following object after the default logging:

```
{
  "Serilog": {
    "MinimumLevel": {
      "Default": "Debug",
      "Override": {
        "Microsoft": "Information",
        "System": "Information"
      }
    }
  }
}
```

14. Open the ProgramExtensions.cs file. This file currently extends the WebApplicationBuilder class's Program.cs file. At the bottom of the ProgramExtensions class, let's add two helper methods that we will need to grab our Seq configuration from appsettings.json.

Let's start by creating a static helper method to get the GetSeqUrl configuration:

```
private static string GetSeqUrl(IConfiguration configuration)
{
    var seqUrl = configuration["Seq:Url"];
    if (string.IsNullOrEmpty(seqUrl))
    {
        seqUrl = Environment.GetEnvironmentVariable("SEQ_URL");
    }
    return string.IsNullOrEmpty(seqUrl) ? "http://
localhost:5341" : seqUrl;
}
```

15. Now, on the next line, let's create a helper method to get our API key from dotnet secrets. If you recall, we set up dotnet secrets after we got our API key from Seq:

```
private static string GetSeqApiKey(IConfiguration configuration)
{
    return configuration["Seq:ApiKey"] ??
            Environment.GetEnvironmentVariable("SEQ_API_KEY") ??
            throw new InvalidOperationException("Seq API key not
found.");
}
```

16. Still in `ProgramExtensions.cs`, modify the main `ConfigureLogging` extension method at the top of the file. We will start by creating the logs directory. Place this on the first line of the `ConfigureLogging` method:

```
public static WebApplicationBuilder ConfigureLogging(this
WebApplicationBuilder builder)
{
Directory.CreateDirectory(Path.Combine(Directory.
GetCurrentDirectory(), "logs"));
```

17. Still in `ProgramExtensions.cs`, on the next line, let's delete the entire `Log.Logger = new LoggerConfiguration()` method chain.

18. On the next line, complete the `ConfigureLogging` method by replacing the existing `builder.Host.UseSerilog();` line with the following code. This configures our Web API to use our server URL and API key:

```
builder.Host.UseSerilog((context, services, configuration) =>
configuration .ReadFrom.Configuration(context.Configuration)
.ReadFrom.Services(services)
.Enrich.FromLogContext()
.WriteTo.Seq(
    serverUrl:GetSeqUrl(context.Configuration),
    apiKey:GetSeqApiKey(context.Configuration)));
  return builder;
  }
}
```

Note that when we use `.ReadFrom.Configuration(context.Configuration)`, Serilog will load most settings from our `appsettings.json` file. This includes `MinimumLevel`, sink configurations (`Console` and `File`), and enrichers. We only need to explicitly configure the Seq sink in code because it needs our helper methods to handle the URL and API key securely.

19. In the `Program.cs` file, verify that the `UseSerilogRequestLogging` middleware is placed before any other middleware in the pipeline:

```
app.UseSerilogRequestLogging();
```

20. Now, run and test our API in the terminal:

```
dotnet run
Invoke-RestMethod "http://localhost:5217/api/books?pageSize=200"
```

Our endpoints should be logged normally via the Serilog middleware.

> **Troubleshooting**
>
> If you encounter any issues running the API, make sure the API key is indeed listed as a secret. You can see what secrets are saved via the dotnet command-line tool. Open the terminal and run the following in the root directory of your project:
>
> ```
> dotnet user-secrets list
> ```

How it works...

We set up Serilog and Seq via our `appsettings.json` file. We also left room for other JSON configuration files based on the environment. Next, we configured global enrichers directly in the JSON file. We then generated an API key and used the built-in .NET CLI tool dotnet secrets to store the key. Finally, we created helper methods for retrieving our API key and other settings.

When it comes to the location of the Seq server, our code is currently checking the `appsettings.json` and `appsettings.Development.json` files and the `SEQ_URL` environment variable. For deployment targets, we can add additional JSON deployment files or set the `SEQ_URL` environment variables in a `.env` file locally. When working with `.env` files, we can use the `dotnet-env` library to load environment configurations into our application.

See also

- For more advanced scenarios, especially when deployed to cloud environments, it is usually a good idea to use something such as Azure Secrets. Setting up Azure Secrets is very similar to what we did here: `https://learn.microsoft.com/en-us/azure/key-vault/secrets/secrets-best-practices`.

- The Seq documentation for setting up secret keys is filled with great information such as generating a secret key from the CLI: `https://docs.datalust.co/docs/secret-key-storage`.

- See the Seq documentation for an overview of working with API keys in Seq: `https://docs.datalust.co/docs/api-keys`.

6

Real-Time Communication with SignalR

This chapter explores **SignalR**, Microsoft's powerful solution for real-time, bidirectional communication that takes us beyond traditional REST APIs. While REST excels at standard request-response patterns, modern applications often demand instant updates and interactive experiences. Think of real-time chat applications, live dashboards displaying IoT sensor data, sports scores updating in real time, or collaborative document editing where multiple users see their changes instantly.

The true power of SignalR lies in how it abstracts away the complexity of WebSocket connections, such as managing the client-server handshake and connection. WebSockets, the primary transport protocol used by SignalR, operates over TCP/IP, providing full-duplex communication that's more efficient than HTTP polling while maintaining TCP's reliability guarantees. While not as low-latency as UDP-based protocols (which are often preferred for video streaming or high-frequency gaming), WebSocket strikes an excellent balance for most real-time web applications where reliable message delivery is crucial.

It gets better: SignalR is not limited to WebSocket. When WebSocket connections are unavailable or disrupted, SignalR will automatically fall back to alternative transport methods, such as long-polling or server-sent events, if the connection is disrupted. This ensures consistent real-time functionality. If the WebSocket connection fails, SignalR has a backup plan.

In this chapter, we're going to cover the following main topics:

- Creating a real-time opinion poll in SignalR
- JWT authentication flow – identity from controller login to SignalR connection
- Invoking a hub method from an HTTP controller – announcing user login
- User customization with `IUserIdProvider`
- Sending direct messages via SignalR
- Implementing admin-controlled group management in SignalR

Technical requirements

For the recipes in this chapter, you'll need the following:

- **.NET 9 SDK**: SignalR is now included out of the box with .NET, so there is nothing to install.

- **Terminal emulator**: A terminal emulator that can perform splits is recommended. To see the power of SignalR, it is useful to be able to connect from multiple clients at once.

- **SQLite**: We will be using SQLite as the database in all recipes in this chapter. If you would like to examine the data manually, we recommend downloading `https://sqlitebrowser.org/`.

Creating a real-time opinion poll in SignalR

In this recipe, we will build a real-time opinion poll system that demonstrates SignalR's ability to broadcast data instantly to multiple connected clients. Our poll will track votes between two classic gaming consoles. Anonymous users will be able to cast their votes and see the results update in real time across all connected clients.

A key feature of this implementation is how it leverages SignalR's connection management to track unique clients without requiring user registration. This allows us to prevent duplicate voting while maintaining anonymity.

Getting ready

We will be using SQLite in this recipe. If you would like to take a look at the data we will be collecting, please download `https://sqlitebrowser.org/`.

Make sure you have the latest version of the EF Core CLI tools installed:

```
dotnet tool update --global dotnet-ef
```

Or you can install it for the first time as follows:

```
dotnet tool install --global dotnet-ef
```

Clone the starter project here: `https://github.com/PacktPublishing/ASP.NET-9-Web-API-Cookbook/tree/main/start/chapter06/OpinionPoll`.

The starter project includes a console application necessary for testing this recipe. We will add our code to the project in the `SignalRServer` subfolder. At this point, it is only a very basic Web API project skeleton. While the completed version in the repository includes a web-based client, we'll focus on the console client for testing during development.

How to do it...

1. In the `SignalRServer` project, open the `Models` folder. Create a `Vote.cs` file. In this file, let's create a model to represent a user vote:

    ```
    namespace OpinionPoll.Data;

    public record Vote
    {
        public int Id { get; set; }
        public int Choice { get; set; }
        public DateTime Timestamp { get; set; }
        public required string ConnectionId { get; set; }
    }
    ```

2. Still in the `Models` folder, let's create a record for voting results in a new file called `VoteResult.cs`:

    ```
    namespace OpinionPoll.Data;

    public record VoteResult(int Choice, int Count);
    ```

3. In the `Data` folder, create a file called `VoteDbContext.cs`.

4. In `VoteDbContext.cs`, add our EF Core database context:

    ```
    using Microsoft.EntityFrameworkCore;

    namespace OpinionPoll.Data;

    public class VoteDbContext : DbContext
    {
        public VoteDbContext(DbContextOptions<VoteDbContext>
            options) : base(options) { }

        public DbSet<Vote> Votes =>Set<Vote>();
    }
    ```

5. Open the `Program.cs` file and import the SQLite namespace:

    ```
    using Microsoft.EntityFrameworkCore;
    ```

6. After `AddControllers()`, specify a local SQLite file to act as our database:

    ```
    builder.Services.AddDbContext<VoteDbContext>(options =>
        options.UseSqlite("Data Source=./Data/Data.db")
    );
    ```

7. Create an initial migration for our database:

    ```
    dotnet ef migrations add InitialCreate
    ```

8. Apply the migration to create the database:

    ```
    dotnet ef database update
    ```

9. Open the `Program.cs` file and add the namespaces we will use for our SignalR hubs and data:

    ```
    using OpinionPoll.Data;
    using OpinionPoll.Hubs;
    ```

10. Still in `Program.cs`, let's import SignalR. SignalR is already included with ASP.NET Core, so there is no need to install any new NuGet packages. We also don't have to import any new namespaces. On a line after `var app = builder.Build()`, register SignalR:

    ```
    builder.Services.AddSignalR();
    ```

11. In the Hubs folder, create a new file called `VotingHub.cs` and pass our database context into the constructor:

    ```
    using Microsoft.AspNetCore.SignalR;
    using Microsoft.EntityFrameworkCore;
    using OpinionPoll.Data;

    namespace OpinionPoll.Hubs;

    public class VotingHub : Hub
    {
        private readonly VoteDbContext _context;

        public VotingHub(VoteDbContext context)
        {
            _context = context;
        }
    }
    ```

12. For our voting method, we only want to accept an input of 1 or 2. If an invalid input is sent by the client, we want to send a message back to them:

    ```
    public async Task Vote(int choice)
    {
    if (choice != 1 && choice != 2)
    {
        await Clients.Caller.SendAsync("ReceiveMessage", "Invalid
        choice. Please vote 1 for Super Nintendo or 2 for Sega
    ```

```
            Genesis.");
             return;
    }
```

13. We also want to stop the same client from voting twice:

```
    var connectionId = Context.ConnectionId;
        if (await _context.Votes.AnyAsync(v => v.ConnectionId ==
            connectionId))
        {
            await Clients.Caller.SendAsync("ReceiveMessage", "You
            have already voted.");
            return;
        }
```

Context versus _context

The Context property (with capital C) comes from the **SignalR Hubs** base class and provides information about the current connection, while _context is our injected database context. The Hub.Context.ConnectionId property gives us a unique identifier for each client connection, which is why we marked it as required in our voting record.

---

14. Finally, let's record the vote and return the current poll results:

```
    try
    {
        var vote = new Vote {
            Choice = choice, Timestamp = DateTime.UtcNow,
            ConnectionId = connectionId };
        _context.Votes.Add(vote);
        await _context.SaveChangesAsync();

        var results = await GetVoteResults();
        await Clients.All.SendAsync("ReceiveVoteResults", results);
        await Clients.Caller.SendAsync(
            "ReceiveMessage",
            $"Your vote for option {choice} has been recorded.");
    }
    }
```

15. To safely record votes, let's use a catch to handle any errors that may occur when trying to record a vote:

```
    catch (Exception ex)
    {
```

```
        Console.WriteLine($"Error recording vote: {ex.Message}");
        await Clients.Caller.SendAsync(
            "ReceiveMessage",
            "An error occurred while recording your vote.
            Please try again.");
    }
}
```

16. Create a helper method to return the current tally of total votes recorded. We then send a message to our attached clients, telling clients to execute their assigned action for `ReceiveVoteResults`:

```
public async Task GetCurrentResults()
{
    var results = await GetVoteResults();
    await Clients.Caller.SendAsync(
        "ReceiveVoteResults", results);
}
```

17. Let's use a simple LINQ group by to get full vote results from the database:

```
private async Task<List<VoteResult>> GetVoteResults()
{
    return await _context.Votes
        .GroupBy(v => v.Choice)
        .Select(g => new VoteResult(g.Key, g.Count()))
        .ToListAsync();
}
```

18. Go back to the `Program.cs` file. Register our new SignalR hub on the line before `app.MapControllers();`:

```
app.MapHub<VotingHub>("/votingHub");
```

19. Open a terminal window, make sure you have navigated to the root of the `SignalRServer` folder, and start the API server:

    dotnet run

    Keep this terminal window open – closing it will stop the server.

20. In a new terminal window, let's navigate to the `SignalRClient` folder included in the starter project and run it:

    dotnet run

The client should automatically connect to the server we created as long as it is running. To test multiple clients, open additional terminal windows (or additional splits in tmux or Windows Terminal) and run `dotnet run` in each. When prompted for the URL, enter `https://localhost:7031/votingHub`. The client will then connect to the SignalR server.

The end project also includes a web-based client if you prefer testing from your web browser (see the following instructions).

When one client casts a vote, all other connected clients instantly receive the updated results in real time. *Figure 6.1* is a screenshot of three clients using the application via terminal splits:

```
SignalR Hub Message: You have already voted.        nt\
Please specify the action:                          C:\my-coding-projects\chapter6c\signalRclient [(m
1 - Cast vote for Super Nintendo                    aster)]> dotnet run
2 - Cast vote for Sega Genesis                      Please enter the URL of your SignalR hub and pres
r - Get current results                             s enter
q - Exit the program                                Please use this format http://myUrl.com/myHub
r                                                   http://localhost:5043/votingHub
Current Results:                                     Connected to the SignalR hub.
Please specify the action:                          Please specify the action:
1 - Cast vote for Super Nintendo                    1 - Cast vote for Super Nintendo
2 - Cast vote for Sega Genesis                      2 - Cast vote for Sega Genesis
r - Get current results                             r - Get current results
q - Exit the program                                q - Exit the program
Super Nintendo: 25 votes                            2
Sega Genesis: 13 votes                              Please specify the action:
Current Results:                                    1 - Cast vote for Super Nintendo
Super Nintendo: 26 votes                            2 - Cast vote for Sega Genesis
Sega Genesis: 13 votes                              r - Get current results
Current Results:                                    q - Exit the program
Super Nintendo: 27 votes                            Current Results:
Sega Genesis: 13 votes                              Super Nintendo: 27 votes
Current Results:                                    Sega Genesis: 14 votes
Super Nintendo: 27 votes                            SignalR Hub Message: Your vote for option 2 has b
Sega Genesis: 14 votes                              een recorded.
```

```
1 - Cast vote for Super Nintendo
2 - Cast vote for Sega Genesis
r - Get current results
q - Exit the program
SignalR Hub Message: You have already voted.
Current Results:
Super Nintendo: 27 votes
Sega Genesis: 13 votes
Current Results:
Super Nintendo: 27 votes
Sega Genesis: 14 votes
```

```
r - Get current results
q - Exit the program
Current Results:
Super Nintendo: 27 votes
Sega Genesis: 14 votes
```

```
Invalid action. Please try again.
Please specify the action:
1 - Cast vote for Super Nintendo
2 - Cast vote for Sega Genesis
```

Figure 6.1 – Multiple clients in the terminal connected to a SignalR hub

How it works...

We created a SignalR hub that allows anonymous connected users to vote in a real-time opinion poll. Multiple clients can connect to the same hub. Clients send their votes via the `Vote()` method. After each vote, the `GetCurrentResults()` hub method broadcasts the current tally to all clients. SignalR takes care of the complexities of maintaining this real-time exchange and spares us the need for setting up complex WebSocket implementations. We mapped this new SignalR hub to the `votingHub` path, similar to a standard REST controller endpoint.

Once connected, a client receives real-time updates of the vote tally through the `GetCurrentResults` method. The `Vote` method ensures that only the inputs we decided to be valid (1 or 2 in this case) will be accepted.

> ### Browser client
>
> You can test the application we just built with a web browser. The end version of this project in the Packt repo already has a web page set up to interact with the application we built. Simply run the `SignalRServer` project with **dotnet run** and point your web browser to `https://localhost:7031/index.html`. Feel free to open multiple browser tabs to connect to our server as multiple clients. You can find the end version of this project here: `https://github.com/PacktPublishing/ASP.NET-9-Web-API-Cookbook/tree/main/end/chapter06/OpinionPoll/SignalRServer`.

JWT authentication flow – identity from controller login to SignalR connection

When building real-time applications with SignalR, a common challenge is maintaining user identity across both HTTP endpoints and WebSocket connections. How do we transfer a user's identity from a normal REST HTTP controller login to a SignalR hub – in such a way that the user's auth information can be used in real-time SignalR communication? In this recipe, we will start with a basic HTTP controller for user registration and login, then pass the authenticated user's identity to a chat room application. We will accomplish this by using SignalR's built-in ability to get a user identity from a JWT `NameIdentifier` claim.

Getting ready

The starter project for this recipe can be found here: `https://github.com/PacktPublishing/ASP.NET-9-Web-API-Cookbook/tree/main/start/chapter06/JWTNameIdentifier`.

Before starting, ensure you have a development certificate installed:

```
dotnet dev-certs https --trust
```

How to do it...

1. We will be working with the `SignalRServer` project. Let's begin by opening the `AuthController.cs` file and add a new claim for `NameIdentifier` right after the existing Name claim:

    ```
    private string GenerateJwtToken(string userName,
        IList<string> roles)
    {
        var claims = new List<Claim>
        {
            new Claim(ClaimTypes.Name, userName),
            new Claim(ClaimTypes.NameIdentifier, userName),

            // ... rest of the method ...
    }
    ```

2. Create a new file in the `Hubs` folder called `MessagingHub.cs`. In this file, let's start implementing a new SignalR hub. We will import the existing `UserConnectionManager` service only for adding and removing connections:

    ```
    using Microsoft.AspNetCore.SignalR;
    using SignalRServer.Services;

    namespace SignalRServer.Hubs;

    public class MessagingHub(IUserConnectionManager
    userConnectionManager) : Hub
    {
    ```

3. Let's create an `OnConnectedAsync` method that reads the `NameIdentifier` claim from the JWT and broadcasts a message:

    ```
    public override async Task OnConnectedAsync()
    {
        var username = Context.UserIdentifier ?? "Anonymous";
        userConnectionManager.AddConnection(
            username, Context.ConnectionId);
        await Clients.All.SendAsync("UserConnected", username);
        await base.OnConnectedAsync();
    }
    ```

    `userConnectionManager.AddConnection` simply wraps SignalR's `connections.Add()`.

4. Now let's create a Hub method for disconnecting a user:

    ```
    public override async Task OnDisconnectedAsync(
        Exception exception)
    {
        var username = Context.UserIdentifier ?? "Anonymous";
        userConnectionManager.RemoveConnection(
            username, Context.ConnectionId);
        await Clients.All.SendAsync(
            "UserDisconnected", username);
        await base.OnDisconnectedAsync(exception);
    }
    ```

    This removes the user from HubConnection.

5. Finally, let's implement a Hub method that can post a message in the chat room:

    ```
    public async Task SendMessage(string message)
    {
        var username = Context.UserIdentifier ?? "Anonymous";
        await Clients.All.SendAsync(
            "ReceiveMessage", username, message);
    }
    ```

6. Open Program.cs and import the namespace for our new hub at the top of the file:

    ```
    using SignalRServer.Services;
    ```

7. Now, register our new hub; after app.MapControllers(), add the following:

    ```
    app.MapHub<MessagingHub>("/messagingHub");
    ```

8. Configure JWT authentication for SignalR in Program.cs. Unlike regular HTTP requests where JWTs are sent in the authorization header, SignalR needs a different approach for its various transport methods (WebSocket, server-sent events, long polling). We'll configure the JWT middleware to also look for tokens in the query string:

    ```
    options.Events = new JwtBearerEvents
    {
        OnMessageReceived = context =>
        {
            var accessToken = context.Request.Query["access_token"];
            var path = context.HttpContext.Request.Path;
            if (!string.IsNullOrEmpty(accessToken) &&
                path.StartsWithSegments("/messagingHub"))
            {
                context.Token = accessToken;
    ```

```
        }
        return Task.CompletedTask;
    }
};
```

This configuration allows clients to connect to our SignalR hub by appending their JWT as a query parameter. This approach works consistently across all SignalR transport methods, whereas the standard authorization header would only work with HTTP-based transports.

9. Run our API from the terminal with the following:

```
dotnet run
```

The starter project comes with two clients for connecting to the repo. You can navigate to `https://localhost:7031/index.html` and use the web browser client (included with the `SignalRServer` project) or start the console app in the `consoleClient` folder. Feel free to use both at the same time, as was done in *Figure 6.2*:

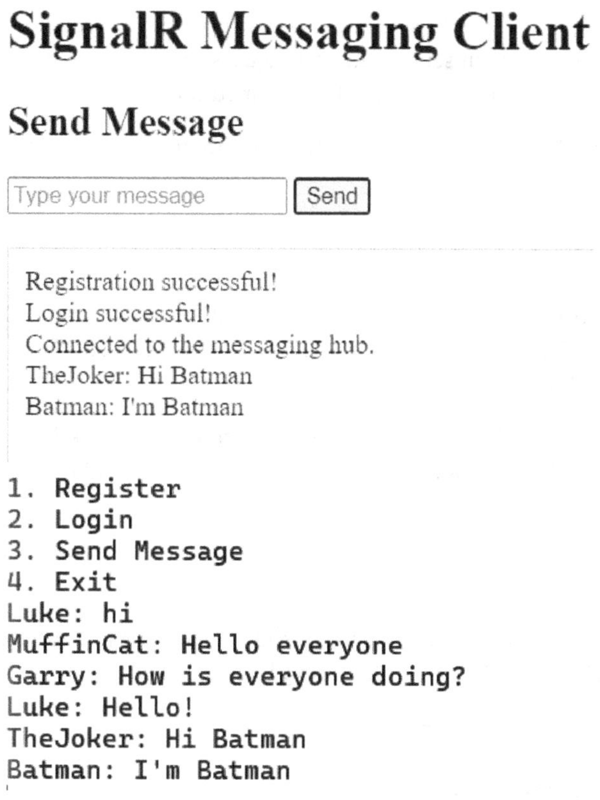

SignalR Messaging Client

Send Message

| Type your message | Send |

Registration successful!
Login successful!
Connected to the messaging hub.
TheJoker: Hi Batman
Batman: I'm Batman

```
1. Register
2. Login
3. Send Message
4. Exit
Luke: hi
MuffinCat: Hello everyone
Garry: How is everyone doing?
Luke: Hello!
TheJoker: Hi Batman
Batman: I'm Batman
```

Figure 6.2 – The same chat room in the browser and the terminal

In addition to the web and console clients shown in *Figure 6.2*, you can interact with the authentication endpoints directly through the OpenAPI documentation at `https://localhost:7031/scalar/chapter6`. Here you can test user registration and generating JWTs without the SignalR client connections.

How it works...

We took a basic Web API authentication controller that implemented ASP.NET Core identity and JWT authentication. We used SignalR's built-in capability to read the `NameIdentifier` claim from a JWT and used that to pass a username via our JWT. The `NameIdentifier` claim is what SignalR will use by default to identify users.

Invoking a hub method from an HTTP controller – announcing user login

In this recipe, we will explore how to invoke hub methods not from a SignalR client but from HTTP Web API controller endpoints on our server. This technique is particularly useful for adding contextual information (such as locale) without cluttering the hub methods.

We will modify our HTTP POST login endpoint to announce to all connected SignalR clients when a new client has logged in.

Getting ready

You can clone the starter project here: `https://github.com/PacktPublishing/ASP.NET-9-Web-API-Cookbook/tree/main/start/chapter06/HubInController` or continue from the preceding recipe.

SignalR is always tightly coupled with a client. In the project folder, there is both a console client you can use in the terminal and a web page in the server project that is set up to work with this example. Use either or both to test this recipe.

How to do it...

1. The first thing we have to do is upgrade the provided messaging hub to a typed hub. Let's create a new file in the Hubs folder called `IMessagingClient.cs`:

    ```
    namespace SignalRServer.Hubs;

    public interface IMessagingClient
    {
        Task ReceiveMessage(string user, string message);
        Task UserConnected(string username);
    ```

```
    Task UserDisconnected(string username);
    Task UserLoggedIn(string username);
}
```

2. Open `MessagingHub.cs` and convert it into a typed hub by inheriting from `Hub<T>` with our new interface as the type:

```
public class MessagingHub(IUserConnectionManager
userConnectionManager) : Hub<IMessagingClient>
```

3. Still in `MessagingHub.cs`, since we are using a typed hub, we can no longer simply use `SendAsync()` followed by the method name. Instead, we must modify each `Clients.All` to directly call the method defined in the interface:

```
public override async Task OnConnectedAsync()
    {
        var username = Context.UserIdentifier ?? "Anonymous";
        userConnectionManager.AddConnection(
            username, Context.ConnectionId);
        await Clients.All.UserConnected(username);
        await base.OnConnectedAsync();
    }
    public override async Task OnDisconnectedAsync(
        Exception exception)
    {
        var username = Context.UserIdentifier ?? "Anonymous";
        userConnectionManager.RemoveConnection(
            username, Context.ConnectionId);
        await Clients.All.UserDisconnected(username);
        await base.OnDisconnectedAsync(exception);
    }
```

4. In the same file, on the next line, we also need to update the `SendMessage` method:

```
public async Task SendMessage(string message)
{
    var username = Context.UserIdentifier ?? "Anonymous";
    await Clients.All.ReceiveMessage(username, message);
}
```

5. In the same folder, create a new file called `MessagingHubExtensions.cs`. In that file, create a simple extension method:

```
using Microsoft.AspNetCore.SignalR;
namespace SignalRServer.Hubs;
```

```
public static class MessagingHubExtensions
{
    public static async Task AnnounceUserLogin(
        this IHubContext<MessagingHub, IMessagingClient>
            hubContext,
        string username)
    {

        var message = $"{username} has logged in.";
        await hubContext.Clients.All.ReceiveMessage(
            "System", message);
    }
}
```

6. Now, import the typed hub into our HTTP AuthController.cs. Import our Hubs namespace and add our typed hub as yet another parameter in our controller's constructor:

```
using Microsoft.AspNetCore.SignalR;
using SignalRServer.Models;
using SignalRServer.Hubs;

namespace SignalRServer.Controllers;

[ApiController]
[Route("api/[controller]")]
public class AuthController(
    UserManager<IdentityUser> userManager,
    SignInManager<IdentityUser> signInManager,
    IConfiguration configuration,
    IHubContext<MessagingHub, IMessagingClient> hubContext)
    : ControllerBase
    {
```

7. Let's adjust the login controller to announce the user right before returning Ok:

```
[HttpPost("login")]
[ProducesResponseType(StatusCodes.Status200OK)]
[ProducesResponseType(StatusCodes.Status401Unauthorized)]
public async Task<IActionResult> Login([FromBody] LoginDTO
model)
{
    var user = await userManager.FindByNameAsync(model.
        Username);
    if (user is not null && await userManager.
        CheckPasswordAsync(user, model.Password))
    {
```

```
        var userRoles = await userManager.GetRolesAsync(user);
        var token = GenerateJwtToken(user.UserName, userRoles);

        await hubContext.AnnounceUserLogin(model.Username);
        return Ok(new { token, user.UserName, Roles = userRoles
            });
    }
    return Unauthorized("Invalid username or password");
}
```

8. Run our `SignalRServer` API in the terminal:

    dotnet run

9. Create a user and log in via your web browser by navigating to `https://localhost:7031/index.html`. You can also use the console application in the `consoleClient` folder. *Figure 6.3* shows the SignalR hub sending a notification right before the login endpoint returns:

> Registration successful!
> Login successful!
> Connected to the messaging hub.
> GarryC: Hello how is everyone doing?
> System: LukeAvedon has logged in.
> LukeAvedon: I finally made it!

Figure 6.3 – Login POST endpoint triggering SignalR to send a message

How it works...

We converted our SignalR hub into a typed hub. We then created an extension method on this hub, which we used to broadcast an announcement that a user has logged in. By importing our new typed hub into our `AuthorizationController`, we could invoke our extension method inside our login endpoint before a JWT was returned. This bridges the gap between REST APIs and real-time updates.

User customization with IUserIdProvider

SignalR's `IUserIdProvider` interface allows you to customize how user information is presented across your SignalR hubs without having to modify individual hub methods. By implementing a custom service that inherits from `IUserIdProvider`, user information will be automatically enhanced when clients connect.

In this recipe, we will enhance our messaging application to include the user's locale, taken from a claim on the JWT, alongside their username. We will do this without having to modify any of our hub methods. Our hub methods will continue to call `Context.UserIdentifier` as normal, receiving both pieces of information automatically.

Getting ready

The starter project can be cloned here: `https://github.com/PacktPublishing/ASP.NET-9-Web-API-Cookbook/tree/main/start/chapter06/IUserProviderLocale`.

Please clone the starter project; the browser client and console client have been customized to test this recipe.

How to do it...

1. Modify our `LoginDTO` to take locale information:

    ```
    namespace SignalRServer.Models;

    public record LoginDTO
    (
        string Username,
        string Password,
        string Locale = "en-US"
    );
    ```

2. Open the `AuthController.cs` file. In the `HttpPost IActionResult` login method, all we have to do is update the `GenerateJwtToken` method signature to accept the locale:

    ```
    var token = GenerateJwtToken(user.UserName, userRoles, model.
    Locale);
    ```

3. In the same file, update `GenerateJwtToken` to accept a string locale parameter and add a locale custom claim:

    ```
    private string GenerateJwtToken(string userName, IList<string>
    roles, string locale)
    {
        ... // other claims
        new Claim("locale", locale),
        new Claim(JwtRegisteredClaimNames.Jti, Guid.NewGuid().
            ToString())
    };
    ```

4. Create a new file in the `Services` folder called `LocaleUserIdProvider.cs`. Create the following class and the `GetUserId` method:

```
using Microsoft.AspNetCore.SignalR;
using System.Security.Claims;

public class LocaleUserIdProvider : IUserIdProvider
{
    public string GetUserId(HubConnectionContext connection)
    {
        var userId = connection.User?.FindFirst(
            ClaimTypes.NameIdentifier)?.Value;
        var locale = connection.User?.FindFirst(
            "locale")?.Value ?? "en-US";

        if (string.IsNullOrEmpty(userId))
            return null;

        return $"{userId} - {locale}";
    }
}
```

Note: We are inheriting from SignalR's `IuserIdProvider`, which is the SignalR interface for getting custom user information.

5. Open `Program.cs` and import the SignalR namespace at the top of `Program.cs`:

```
using Microsoft.AspNetCore.SignalR;
```

6. Register the service in our `Program.cs` file, on the line after `IUserConnectionManager` is registered:

```
builder.Services.AddSingleton<IUserIdProvider,
LocaleUserIdProvider>();
```

7. Run the application with the `dotnet run` command in the terminal:

```
dotnet run
```

8. Test the application via the browser in `https://localhost:7031/index.html` or via the included console application in the `consoleClient` folder. When logging in, provide a locale in the locale text box.

Figure 6.4 shows two users talking, with locale information displayed next to their username:

> System: LukeAvedon has logged in.
> LukeAvedon-fr-CA: Good evening
> System: LukeAvedon has logged in.
> LukeAvedon - fr-CA: hello
> System: GarryC has logged in.
> GarryC - es-US: Good evening
> LukeAvedon - fr-CA: Hello

Figure 6.4 – Username customized by custom IUserProviderId service

How it works...

We created a custom JWT claim that stored the user locale on login. When that user connects to our SignalR hub, the normal way SignalR gets the user identification is modified by our `LocaleUserIdProvider` service, which inherits from SignalR's `IUserIdProvider` interface. This interface requires a `GetUserId` method to be implemented. We used this method to add locale information to our `userId`, which is displayed in the username when a message is sent.

The main benefit of using `IUserIdProvider` is that existing hub methods don't need modification to access this additional information – they continue to use `Context.UserIdentifier` as normal, automatically receiving the enhanced user information. Of course, we could have passed other custom information, not just a custom claim from a JWT.

The downside of this approach is that this custom information is only created on connection. To dynamically work with custom claims in the hub, it would be better to directly access the claims via `Context.User.Claims`.

Sending direct messages via SignalR

In this recipe, we will learn how to send direct messages to individual SignalR clients. We will still be working with JWT claims. We will look through the claims associated with each connected client and send a private message to those clients with our target username.

Getting ready

The starter project can be found here: `https://github.com/PacktPublishing/ASP.NET-9-Web-API-Cookbook/tree/main/start/chapter06/DirectMessage/SignalRServer`.

The starter project comes with both a console application and a web page configured for testing this project.

How to do it...

1. Open `IMessagingClient.cs` in the Hubs folder. Let's add a new method after `ReceiveMessage` called `ReceiveDirectMessage`. This interface defines all the methods our server can call on connected clients:

```
namespace SignalRServer.Hubs;

public interface IMessagingClient
{
    Task ReceiveMessage(string user, string message);
    Task ReceiveDirectMessage(string user, string message);
    ... // interface continues
```

2. In the starter project, open `MessagingHub.cs`. First, add the namespace for working with claims:

```
using System.Security.Claims;
```

3. In the same file, let's start filling in an `async` method that can send a message to an individual user. The first step is retrieving the sender's username from SignalR's hub context:

```
public async Task SendToIndividual(string targetUsername,
    string message)
{
    var senderUsername = Context.User?.FindFirst(
        ClaimTypes.Name)?.Value ?? Context.User?
        .FindFirst(ClaimTypes.NameIdentifier)?.Value;
```

Note: The `SendToIndividual` method does not need to be defined in the `IMessagingClient` interface. Methods in `MessagingHub` define what clients can call on our server, while the `IMessagingClient` interface only defines methods that flow from server to client (such as `ReceiveDirectMessage`).

4. On the next line, we will retrieve the individualized, unique `connectionIds` values for each client with that username:

```
var targetConnectionIds = userConnectionManager.
GetConnections(targetUsername).ToList();
```

5. If any `connectionIds` values are found, send a message to those IDs:

```
if (targetConnectionIds.Any())
{
    foreach (var connectionId in targetConnectionIds)
    {
        await Clients.Client(connectionId).
        ReceiveDirectMessage(senderUsername, message);
        Console.WriteLine($"Sent message to {
            targetUsername} on connection {connectionId}");
    }
}
else
{
    await Clients.Caller.ReceiveMessage("System",
        $"User {targetUsername} is not connected.");
    Console.WriteLine($"User {
        targetUsername} is not connected");
}
```

6. Open `IUserConnectionManager.cs` in the `Services` folder. We need to update our `IUserConnectionManager` interface to include the contract for retrieving user connections. Add the new method signature after the others:

```
public interface IUserConnectionManager {
{
    ...
    IEnumerable<string> GetConnections(string username);
}
```

7. Finally, in our `UserConnectionManager` service, we need to implement a helper method that retrieves all current client connections and adds them to a collection:

```
public IEnumerable<string> GetConnections(string username)
{
    lock (connections)
    {
    if (connections.TryGetValue(username, out HashSet<string>
        connections))
    {
    Console.WriteLine($"Found {connections.Count} connections
        for user {username}");
     return connections.ToList();
    }
    Console.WriteLine($"No connections found for user
```

```
        {username}");
        return Enumerable.Empty<string>();
    }
}
```

Notice we used `lock` to ensure thread-safe access when multiple clients are connecting/disconnecting simultaneously.

Run the project in the terminal:

```
dotnet run
```

You can log in to the application from both the web page at `https://localhost:7031/index.html` and the `consoleClient` project. Try registering multiple users and then sending direct messages between them.

Figure 6.5 shows receiving a direct message in the web page client:

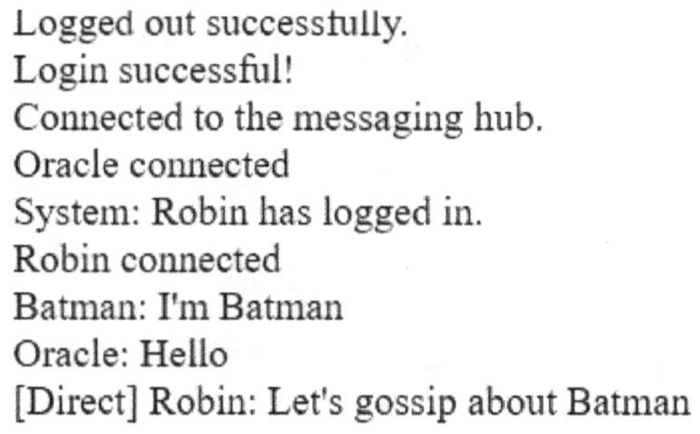

Logged out successfully.
Login successful!
Connected to the messaging hub.
Oracle connected
System: Robin has logged in.
Robin connected
Batman: I'm Batman
Oracle: Hello
[Direct] Robin: Let's gossip about Batman

Figure 6.5 – Receiving a direct message

How it works...

We implemented a hub method for sending direct messages from one user to another. We relied on reading the username from the JWT claim when the user logs in. We created a collection of all connected users with this name and then retrieved their unique connection IDs. A mapping of usernames to connection IDs is crucial for direct messaging, as a single user might be connected from multiple devices or browsers simultaneously. In a production scenario, consider improving the user lookup process by either normalizing usernames (trimming whitespace or converting to lowercase) or using a strongly typed dictionary approach. Finally, we sent our message only to `connectionId` and not to all clients by using `Clients.Client()` instead of `Clients.All()`.

Implementing admin-controlled group management in SignalR

In this recipe, we will explore SignalR groups. Groups can be a way to not only organize users but also isolate their interactions from one another. We will also have a special admin user – who is the only one who can add and remove users from a group.

Getting ready

The starter project for this recipe can be found here: https://github.com/PacktPublishing/ASP.NET-9-Web-API-Cookbook/tree/main/start/chapter06/Groups/SignalRServer.

How to do it...

1. In the Services folder, create a file called ICustomGroupManager.cs and fill in the ICustomGroupManager interface:

    ```
    public interface ICustomGroupManager
    {
        Task AddUserToGroup(string username, string groupName);
        Task RemoveUserFromGroup(string username, string groupName);
        Task<IEnumerable<string>> GetUserGroups(string username);
    }
    ```

2. In the same folder, create a file called CustomGroupManager.cs. Allow this class to receive a dictionary of unique usernames:

    ```
    #nullable enable
    public class CustomGroupManager(
        Dictionary<string, HashSet<string>>? groupUserMap = null) :
            ICustomGroupManager
    {
        private readonly Dictionary<string, HashSet<string>>
        _groupUserMap = groupUserMap ?? new Dictionary<
            string,HashSet<string>>();
    ```

You will notice we enabled a nullable reference checking for this specific class to ensure type safety when handling the optional dictionary parameter. Most of this chapter has nullables disabled to focus on SignalR concepts, but this shows you how to use nullable safety checks selectively.

3. On the next line, implement the method for adding a user to a group:

```
public Task AddUserToGroup(string username, string groupName)
    {
        lock (_groupUserMap)
        {
            if (!_groupUserMap.ContainsKey(groupName))
            {
                _groupUserMap[groupName] =
                    new HashSet<string>();
            }
            _groupUserMap[groupName].Add(username);
        }
        return Task.CompletedTask;
    }
```

4. On the next line, implement the RemoveUserFromGroup method:

```
public Task RemoveUserFromGroup(string username, string
groupName)
    {
        lock (_groupUserMap)
        {
            if (_groupUserMap.ContainsKey(groupName))
            {
                _groupUserMap[groupName].Remove(username);
                if (_groupUserMap[groupName].Count == 0)
                {
                    _groupUserMap.Remove(groupName);
                }
            }
        }
        return Task.CompletedTask;
    }
```

5. We will finish our work on CustomUserGroup.cs by adding a method to retrieve all groups using LINQ:

```
public Task<IEnumerable<string>> GetUserGroups(string username)
{
    lock (_groupUserMap)
    {
        return Task.FromResult(_groupUserMap
            .Where(g => g.Value.Contains(username))
            .Select(g => g.Key));
```

```
        }
    }
}
```

6. Open our `Program.cs` file and register our new service as a singleton. We will choose a singleton lifetime to maintain the group state across connections. Let's register it on the line after the `IUserConnectionManager` registration:

    ```
    builder.Services.AddSingleton<ICustomGroupManager,
    CustomGroupManager>();
    ```

7. In our hub, we now need to implement the same ability to add and remove users from a group at the hub level. Open `MessagingHub.cs` and implement an `AddUserToGroup` method, which first searches for relevant usernames and then grabs their connection IDs:

    ```
    public async Task AddUserToGroup(string username, string
    groupName)
    {
        await _groupManager.AddUserToGroup(username, groupName);
        var connectionIds = _userConnectionManager.
            GetConnections(username);
        foreach (var connectionId in connectionIds)
        {
            await Groups.AddToGroupAsync(connectionId, groupName);
        }
        await Clients.All.UserAddedToGroup(username, groupName);
    }
    ```

8. Next, add a similar `RemoveUserFromGroup` method, which searches for a username and then calls `RemoveFromGroupAsync` on SignalR's `Groups` class:

    ```
    public async Task RemoveUserFromGroup(
        string username, string groupName)
    {
        await _groupManager.RemoveUserFromGroup(
            username,groupName);
        var connectionIds = _userConnectionManager.
            GetConnections(username);
        foreach (var connectionId in connectionIds)
        {
            await Groups.RemoveFromGroupAsync(
                connectionId, groupName);
        }
        await Clients.All.UserRemovedFromGroup(
            username,groupName);
    }
    ```

9. Decorate both methods with an `Authorize` attribute, which only makes these hub methods accessible to admins:

```
[Authorize(Roles = "Admin")]
public async Task AddUserToGroup(string username, string
groupName)
...

[Authorize(Roles = "Admin")]
```

10. Finally, let's implement a method that first grabs the sender's username. Next, the method uses that username along with the group name. It will then send a message to all group members:

```
public async Task SendToGroup(string groupName, string message)
{
    var senderUsername = Context.User?.FindFirst(ClaimTypes.
        Name)?.Value
  ?? Context.User?.FindFirst(ClaimTypes.NameIdentifier)?.Value;

    await Clients.Group(groupName).ReceiveGroupMessage(
        senderUsername, groupName, message);
}
```

Note that we do not have to send a message to individual users – we can send a message to all group members using SignalR's `Group` class.

11. Update the `IMessagingClient` interface to make our new SignalR methods available:

```
public interface IMessagingClient
{
    ...

    Task ReceiveGroupMessage(string user, string groupName,
        string message);
    Task UserAddedToGroup(string username, string groupName);
    Task UserRemovedFromGroup(string username, string
        groupName);
```

To test this recipe, run the `SignalRServer` project and navigate to `https://localhost:7031/index.html`. You can also use the provided console client project. Log in as the admin user with the username `adamTheAdmin` and the password `AdminPassword123!` to manage groups. Open additional browser tabs and create new accounts for regular users – each tab represents a separate user connection.

Using the admin account, you can add and remove users from groups, as shown in *Figure 6.6*, while regular users can only send messages to the groups they belong to:

adamTheAdmin: Hello the admin is here
System: ThirdUser has logged in.
ThirdUser connected
User Batman added to group JusticeLeague
User Robin added to group JusticeLeague
User Oracle added to group JusticeLeague

Figure 6.6 – Adding users to a group

How it works...

SignalR groups are a powerful feature that allows you to organize and manage connections, with messages only reaching members of the specified group. We implemented a dual-layer group management system: our `CustomGroupManager` maintains group membership data, while SignalR's built-in groups handle the actual message routing. Our `AddToGroup` method first updates the membership in our custom manager and then associates the user's connection ID with SignalR's group system.

Security is managed through the `[Authorize(Roles = "Admin")]` attribute, ensuring only users with the `Admin` role can add or remove users to groups. The `AuthController.cs` class assigns roles to our JWT. SignalR allows us to decorate our hub methods with `[Authorize]` and other security attributes just like we do in our standard HTTP controllers.

We implemented sending messages to all group members using `Clients.Group(groupName)` rather than having to go through the trouble of sending specific messages to each group member. The `AddUserToGroup` method first updates the group membership in our custom `_groupManager` and then associates the user's connection IDs with the specified SignalR group. The `RemoveUserFromGroup` method detaches the user's connections from the group.

Learn more on Discord

To join the Discord community for this book – where you can share feedback, ask questions to the authors, and provide solutions to other readers – scan the QR code or visit the link:

`https://packt.link/aspdotnet9WebAPI`

7

Building Robust API Tests: a Guide to Unit and Integration Testing

This chapter delves into best practices for testing ASP.NET Core 9 web APIs. We begin by exploring unit testing and the foundations of **xUnit**. We then layer in the powerful and essential libraries required for writing clean and maintainable tests: **AutoFixture**, **NSubstitute**, and **FluentAssertions**. We will also tackle common real-world controller testing scenarios such as testing pagination and stubbing **UrlHelper** for URL generation. These are essential skills for unit testing controllers.

The later part of the chapter focuses on integration testing. We will set up and execute web API integration tests that interact with the entire stack. You can be confident that all parts of your application work together as intended. Finally, we will confront one of the toughest challenges in integration testing: handling authentication in your integration test suite.

In this chapter, we're going to cover the following main topics:

- Unit testing an API service method with xUnit
- Unit testing with `AutoFixture`, `NSubstitute`, and `FluentAssertions`
- Organizing unit tests with a base service class
- Testing pagination with custom `UrlHelper` and `NSubstitute`
- Controller unit tests with custom fixtures
- Web API integration testing
- Authentication in integration testing

Technical requirements

For the recipes in this chapter, you'll need the following:

- **.NET 9 SDK**: `Microsoft.NET.Test.SDK` is included out of the box. We will be creating most of our tests with the xUnit template, which is already included. We will be installing the needed packages as we go.

- **IDE**: Almost all of the unit and integration test recipes also work out of the box with Visual Studio, Rider, or VS Code's test runner thanks to `xunit.runner.visualstudio`. The recipes in this chapter will use `dotnet test` to keep them as cross-platform as possible. Keep in mind they can also just as easily be run in the IDE of your choice.

Unit testing an API service method with xUnit

xUnit makes it easy to unit test the individual discrete pieces of our application. In this first recipe, we will focus solely on xUnit's built-in functionality – which is quite powerful on its own – before introducing the additional testing libraries: `AutoFixture`, `NSubstitute`, and `FluentAssertions`. This approach helps us appreciate what xUnit can do on its own before adding more specialized tools.

Getting ready

Clone the starter project here: `https://github.com/PacktPublishing/ASP.NET-9-Web-API-Cookbook/tree/main/start/chapter07/UnitTests1`.

The starter project includes a simple web API that uses **Entity Framework Core (EF Core)**. Although it uses EF Core, there is also a separate repository layer. We will focus on testing the service layer and mocking the repository layer for this series of unit tests.

How to do it...

1. Create a new xUnit test project using the built-in xUnit template. Run this command in the root `UnitTests1` folder. Do not run it inside the `BooksAPI` folder:

   ```
   dotnet new xunit -n Unit.Tests
   ```

   It is critical that this new tests folder is a sibling of the `BooksAPI` folder. Do not create the tests project inside the `BooksAPI` folder. The main project and tests project folders must be siblings in the system file structure.

2. Navigate to your new tests project folder and add a reference to the main project:

   ```
   cd Unit.Tests
   dotnet add reference ..\BooksAPI\chapter7.csproj
   ```

3. Delete the auto-generated `UnitTest1.cs` file.

4. First, we will manually mock our repository layer. Create a file called `FakeBooksRepository.cs`, and then create a constructor that initializes a `Book` field:

```
using Books.Repositories;
using Books.Models;

namespace Tests.Services;

public class FakeBooksRepository : IBooksRepository
{
    private readonly Book _bookToReturn;

    public FakeBooksRepository(Book bookToReturn)
    {
        _bookToReturn = bookToReturn;
    }

}
```

5. Now, mock the method that our service test depends on:

```
public Task<Book?> GetBookByIdAsync(int id)
{

  if (_bookToReturn != null && _bookToReturn.Id == id)
  {
    return Task.FromResult<Book?>(_bookToReturn);
  }
    return Task.FromResult<Book?>(null);
}
```

6. We also have to stub out the remaining `IBooksRepository` function:

```
public Task<IReadOnlyCollection<Book>> GetBooksAsync(
    int pageSize, int lastId)
{
    throw new NotImplementedException(
        "GetBooksAsync is not implemented in
FakeBooksRepository.");
}
public Task<Book> CreateBookAsync(Book book)
{
    throw new NotImplementedException("CreateBookAsync is
    not implemented in FakeBooksRepository.");
}
```

7. Next, create a file called `BookServiceTests.cs`.

At the top of `BookServiceTests.cs`, import the relevant namespaces from the main API project. We will also set the namespace for our test class:

```
using Xunit;
using Books.Repositories;
using Books.Models;
using Books.Services;
using Microsoft.AspNetCore.Mvc;


namespace Tests.Services;
```

8. Our first test will be to make sure that the **Data Transfer Object (DTO)** our service creates has the correct properties. We will create a full mock `Book` object and compare it to the generated DTO:

```
public class BooksServiceTests
{
    [Fact]
    public async Task GetBookById_ReturnsBookDTO_
    WhenBookExists()
    {
    // Arrange
    int testBookId = 1;
    var bookFromRepository = new Book
    {
        Id = testBookId,
        Title = "Test Book",
        Author = "Test Author",
        PublicationDate = new DateTime(2020, 1, 1),
        ISBN = "1234567890123",
        Genre = "Test Genre",
        Summary = "Test Summary"
    };
```

9. Next, we can define the properties we expect to be returned:

```
var expectedBookDto = new BookDTO
    {
        Id = testBookId,
        Title = "Test Book",
        Author = "Test Author",
        PublicationDate = new DateTime(2020, 1, 1),
        ISBN = "1234567890123",
```

```
        Genre = "Test Genre",
        Summary = "Test Summary"
    };
```

10. Initialize the repository and the *system under test* – our service:

```
var repository = new FakeBooksRepository(bookFromRepository);
var service = new BooksService(repository);
```

11. Let's return one single book from our service:

```
// Act
var result = await service.GetBookByIdAsync(testBookId);
```

12. Finally, let's assert that our model and DTO match:

```
// Assert
Assert.NotNull(result);
Assert.Equal(expectedBookDto.Id, result.Id);
Assert.Equal(expectedBookDto.Title, result.Title);
Assert.Equal(expectedBookDto.Author, result.Author);
Assert.Equal(expectedBookDto.PublicationDate,
    result.PublicationDate);
Assert.Equal(expectedBookDto.ISBN, result.ISBN);
Assert.Equal(expectedBookDto.Genre, result.Genre);
Assert.Equal(expectedBookDto.Summary, result.Summary);
}
}
```

13. Now, run the test:

```
dotnet test
```

How it works...

We created a minimum unit test of one service method, using only the features of xUnit. We manually created test data and manually mocked our repository layer, which was a dependency for our test. We also used the built-in xUnit assertions to compare the generated object to the object we expected.

Unit testing with AutoFixture, NSubstitute, and FluentAssertions

xUnit is a powerful testing framework, but it has some limitations. xUnit, by itself, lacks a concise assertion syntax, built-in dependency mocking, and the ability to generate random test data. In this recipe, we will learn how to automatically mock our dependencies with `NSubstitute`. We will also make our tests much more robust by automatically creating test data to assert against using `AutoFixture`. Automatic test data makes our tests more robust; the data pushed through our system is not only limited to what we happen to think up. Finally, we will write more expressive assertions using the `FluentAssertions` library.

Getting ready

The starter project for this recipe can be found here: `https://github.com/PacktPublishing/ASP.NET-9-Web-API-Cookbook/tree/main/start/chapter07/UnitTests2`.

You can also just pick up from where the preceding recipe left off.

How to do it...

1. Open `BookServiceTests.cs`. Copy and paste our `GetBookById_ReturnsBookDTO_WhenBookExists()` unit test. We will give it a new name. Delete the `Fact` attribute and decorate the method with `Theory` and `InlineData` instead, as follows:

   ```
   [Theory]
   [InlineData(999)]
   [InlineData(5)]
   [InlineData(1)]
   public async Task GetBookByIdTheory_ReturnsBookDTO_
   WhenBookExists(int testBookId)
   {
   ```

   We have also changed `testBookId` to be passed as a parameter.

   If you run `dotnet test` now in the terminal, you should see that three additional tests have been created.

2. Let's install `AutoFixture`. This will free us from having to manually generate the test data. In the terminal, run the following:

   ```
   dotnet add package AutoFixture
   dotnet add package AutoFixture.Xunit2
   ```

3. Import the `AutoFixture` namespace at the top of the file:

   ```
   using AutoFixture;
   ```

4. Let's change our test to use `InlineAutoData`. Here, we mix automatic data with manual data generation. We manually specify `testBookId` but `AutoFixture` takes care of the rest:

```
using AutoFixture.Xunit2;

[Theory]
[InlineAutoData(1)]
[InlineAutoData(2)]
[InlineAutoData(3)]
public async Task GetBookById_ReturnsBookDTO_WhenBookExists(int
testBookId, Book bookFromRepository, BookDTO expectedBookDto)
{
```

We have also changed our test method signature to pass a `Book` class and `BookDTO` as parameters.

5. Now, install `NSubstitute`:

```
dotnet add package NSubstitute
```

6. Import the `NSubstitute` namespace at the top of our file:

```
using NSubstitute;
```

7. Delete the manual test data creation (the `bookFromRepository` and `expectedDto` blocks) in our `arrange` step. In our new `arrange` step, the only thing we are manually going to map is the passed in `testBookId`:

```
// Arrange
bookFromRepository.Id = testBookId;
```

8. On the next line, we will automatically mock `BooksRepository` from its interface. First, remove the existing `FakeBooksRepository` initialization. Then, specify the `GetBookByIdAsync` method, and instantiate our service to use the mocked repository:

```
var repository = Substitute.For<IBooksRepository>();
repository.GetBookByIdAsync(testBookId).
Returns(bookFromRepository);

var service = new BooksService(repository);
```

9. Now, it's time to update our assertions. We are going to install the `FluentAssertions` library to enable much more expressive and powerful assertions:

```
dotnet add package FluentAssertions
```

10. Import the `FluentAssertions` namespace at the top of our file:

```
using FluentAssertions;
```

11. Replace the current assertions with `FluentAssertion`, which checks that the resulting DTO is the same as the original class that created it, except for the properties that the DTO does not include:

```
result.Should().BeEquivalentTo(bookFromRepository, options =>
options.ExcludingMissingMembers());
```

12. Run `dotnet test` or your test runner of choice and observe our three new passing tests:

How it works...

In this recipe, we enhanced xUnit with three libraries – `AutoFixture`, `NSubstitute`, and `FluentAssertions`:

- `AutoFixture` automates the creation of test data. We used the `InlineAutoData` attribute to combine a manually specified parameter with an automatically generated one. This allows us to test our methods with a variety of inputs effortlessly.

- `NSubstitute` simplifies our mocking of dependencies, eliminating the need for a `FakeRepository` class.

- Finally, the `FluentAssertions` library provides a more readable and expressive way to write assertions. We were able to replace multiple `Assert.Equal` statements with a single `BeEquivalentTo` assertion.

See also...

- This cheat sheet illustrates many ways of generating mock data with `AutoFixture`: `https://github.com/AutoFixture/AutoFixture/wiki/Cheat-Sheet`

- This is a worthwhile project that opens up more possibilities for using `AutoFixture` with various mocking libraries, including `Nsubstitute`: `https://github.com/Accenture/AutoFixture.XUnit2.AutoMock`

Organizing unit tests with a base service class

We can better organize our tests by creating an abstract class. This abstract class establishes a framework for mocking our repositories, services, or anything else we need to share among tests. This pattern can work well with either a test fixture or a series of independent tests.

Getting ready

You can download the starter project here: `https://github.com/PacktPublishing/ASP.NET-9-Web-API-Cookbook/tree/main/start/chapter07/UnitTests3`.

You can also continue from the preceding recipe.

How to do it...

1. Create a new file called `BookServiceTestsBase.cs`. Import the namespaces for our API services and repositories as well as the `NSubstitute` library:

   ```
   using Books.Repositories;
   using Books.Services;
   using NSubstitute;

   namespace Tests.Services;
   ```

2. Implement protected properties to hold `Service` and `Repository`:

   ```
   public abstract class BooksServiceTestsBase
   {
       protected IBooksRepository Repository { get; }
       protected BooksService Service { get; }
   ```

3. In the constructor, create a mock of `Repository` using `NSubstitute`. Then, initialize `Service` to use the repository mocked by `Nsubstitute`:

   ```
   protected BooksServiceTestsBase()
       {
           Repository = Substitute.For<IBooksRepository>();
           Service = new BooksService(Repository);
       }
   }
   ```

4. Open our `BooksServiceTests.cs` file. Have our class of tests inherit from our new abstract class:

   ```
   public class BooksServiceTests : BooksServiceTestsBase
   ```

5. We can now delete where we instantiate our local repository and service variables. Since these are now provided by the `BooksServiceTestBase` class, anywhere we use `Service` and `Repository`, make sure they are capitalized. We can simplify the `GetBookByIdTheory_` test as follows:

   ```
   [Theory]
   [InlineAutoData(1)]
   [InlineAutoData(2)]
   [InlineAutoData(3)]
   ```

```
public async Task GetBookByIdTheory_ReturnsBookDTO_
WhenBookExists(int testBookId, Book bookFromRepository)
  {

    // Arrange
    bookFromRepository.Id = testBookId;

    Repository!.GetBookByIdAsync(testBookId).Returns(
        bookFromRepository);
    // Act
    var result = await Service!.GetBookByIdAsync(testBookId);

    // Assert
    result.Should().BeEquivalentTo(bookFromRepository,
        options => options.ExcludingMissingMembers());

  }
```

How it works...

By creating an abstract base class, BooksServiceTestsBase, we centralized the setup of common dependencies required by our tests. We declared properties for Repository and Service. Our abstract class uses NSubstitute to create a mock of the IBooksRepository interface. Any class that inherits from BooksServiceTestsBase gains access to the Repository and Service properties, which eliminates the need to declare and initialize them in each test method.

Testing pagination with custom UrlHelper and NSubstitute

In this recipe, we will focus on testing pagination at the service layer, which involves two distinct challenges. First, we need to verify that our paging GET endpoint correctly handles page sizes and navigation between pages. Second, we need to tackle URL generation in our test environment, which requires special handling of ASP.NET Core's UrlHelper. We'll enhance our abstract base class to handle both these challenges while maintaining clean, readable tests.

Getting ready

The starter project for this recipe can be found here: https://github.com/PacktPublishing/ASP.NET-9-Web-API-Cookbook/tree/main/start/chapter07/UnitTests4.

You can also continue from the preceding recipe.

How to do it...

1. In the terminal, install `AutoNSubstitute` for `AutoFixture`:

    ```
    dotnet add package AutoFixture.AutoNSubstitute
    ```

2. Let's expand our `BooksServiceTestsBase()` class. The first thing we will do is import the new `AutoNSubstitute` library:

    ```
    using AutoFixture;
    using AutoFixture.AutoNSubstitute;
    using Microsoft.AspNetCore.Mvc;
    ```

3. Add a new `Fixture` property where we will set up a common fixture for use across tests:

    ```
    public abstract class BooksServiceTestsBase {
        protected Fixture Fixture { get; }
        protected IUrlHelper UrlHelper { get; }
        protected IBooksRepository Repository { get; }
        protected BooksService Service { get; }
        ...
    ```

4. In the constructor, initialize our new `Fixture` with `AutoNSubstitute`:

    ```
    protected BooksServiceTestsBase() {
        Fixture = new Fixture();
        Fixture.Customize(new AutoNSubstituteCustomization());
    ```

    The `Fixture` instance is customized using `AutoNSubstituteCustomization`. This allows `AutoFixture` to automatically create mocks using `NSubstitute` for interfaces and abstract classes.

5. Finish off the constructor. We are now going to create a new mocked `UrlHelper` that will simulate full URLs such as those generated by our API for the next page and previous page:

    ```
            Repository = Substitute.For<IBooksRepository>();
            UrlHelper = Substitute.For<IUrlHelper>();
            Service = new BooksService(Repository);
        }
    }
    ```

6. In `BooksServiceTests`, let's create a test that makes sure our service layer is correctly formulating pagination information. First, we have to make sure `BooksServiceTests` has access to `AutoFixture`:

    ```
    using AutoFixture;
    ```

7. In this example, we are going to test returning a page size of 2 and no last ID supplied. First, let's arrange the test. We will use our new `Fixture` property to produce the page of results:

```
public class BooksServiceTests : BooksServiceTestsBase
{
    [Fact]
    public async Task GetBooksAsync_ReturnsPagedResult_
        WhenNoPreviousOrNextPage()
    {
        // Arrange
        int pageSize = 2;
        int lastId = 0;

        var booksFromRepository = Fixture.
            CreateMany<Book>(pageSize).ToList();
        Repository.GetBooksAsync(
            pageSize + 1, lastId).Returns(booksFromRepository);
```

8. Next, let's create an object of what we expect to be returned by our service:

```
var expectedItems = booksFromRepository.Select(b => new BookDTO
    {
        Id = b.Id,
        Title = b.Title,
        Author = b.Author,
        PublicationDate = b.PublicationDate,
        ISBN = b.ISBN,
        Genre = b.Genre,
        Summary = b.Summary
    }).ToList();

    // Act
    var result = await Service.GetBooksAsync(
        pageSize, lastId, UrlHelper);
```

9. Finally, assert that the returned data is what we expect to see:

```
// Assert
result.Items.Should().BeEquivalentTo(expectedItems, options =>
options.WithStrictOrdering());
result.HasPreviousPage.Should().BeFalse();
result.HasNextPage.Should().BeFalse();
result.PreviousPageUrl.Should().BeNull();
result.NextPageUrl.Should().BeNull();
result.PageSize.Should().Be(pageSize);
```

In this test, we decided to not mock `UrlHelper` and we do not expect URLs to be generated. The goal of this test is to isolate the other pagination logic.

10. Confirm that this test works with `dotnet test`:

    ```
    dotnet test
    ```

    We should see five passing tests.

11. Now, let's test the pagination URLs. Our method uses extension methods on `UrlHelper` – extension methods that `NSubstitute` cannot mock. The problem we have is that our service method has a dependency on `UrlHelper` to generate the URLs. We need to have a way to provide that dependency. Let's expand our `TestBaseAbstract` class further. Let's change the constructor so that `UrlHelper` is using a custom mock we are about to create:

    ```
    protected BooksServiceTestsBase()
    {
        Fixture = new Fixture();
        Fixture.Customize(new AutoNSubstituteCustomization());
        Repository = Substitute.For<IBooksRepository>();
        UrlHelper = new TestUrlHelper();
        Service = new BooksService(Repository);
    }
    ```

12. At the top of the `BooksServiceTestBase.cs` file, import the namespace that will give us access to `UrlActionContext`:

    ```
    using Microsoft.AspNetCore.Mvc.Routing;
    ```

13. Next, still in the `BooksServiceTestBase.cs` file, create a helper method that our service can use to generate URLs:

    ```
    private class TestUrlHelper : IUrlHelper
    {
        public ActionContext ActionContext => throw new
            NotImplementedException();
        public string? Action(UrlActionContext actionContext)
        {
            var pageSize = actionContext.Values?.GetType()
                .GetProperty("pageSize")?
                .GetValue(actionContext.Values);
            var lastId = actionContext.Values?.GetType()
                .GetProperty("lastId")?
                .GetValue(actionContext.Values);

            return $"/api/books?action={actionContext.
            Action}&controller={actionContext.
    ```

```
                    Controller}&pageSize={pageSize}&lastId={lastId}";
        }
        public string? Content(string? contentPath) =>
            throw new NotImplementedException();
        public bool IsLocalUrl(string? url) =>
            throw new NotImplementedException();
        public string? Link(string? routeName, object? values) =>
            throw new NotImplementedException();
        public string? RouteUrl(UrlRouteContext routeContext) =>
            throw new NotImplementedException();
}
```

14. Let's create a test that makes sure the URLs returned by the service have the navigation data we expect. We can set up the test with a simple arrangement:

```
        [Fact]
        public async Task GetBooksAsync_
ShouldReturnCorrectPagedResult()
        {
            // Arrange
            int pageSize = 2;
            int lastId = 0;

            var books = new List<Book>
            {
                new Book { Id = 1, Title = "Book 1" },
                new Book { Id = 2, Title = "Book 2" },
                new Book { Id = 3, Title = "Book 3" },
            };

            Repository.GetBooksAsync(pageSize + 1, lastId).
                Returns(books);
```

15. For the Act section, we make a simple call to the method:

```
        // Act
        var result = await Service.GetBooksAsync(pageSize, lastId,
        UrlHelper);
```

16. For the Assert section, let's make sure the URLs contain what we expect them to:

```
        // Assert
        result.Items.Should().HaveCount(2);
        result.Items.Should().BeEquivalentTo(
            books.Take(2).Select(b => new BookDTO
                {
```

```
        Id = b.Id,
        Title = b.Title,
    }), options => options.ExcludingMissingMembers());

    result.HasPreviousPage.Should().BeFalse();
    result.HasNextPage.Should().BeTrue();
    result.PreviousPageUrl.Should().BeNull();
    result.NextPageUrl.Should().NotBeNull(
        "NextPageUrl should not be null when
        HasNextPage is true");
    if (result.NextPageUrl != null)
    {
        result.NextPageUrl.Should().Contain(
            "action=GetBooks",
            "The action should be GetBooks");
        result.NextPageUrl.Should().Contain(
            $"pageSize={pageSize}",
            "The pageSize should be included");
        result.NextPageUrl.Should().Contain(
            $"lastId={books[1].Id}",
            "The lastId should be the ID of
            the last item on the current page");
    }
    result.PageSize.Should().Be(pageSize);
}
```

17. If you run `dotnet test` in the terminal, you should see six passing tests.

How it works...

We created two tests of our pagination on the service layer. The challenge we have is our service layer pagination generates URLs via ASP.NET Core's `UrlHelper`. This creates a dependency for our pagination method that other service methods do not have. We expanded our abstract class to provide a basic mocked `UrlHelper` stub and wrote a test to make sure the non-URL-related logic worked. Then, we expanded our `UrlHelper` stub and created a test that made sure the service layer was providing URLs with the correct logic. We also set up `AutoFixture` to work with `NSubstitute` via the `AutoNSubstituteCustomization()` class.

Controller unit tests with custom fixtures

In this recipe, we will set up unit testing on the `Controller` layer. We will explore the expanded version of the `FluentAssertions` library, `FluentAssertions.AspNetCore.Mvc`, which will allow us to assert against HTTP results and not only internal method logic. We will provide dependencies to the controller via `AutoNSubstitute`. Also, we will create a custom fixture to provide a consistent environment for our controller tests.

Getting ready

The starter project for this recipe can be found here: `https://github.com/PacktPublishing/ASP.NET-9-Web-API-Cookbook/tree/main/start/chapter07/UnitTestsController`.

You can also continue from the preceding recipe.

How to do it...

1. First, let's import the expanded `FluentAssertions` package for testing the controller's action methods. Make sure you add this only in the `Unit.Tests` project.

> **Important note**
>
> `FluentAssertions.AspNetCore.Mvc` cannot coexist with the standard `FluentAssertions` package in the same project; you must first remove the normal `FluentAssertions` package.

    Navigate to the `Unit.Tests` subfolder and run the following in the terminal:

    ```
    dotnet remove package FluentAssertions
    dotnet add package FluentAssertions.AspNetCore.Mvc
    ```

2. In this recipe, instead of an abstract base class, we will explore another popular technique: using a custom attribute to automatically inject mocked dependencies. Create a folder called `Attributes`. In this `Attributes` folder, create a new file called `AutoNSubstituteDataAttribute.cs`.

3. Let's fill in the code for our new attribute. The only new thing we are going to do is provide a custom `AutoNSubstitute` fixture:

    ```
    using AutoFixture;
    using AutoFixture.AutoNSubstitute;
    using AutoFixture.Xunit2;

    public class AutoNSubstituteDataAttribute : AutoDataAttribute
    {
    ```

```
    public AutoNSubstituteDataAttribute()
        : base(() => new Fixture().Customize(
            new AutoNSubstituteCustomization()))
    {
    }
}
```

4. Create a file called `BooksControllerFixture.cs` in a `Fixtures` directory.

5. Let's fill in the code for our fixture:

```
using books.Repositories;
using Books.Models;
using Books.Services;
using Books.Controllers;
using AutoFixture;
using NSubstitute;

namespace Tests.Controllers;

public class BooksControllerFixture
{
    public BooksController BooksController { get; }
    public Fixture Fixture { get; }
    public IBooksService BooksService { get; }

    public BooksControllerFixture()
    {
        Fixture = new Fixture();
        BooksService = Substitute.For<IBooksService>();
        BooksController = new BooksController(BooksService);
    }
}
```

Now, any test class that uses this fixture will have a mocked `Services` class provided to them. A fixture creates a common foundation for a suite of tests, and it prevents tests from being run in parallel with other tests in the fixture.

6. In the `Attributes` directory, create a file called
    `BooksControllerDefinitionAttributeTest.cs`:

    ```
    namespace Tests.Controllers;


    [CollectionDefinition("BooksController Tests")]
    public class BooksControllerCollection :
    ICollectionFixture<BooksControllerFixture>
    {}
    ```

7. In the main testing folder, create a file called `BooksControllerTests.cs`. In this file,
    import the required namespaces and libraries:

    ```
    using Xunit;
    using AutoFixture;
    using AutoFixture.Xunit2;
    using FluentAssertions.Mvc;
    using Books.Controllers;
    using Books.Services;
    using Books.Models;
    using NSubstitute;
    using Microsoft.AspNetCore.Mvc;
    ```

8. In this `BooksControllerTests` class, we will only test the `GetBookById` method. Let's
    start off by using `[AutoNSubstituteData]` to provide dependencies:

    ```
    [Collection("BooksController Tests")]
    public class BooksControllerTests
    {
        [Theory]
        [AutoNSubstituteData]
        public async Task GetBookById_ReturnsOk_WhenBookExists(
            int testBookId,
            BookDTO bookDto,
            IBooksService booksService)
        {
    ```

9. Finish this first test method by testing that the `GET /books/{id}` endpoint returns `200`:

    ```
    // Arrange
            booksService.GetBookByIdAsync(testBookId).
    Returns(bookDto);
    var controller = new BooksController(booksService);

    // Act
    var result = await controller.GetBookById(testBookId);
    ```

```
// Assert
Result.Should()
   .BeOkObjectResult()
   .WithValueEquivalentTo<BookDTO>(bookDto);
}
```

10. Let's also add a test that if no book is found, then a bad request should be returned:

```
[Theory]
[AutoNSubstituteData]
public async Task GetBookById_ReturnsNotFound_
WhenBookDoesNotExist(
    int testBookId,
    IBooksService booksService)
{
// Arrange
booksService.GetBookByIdAsync(testBookId).Returns((BookDTO)
null!);
var controller = new BooksController(booksService);

// Act
var result = await controller.GetBookById(testBookId);

// Assert
result.Should().BeNotFoundResult();
    }
}
```

11. Run dotnet test in your terminal or use your IDE's test runner. You should see eight passing tests.

How it works...

We set up controller testing by taking advantage of some of the most powerful features of xUnit. We set up a collection for our test to provide a common platform to our test class (instead of using an abstract base class). We customized the AutoNSubstitute attribute to provide dependencies and mock data for our tests. We also created CollectionDefinition for our suite of tests, to keep these tests organized as our test suite grows. We created a custom BooksControllerFixture to provide a consistent, mocked BooksService across our tests. Finally, we used the expanded FluentAssertions library, FluentAssertions.AspNetCore.Mvc, to very easily write assertions against things such as HTTP status codes.

Web API integration testing

In this recipe, we will set up integration tests for our web API. Unlike unit tests, integration tests use real dependencies and test that the entire system or parts of the system work together. The controversial issue in unit tests is this: What do we do about the database? An automated test system that modifies our actual database can be dangerous. Avoiding the database issue entirely and only mocking and stubbing the repository layer (as we did in unit tests) isn't sufficient for true integration testing.

EF Core provides an in-memory database provider, but this provider was designed for rapid prototyping, not integration testing, as it doesn't properly simulate a real SQL database's behavior. Instead, Microsoft recommends using SQLite's in-memory mode for integration testing. SQLite in-memory provides a lightweight yet real database engine that properly simulates SQL behavior while remaining isolated and ephemeral. This solution works well for web APIs using standard EF Core features through `IQueryable<T>`, but if your project uses raw SQL queries, manually specified complex joins, stored procedures, or data access outside of EF Core (such as Dapper), you'll need to consider alternatives such as Docker containers running SQL Server.

In this recipe, we will learn to set up an *integration test suite* with `WebApplicationFactory<T>`, which can run our ASP.NET Core web API entirely in memory. We will then execute real HTTP calls to our endpoints and make sure all components of our system work together.

Getting ready

The starting project for this recipe can be found here: `https://github.com/PacktPublishing/ASP.NET-9-Web-API-Cookbook/tree/main/start/chapter07/IntegrationTests`.

How to do it...

1. Create a new xUnit project called `Integration.Tests`. This folder should be a sibling to our main project folder and our unit test folder.

    This is our desired folder structure:

    - `BooksAPI`
    - `Unit.Tests`
    - `Integration.Tests`

    In the root folder, create the new test project:

    ```
    dotnet new xunit -n Integration.Tests
    ```

2. Add a reference to our API:

    ```
    cd Integration.Tests
    dotnet add reference ..\BooksAPI\chapter7.csproj
    ```

3. Let's add our project, unit tests, and integration tests to a solution file so that is easier to test all of them at once. In the main folder, type the following in the terminal to create a new solution:

    ```
    dotnet new sln
    dotnet sln add .\BooksAPI\chapter7.csproj
    dotnet sln add .\Integration.Tests\Integration.Tests.csproj
    dotnet sln add .\Unit.Tests\Unit.Tests.csproj
    ```

4. WebApplicationFactory requires access to our API's Program class. There are two ways to accomplish this. The first involves changing the access specifier on the main Program class of the API we are testing to public partial. The disadvantage of this technique is we are modifying the code of the system under test. The second technique is to modify our API's csproj file to allow our testing project access to its internals. For this recipe, we will go with the second method. Let's modify our Integration Tests project to give visibility into our API's internal files. In chapter7.csproj in the BooksAPI folder, add the following:

    ```
    <ItemGroup>
        <InternalsVisibleTo Include="Integration.Tests" />
    </ItemGroup>
    ```

    The nice thing about this approach is it requires no modification of the code of the project we are testing, only its project file.

5. Rebuild the API project for these changes to take effect. In the terminal, run the following command:

    ```
    dotnet build
    ```

6. In the Integration.Tests folder, let's add Microsoft's library for comprehensive integration testing:

    ```
    dotnet add package Microsoft.AspNetCore.Mvc.Testing
    ```

7. Create a file called CustomIntegrationTestsFixture.cs. Let's code our fixture for integration tests:

    ```
    using Microsoft.AspNetCore.Mvc.Testing;
    using Microsoft.Extensions.DependencyInjection;
    using Microsoft.Data.Sqlite;
    using Microsoft.EntityFrameworkCore;
    using Books;
    using Books.Data;
    using System.Net.Http;
    ```

```
using Microsoft.AspNetCore.Hosting;

namespace Tests.Integration;

public class CustomIntegrationTestsFixture :
WebApplicationFactory<Program>
{
}
```

All this fixture does is use `WebApplicationFactory` to start our API and integration tests in memory.

8. Now, we will replace our original project's `DbContext` registration:

```
namespace Tests.Integration;

public class CustomIntegrationTestsFixture :
WebApplicationFactory<Program>
{
    private SqliteConnection? _connection;

    protected override void ConfigureWebHost(
        IWebHostBuilder builder)
    {
        builder.ConfigureServices(services =>
        {
            var descriptor = services.SingleOrDefault(
                d => d.ServiceType == typeof(
                    DbContextOptions<AppDbContext>));

            if (descriptor != null)
            {
                services.Remove(descriptor);
            }
```

9. On the next line, create a new connection to the SQLite in-memory database:

```
_connection = new SqliteConnection("DataSource=:memory:");
_connection.Open();
```

10. Finish setting up `DbContext` and initialize the database. Replace the API's `AppDbContext` with our own:

```
services.AddDbContext<AppDbContext>(options =>
{
    options.UseSqlite(_connection);
});
```

11. Next, enter the code that will eventually seed the database:

```
var sp = services.BuildServiceProvider();

using (var scope = sp.CreateScope())
{
    var scopedServices = scope.ServiceProvider;
    var db = scopedServices.
    GetRequiredService<AppDbContext>();
    db.Database.EnsureCreated();
    Utilities.InitializeDatabase(db);
}
});
}
```

12. On the next line, let's create a method for returning `HttpClient` so we can support full HTTP requests:

```
public HttpClient GetClient()
{
    return CreateClient();
}
```

13. Now, implement `IDisposable` so we can correctly clean up each test:

```
protected override void Dispose(bool disposing)
{
    base.Dispose(disposing);
    if (disposing)
    {
        _connection?.Close();
    }
}
```

14. Next, create a file called `Utilities.cs`. In this `Utilities` class, we will do any of the custom database seeding we may want to perform:

```
using Books.Data;
using Books.Models;

namespace Tests.Integration;

public static class Utilities
{
    public static void InitializeDatabase(AppDbContext context)
    {
        context.Books.RemoveRange(context.Books);
        context.SaveChanges();
        context.Books.AddRange(
            new Book { Title = "Test Book 1", Author = "Author
                       1", ISBN = "1234567890" },
            new Book { Title = "Test Book 2", Author = "Author
                       2", ISBN = "0987654321" }
        );

        context.SaveChanges();
    }
}
```

We will only seed two books for this recipe.

15. Make sure the `FluentAssertions` library is installed in the `Integration.Tests` project:

```
dotnet add package FluentAssertions
```

16. Finally, create a file for our integration tests called `IntegrationTests.cs`.

Start to set up our tests by inheriting from our custom fixture:

```
using System.Net;
using System.Net.Http.Json;
using Books.Models;
using FluentAssertions;
using Microsoft.AspNetCore.Mvc.Testing;
using Xunit;

namespace Tests.Integration;

public class BooksControllerIntegrationTests :
IClassFixture<CustomIntegrationTestsFixture>
{
```

```
        private readonly HttpClient _client;

        public BooksControllerIntegrationTests(
            CustomIntegrationTestsFixture fixture)
        {
            _client = fixture.CreateClient();
        }
```

17. Create an integration test for the happy path:

```
    [Fact]
    public async Task GetBookById_ReturnsCorrectBook()
    {
        // Arrange
        var expectedBookId = 1; // Assuming the first seeded book
                                 // has ID 1
        // Act
        var response = await _client.GetAsync(
            $"/api/Books/{expectedBookId}");
        // Assert
        response.StatusCode.Should().Be(HttpStatusCode.OK);
        var book = await response.Content.ReadFromJsonAsync<
        BookDTO>();
        book.Should().NotBeNull();
        book!.Id.Should().Be(expectedBookId);
        book.Title.Should().Be("Test Book 1");
        book.Author.Should().Be("Author 1");
        book.ISBN.Should().Be("1234567890");
    }
```

18. Now, add an integration test for the unhappy path:

```
    [Fact]
    public async Task GetBookById_ReturnsNotFound_
    ForNonExistentBook()
    {
        // Arrange
        var nonExistentBookId = 9999;
        // Act
        var response = await _client.GetAsync($"/api/Books/
            {nonExistentBookId}");

        // Assert
        response.StatusCode.Should().Be(HttpStatusCode.NotFound);
    }
```

How it works...

We set up integration testing for our web API. We created a test fixture for our integration tests. In this test fixture, we customized the behavior of `WebApplicationFactory<T>`. This class has the ability to run our entire web API in memory. `WebApplicationFactory<T>` also gives us the ability to override or replace registrations and other startup code in our API with our own configuration when we run the test. We unregistered the real database context from our API and instead loaded our own mock database in memory using Microsoft's SQLite in-memory provider. We then created a static `Utilities` class to see this database with our own data.

> **Note**
>
> If we were dependent on SQL Server, or using a mapper such as Dapper, the SQLite in-memory database would not be sufficient (there can be no stored procedures for one thing, as it is SQLite). In that case, a better approach is to spin up an instance of SQL Server isolated in a Docker container.

Authentication in integration testing

The most frustrating part of creating integration tests is working with authentication. There are two approaches. The first approach is this: we simply duplicate the same authentication code that is in our API. This is especially straightforward if we are using a stateless JWT authentication token. We create the same token in the same way as we do in our API and add it to `HttpContext`. Then, we use normal HTTP requests in our integration tests. The system under test goes through its normal authentication process. The advantage is we have a lot of fine-grained control. The disadvantage to this setup is that it is extremely brittle. If any detail of authentication changes in our API, we have to duplicate that same code exactly the same way in our integration tests.

The other option is to create a custom authentication handler. When `WebApplicationFactory<T>` starts our API in test, we temporarily override the normal authentication service. We then bypass the reading of tokens and such, and simply add claims. Essentially, we bypass the normal security and directly add whatever claims we like to `ClaimsPrincipal`. Then, we instruct the system under test to create an authentication ticket from that claims principal. The system pretends that we are a logged-in user with claims that we specify (if we are using claims-based authentication).

It can be extremely frustrating to correctly set this up in ASP.NET Core, but once it is working, it is generally the recommended approach.

In this recipe, we will focus on the custom authentication handler approach. The end project for this recipe on GitHub includes both, if you are also curious about using the JWT approach.

Getting ready

The starter project for this recipe can be found here: `https://github.com/PacktPublishing/ASP.NET-9-Web-API-Cookbook/tree/main/start/chapter07/AuthHandler`.

How to do it...

1. The first thing we will have to do is change the `Program` class in our API to have the access modifier of `partial`. In the `BookAPI` folder, open `Program.cs` and change the public `Program` to this:

    ```
    public partial class Program {}
    ```

    While we previously discussed using `InternalsVisibleTo` in the API project's `csproj` file to grant access to internal members, this approach has limitations when working with custom authentication handlers in integration tests. In practice, setting claims on the client object via a custom authentication handler often fails unless the API's `Program` class is explicitly made partial.

    In `Integration.Tests`, create a new file called `CustomWebApplicationFactory.cs`. In this file, we will do the basic setup needed so `WebApplicationFactory` can start our system under test:

    ```
    Public class CustomWebApplicationFactory :
    WebApplicationFactory<Program>
    {
        private DbConnection? _connection;
    ```

2. Define a method called `ConfigureWebHost`; this unregisters the system under test's database, among other things:

    ```
    protected override void ConfigureWebHost(IWebHostBuilder
    builder)
        {
            builder.ConfigureServices(services =>
            {
                var descriptor = services.SingleOrDefault(
                    d => d.ServiceType == typeof(
                        DbContextOptions<AppDbContext>));
                if (descriptor != null)
                {
                    services.Remove(descriptor);
                }

                connection = new SqliteConnection(
    ```

```
        "DataSource=:memory:");
    _connection.Open();
      services.AddDbContext<AppDbContext>(options =>
    {
        options.UseSqlite(_connection);
    });
```

3. Continuing with this method, we need to explicitly register CORS and controllers for our test environment. `WebApplicationFactory<T>` doesn't automatically include these services from the application under test, so we must add them here:

```
services.AddCors(options =>
  {
     options.AddDefaultPolicy(builder =>
       {
         builder.AllowAnyOrigin()
            .AllowAnyHeader()
            .AllowAnyMethod();
       });
    });
    services.AddControllers();
    services.AddEndpointsApiExplorer();

    // Build the service provider.
    var sp = services.BuildServiceProvider();
```

4. We can close our `ConfigureWebHost` method by registering our testing database and setting the environment:

```
var sp = services.BuildServiceProvider();

        // Create a scope to obtain a reference to the database
        //context
        using (var scope = sp.CreateScope())
        {
            var scopedServices = scope.ServiceProvider;
            var db = scopedServices.
                    GetRequiredService<AppDbContext>();
            db.Database.EnsureCreated();
            Console.WriteLine("Database created and seeded.");
        }
    });

    builder.UseEnvironment("Development");
}
```

5. Finally, finish this class up by implementing `dispose`; we can tear down between tests without breaking anything:

```
protected override void Dispose(bool disposing)
{
    base.Dispose(disposing);
    if (disposing)
    {
        _connection?.Dispose();
    }
}
```

6. Create a file called `TesthandlerOptions.cs`; in this file, define simple types that will be used by `TestAuthHandler`:

```
using Microsoft.AspNetCore.Authentication;

public class TestAuthHandlerOptions :
AuthenticationSchemeOptions
{
    public string UserName { get; set; } = "testuser123";
    public List<string> Roles { get; set; } = new
        List<string>();
}
```

7. Create a file called `TestAuthHandler`. Define the `TestAuthHandler` class and inherit from `AuthenticationHandler`:

```
public class TestAuthHandler :
AuthenticationHandler<AuthenticationSchemeOptions>
{
    public const string AuthenticationScheme = "Test";
```

8. Create the constructor and a method that overrides ASP.NET Core's `HandleAuthenticateAsync()` method:

```
public TestAuthHandler(
    IOptionsMonitor<AuthenticationSchemeOptions> options,
    ILoggerFactory logger,
    UrlEncoder encoder,
    TimeProvider clock) : base(options, logger, encoder)
{
}
```

```
protected override Task<AuthenticateResult>
    HandleAuthenticateAsync()
{
```

9. In this method, we manually add our own claims. The minimum we can add is a Name and NameIdentifier claim. We then create our own AuthenticationTicket that tells the system that we are signed in:

```
var claims = new[]
{
    new Claim(ClaimTypes.Name, "testuser123"),
    new Claim(ClaimTypes.NameIdentifier, "testuser123"),
};

var identity = new ClaimsIdentity(
    claims, AuthenticationScheme);
var principal = new ClaimsPrincipal(identity);
var ticket = new AuthenticationTicket(
    principal, AuthenticationScheme);

var result = AuthenticateResult.Success(ticket);

return Task.FromResult(result);
}
```

10. Create a file called WebApplicationFactoryExtensions.cs. Here is where we will define the various extension methods we use to create HttpClient with the ability to simulate being signed in:

```
public static class WebApplicationFactoryExtensions
{
    public static HttpClient CreateClientWithTestAuth<
        TProgram>(this WebApplicationFactory<TProgram> factory)
        where TProgram : class
    {
        return factory.WithWebHostBuilder(builder =>
        {
            builder.ConfigureTestServices(services =>
            {
                services.AddSingleton(TimeProvider.System);
                services.AddAuthentication(options =>
                {
                    options.DefaultAuthenticateScheme =
                        TestAuthHandler.AuthenticationScheme;
```

```
                options.DefaultScheme =
                    TestAuthHandler.AuthenticationScheme;
                options.DefaultChallengeScheme =
                    TestAuthHandler.AuthenticationScheme;
            })
            .AddScheme<AuthenticationSchemeOptions,
                TestAuthHandler>(
                TestAuthHandler.AuthenticationScheme,
                options => { });
        });
    })
    .CreateClient(new WebApplicationFactoryClientOptions
    {
        AllowAutoRedirect = false
    });
}
```

11. We then define a method that returns the actual client with the `TestAuth` claims:

```
public static HttpClient
CreateAuthenticatedClient<TProgram>(this
WebApplicationFactory<TProgram> factory)
    where TProgram : class
    {
        var client = factory.CreateClientWithTestAuth();
        client.DefaultRequestHeaders.Authorization =
            new AuthenticationHeaderValue(
                TestAuthHandler.AuthenticationScheme);
        return client;
    }
```

If you want to use JWT claims, simply create extension methods that copy the token creation code from the API (the end project in GitHub has these examples).

12. We can now create our integration. Create an `Integration.Tests.cs` file. Define an integration tests class that inherits from a class fixture that uses the `CustomWebApplicationFactory` we created earlier:

```
public class AuthenticationTests :
IClassFixture<CustomWebApplicationFactory>
{
    private readonly CustomWebApplicationFactory _factory;

    public AuthenticationTests(CustomWebApplicationFactory
        factory)
    {
```

```
        _factory = factory;
    }
```

13. Let's create a test that calls a protected endpoint. This test uses the extension method we created to authenticate the client:

```
[Fact]
public async Task Auth_ShouldGetPastAuthEndpoint()
{

    var client = _factory.CreateAuthenticatedClient();

    // Act
    var response = await client.GetAsync("/api/Auth/testAuth");
        response.IsSuccessStatusCode.Should().BeTrue(
            "the request should be successful");

    var content = await response.Content.ReadAsStringAsync();

}
```

How it works...

We created our own `TestAuthHandler` that overrides the normal authentication system in our API. This handler simulates a logged-in authenticated user by skipping the normal authentication process and directly creating an `AuthenticationTicket` that includes the claims we specify.

See also...

The folder for this chapter in the book's GitHub repository includes many more examples, which were omitted for space, including extension methods for using a JWT directly with the client: `https://github.com/PacktPublishing/ASP.NET-9-Web-API-Cookbook/tree/main/end/chapter07/AuthHandler`.

8

GraphQL: Designing Flexible and Efficient APIs

This chapter is about building APIs with **GraphQL**. GraphQL offers a more flexible approach to creating APIs when compared to REST. GraphQL gives clients the ability to query only the data they need—no additional or unnecessary data is returned.

We start off by exploring real-time updates via GraphQL subscriptions. Real-time updates are something entirely absent from REST. REST APIs require us to use infrastructure such as SignalR or raw WebSocket implementations for real-time features. In contrast, GraphQL subscriptions provide this capability as a native feature of the protocol. While SignalR excels at real-time communication with features such as groups and connection management, GraphQL subscriptions offer a more integrated approach when you need real-time updates within your data query layer. The main benefit is that it is easy to send real-time updates using the same GraphQL schema and type system you use for your queries and mutations.

After that, we cover mutations for modifying data in GraphQL. Just as GraphQL queries give clients control over reading data, mutations provide a consolidated approach to modifying data – replacing REST's separate POST, PUT, and PATCH endpoints. This streamlined way of handling data modifications still allows clients to specify the exact shape of the response data they need.

We then explore pagination, sorting, and filtering capabilities. Both capabilities work seamlessly with Entity Framework's IQueryable<T> type, enabling efficient and flexible data retrieval directly from the database without loading unnecessary data into memory.

Finally, we explore federating separate GraphQL APIs using **Fusion**, a modern approach to combining multiple GraphQL schemas into a unified API. This gateway pattern is particularly beneficial in microservice architectures, allowing independent services to expose their own GraphQL endpoints while presenting clients with a single, cohesive API. Throughout this chapter, we'll use **Hot Chocolate**, a production-ready GraphQL server and library for .NET.

In this chapter, we're going to cover the following main topics:

- Real-time updates via GraphQL subscriptions

- Mutations for modifying data in GraphQL

- Implementing efficient pagination in GraphQL

- Filtering and sorting with GraphQL

- Distributed GraphQL with Hot Chocolate Fusion

Technical requirements

For the recipes in this chapter, you'll need the following:

- **.NET 9 SDK**: You'll need the latest version to work with the packages and features demonstrated. You can download the .NET 9 SDK here: `https://dotnet.microsoft.com/en-us/download/dotnet/9.0`.

- **Hot Chocolate packages**: We'll be installing these via the `dotnet` CLI as we go through each recipe. Hot Chocolate is the leading GraphQL server for .NET.

Real-time updates via GraphQL subscriptions

In this recipe, we will enhance, not replace, our REST API using **GraphQL** subscriptions. GraphQL subscriptions are an excellent option for adding real-time notifications to our APIs without SignalR or configuring raw WebSocket. Further, we will learn how to integrate a REST API controller with GraphQL services. We will take an ordinary REST `POST` endpoint and enhance it by sending a real-time update with information on a newly added resource via a GraphQL subscription. A change to our `POST` endpoint will call a subscription on our GraphQL service. This can be the basis of an integrated approach – so you can start using GraphQL in your Web API while still retaining REST endpoints. Finally, we will explore observing our GraphQL endpoints with Banana Cake Pop, which is provided for us with Hot Chocolate.

Getting ready

Clone the starter project here: `https://github.com/PacktPublishing/ASP.NET-9-Web-API-Cookbook/tree/main/start/chapter08/Subscription/Subscription`.

We will be running and testing our API via the terminal and the web browser. When we add Hot Chocolate to our project, it will automatically provide **Banana Cake Pop** – a built-in GraphQL IDE accessible at the `/graphql` endpoint. This gives us a powerful interface for testing our GraphQL endpoints and subscriptions.

How to do it...

1. Let's install the necessary HotChocolate packages so we can get started using GraphQL. In the BooksAPI folder, run the following:

    ```
    dotnet add package HotChocolate.AspNetCore
    dotnet add package HotChocolate.Subscriptions
    ```

2. First, we have to create a class for our subscription. Create a new folder called GraphQL. In the GraphQL folder, create a file called Subscription.cs. This class will define an OnNewBookAdded method to hold a newly created book resource:

    ```
    using Books.Models;
    namespace Books.GraphQL;

    public class Subscription
    {
        public BookDTO OnNewBookAdded([EventMessage] BookDTO book)
            => book;

    }
    ```

3. Add the [Subscribe] and [Topic] attributes to the OnNewBookAdded method:

    ```
    public class Subscription
    {
        [Topic]
        [Subscribe]
        public BookDTO OnNewBookAdded([EventMessage] BookDTO book)
            => book;
    }
    ```

    The [Subscribe] attribute designates the OnNewBookAdded method as a GraphQL endpoint. The [Topic] attribute defines what updates this subscription listens for – in this case, new books. The [EventMessage] attribute marks the parameter as the payload that will be sent to subscribers. When our REST API creates a new book, it will publish to this topic and all active subscribers will receive the book data in real time.

4. Next, we need to create a Query class. Create a new file in this folder called Query.cs. To set up GraphQL, we need to define a root Query object:

    ```
    namespace Books.GraphQL;

    public class Query
    {
        public string Hello() => "Hello";
    }
    ```

There must be at least one method defined. If you keep the class entirely empty, Banana Cake Pop will have trouble detecting a schema, as shown by the error message in *Figure 8.1*:

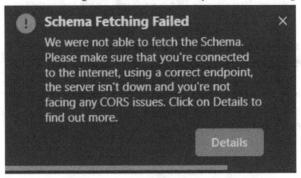

Figure 8.1 – Banana Cake Pop error caused by an empty Query class

5. Now, let's set up our API to use GraphQL with subscriptions. Navigate to the `Startup.cs` file. Import our GraphQL namespace so we have access to the `Query` and `Subscription` classes we just created:

    ```
    using Books.GraphQL;
    ```

6. Now, let's set up our project to use GraphQL with subscriptions. Still in the `Startup.cs` file, navigate to the `ConfigureServices` method in the `Startup.cs` file. On the line after `services.AddControllers`, we will register GraphQL as a service with the root query type and subscriptions enabled:

    ```
    services.AddGraphQLServer()
        .AddQueryType<Query>()
        .AddSubscriptionType<Subscription>()
        .AddInMemorySubscriptions();
    ```

First, we defined the root query type. We then defined our custom `Subscription` class as the class that holds all our `Subscription` endpoints. We specified we are going to use the in-memory subscription provider as opposed to Redis or one of the other providers, such as PostgreSQL. In-memory is a great choice for development and testing.

Startup.cs versus Program.cs

This project uses the traditional `Startup.cs` pattern instead of the minimal `Program.cs` hosting model used in previous recipes. We've chosen this approach to demonstrate that GraphQL works equally well with both patterns, and because many real-world projects still use this structure. The GraphQL configuration shown here can be easily adapted to the minimal hosting model by moving the service registration and middleware configuration to `Program.cs`.

7. Next, on the line after `app.UseRouting`, we will specify that WebSocket is to be used as the transport layer. We should place this before `UseEndpoints()`:

```
app.UseWebSockets();
```

8. Now, map the GraphQL endpoints after and alongside our REST endpoints:

```
app.UseEndpoints(endpoints =>
{
    endpoints.MapControllers();
    endpoints.MapGraphQL();
});
```

9. Let's update `BooksController` to enable real-time notifications.

   We want our REST `POST` endpoint to trigger a notification via our GraphQL subscription. Navigate to `BooksController.cs` and add the following `using` directives:

```
using HotChocolate.Subscriptions;
using Books.GraphQL;
```

This gives us access to Hot Chocolate's subscription library and our custom `Subscription` class.

10. Add a field to our `BooksController` to hold the event sender, which will trigger the subscription:

```
private readonly IBooksService _service;
private required readonly ITopicEventSender _eventSender =
null!;

public BooksController(
    IBooksService service, ITopicEventSender eventSender)
{
    _service = service ?? throw new ArgumentNullException(
        nameof(booksService));
    _eventSender=eventSender ?? throw new ArgumentNullException(
        nameof(eventSender));
}
```

Since our controller has grown more complex, we have set the constructor to throw an error if either our service or event sender is missing. This will make it easier to debug if anything ever goes wrong.

11. Finally, let's update our POST endpoint's action method to send an event right before the endpoint returns:

```
[HttpPost]
public async Task<IActionResult> CreateBook([FromBody] BookDTO
bookDto)
{
    if (!ModelState.IsValid)
    {
        return BadRequest(ModelState);
    }
    try
    {
        var createdBook = await _service.CreateBookAsync(bookDto);
        await _eventSender.SendAsync(nameof(Subscription.
          OnNewBookAdded), createdBook);
        return CreatedAtAction(nameof(GetBookById), new { id =
          createdBook.Id }, createdBook);
}
```

12. Run the project via the terminal or your IDE of choice:

```
dotnet ru.
```

13. While the API project is running, open your web browser. Navigate to http://localhost:5217/graphql to access the interactive Banana Cake Pop IDE.

14. In the **Request** window, run the following subscription query:

```
subscription {
  onNewBookAdded {
    id
    title
    author
  }
}
```

Figure 8.2 shows our subscription activated in Banana Cake Pop:

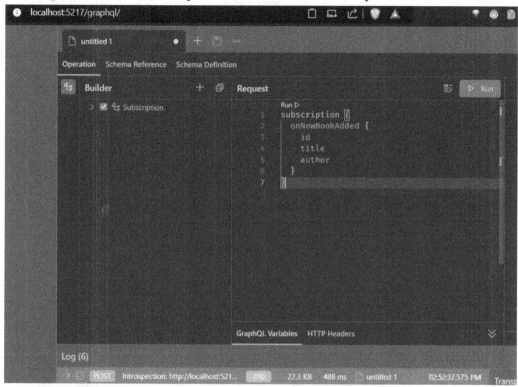

Figure 8.2 – Connecting to a subscription in Banana Cake Pop

15. Hit the **Run** button. Our subscription is now active.

Let's test that creating a resource in REST will trigger real-time updates from GraphQL. Although we can use any client to send the POST request, here is a simple way to do it in the terminal with PowerShell using Invoke-RestMethod:

```
$uri = "http://localhost:5217/api/books";
$headers = @{ "Content-Type" = "application/json" };
$body = @{
    Title = "The Great Gatsby"
    Author = "F. Scott Fitzgerald"
    PublicationDate = "1925-04-10"
    ISBN = "9780743273565"
    Genre = "Classic Fiction"
    Summary = "The story of the fabulously wealthy Jay Gatsby
        and his love for the beautiful Daisy Buchanan."
} | ConvertTo-Json
```

```
$response = Invoke-RestMethod -Uri $uri -Method Post -Body $body
-Headers $headers
```

16. In Banana Cake Pop, we can see the subscription immediately receiving information on the newly created resource, as shown in *Figure 8.3*:

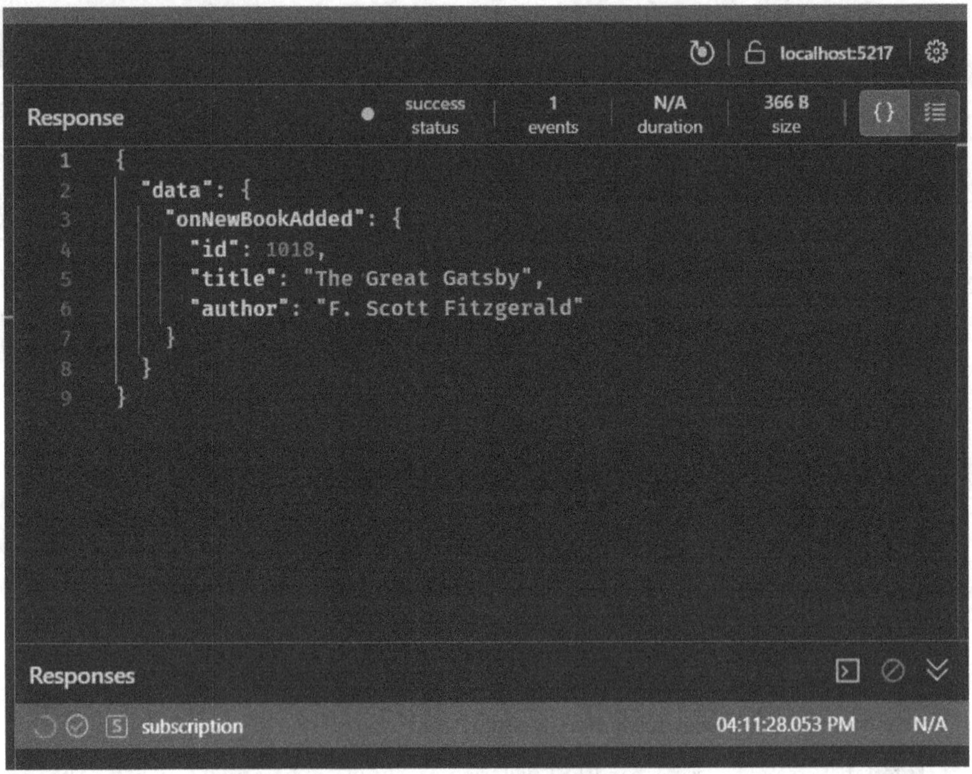

Figure 8.3 – A real-time GraphQL response in Banana Cake Pop

How it works...

We set up the Hot Chocolate implementation of GraphQL for .NET. Hot Chocolate comes with many wonderful community tools, such as the interactive Banana Cake Pop IDE. We registered our GraphQL server and set a root query object and an in-memory subscription. Then, we made sure that ASP.NET Core chose WebSocket as the transport layer for our subscription. We mapped our new GraphQL subscription endpoint alongside our REST endpoints. Then, we updated our REST POST endpoint to send an event to GraphQL using ITopicEventSender. This successfully sends a real-time update whenever a new resource is created.

Mutations for modifying data in GraphQL

In this recipe, we will learn how to modify data using GraphQL. GraphQL mutations are analogous to POST, PUT, and PATCH methods in REST. GraphQL mutations allow us to perform data modifications and at the same time return the modified data. In GraphQL, mutations are operations that cause side effects on the server and return the modified data, allowing clients to specify exactly what data they need in the response.

We will also use type extensions to organize our mutations. In GraphQL schemas, there's a single root mutation type. We can define multiple mutation fields within this type. In this recipe, we'll use type extensions to organize our mutations into separate classes for better code maintainability.

Getting ready

- The startup project can be cloned here: `https://github.com/PacktPublishing/ASP.NET-9-Web-API-Cookbook/tree/main/start/chapter08/Mutations`

How to do it...

1. We already have Hot Chocolate installed in our project, but we will need the NuGet data package. In the terminal, navigate to the `BooksAPI` folder and install the following:

```
dotnet add package HotChocolate.Data
```

2. Let's create an input class for our mutation. Create a new file in `AddBookInput.cs` in the `GraphQL` folder. Let's fill in the `AddBookInput` class:

```
using System.ComponentModel.DataAnnotations;

namespace Books.GraphQL;

public record AddBookInput(
    [Required] [MaxLength(200)] string Title,
    [Required] [MaxLength(100)] string Author,
    [Required] DateTime PublicationDate,
    [Required] [StringLength(13, MinimumLength = 10)] string
        ISBN,
    [Required] [MaxLength(50)] string Genre,
    [MaxLength(1000)] string? Summary);
```

Still in the `GraphQL` folder, let's create a file called `IUserError.cs`.

This custom error interface will map our error classes to user-friendly errors we specify:

```
namespace Books.GraphQL;

public interface IUserError
{
    string Message { get; }
    string Code { get; }
}
```

3. Create an `AddBookPayload.cs` file in the `GraphQL` folder. We will create an `AddBookPayload` class to represent the mutation's response:

```
using Books.Models;

namespace Books.GraphQL;

public class AddBookPayload
{
    public BookDTO? Book { get; }

    public AddBookPayload(BookDTO book)
    {
        Book = book;
    }
}
```

Since we are going to configure `MutationConvention`, we don't have to create a property to store our payload errors.

4. Create a `BookAlreadyExists.cs` file in the `GraphQL` folder:

```
namespace Books.GraphQL;

public class BookAlreadyExistsError : IUserError
{
    public string Message { get; }
    public string Code => "BOOK_ALREADY_EXISTS";
    public BookAlreadyExistsError(string isbn)
    {
        Message = $"A book with ISBN '{isbn}' already exists.";
    }
}
```

5. Let's create a full exception that is inherited from .NET's `Exception` class. Still in the GraphQL folder, create a file called `BookAlreadyExistsException.cs` and fill in the following class:

```
namespace Books.GraphQL;

public class BookAlreadyExistsException : Exception
{
    public string ISBN { get; }

    public BookAlreadyExistsException(string isbn)
        : base($"A book with ISBN '{isbn}' already exists.")
    {
        ISBN = isbn;
    }
}
```

Following GraphQL best practices, when there is a problem, we will throw a full exception. This differs from REST, where some developers choose not to throw an error but just return a failed `StatusCode` if there is a problem with the operation an action method is supposed to perform.

6. Now we will create our `Mutation` class in a file called `BookMutations.cs` and have it use the same `CreateBookAsync` service method our REST API uses to create resources:

```
using Books.Models;
using Books.Services;
using HotChocolate;
using HotChocolate.Subscriptions;
using HotChocolate.Types;

namespace Books.GraphQL;

[ExtendObjectType("Mutation")]
public class BookMutations
{
    [Error(typeof(BookAlreadyExistsException))]
    public async Task<AddBookPayload> AddBookAsync(
        AddBookInput input,
        [Service] IBooksService booksService,
        [Service] ITopicEventSender eventSender)
    {
    }

}
```

7. Now let's fill in the center of our `BookMutations` class. The service method for checking whether a book already exists or not is already included in the starter project:

```
if (await booksService.BookExistsAsync(input.ISBN))
{
    throw new BookAlreadyExistsException(input.ISBN);
}

var bookDto = new BookDTO
{
    Title = input.Title,
    Author = input.Author,
    PublicationDate = input.PublicationDate,
    ISBN = input.ISBN,
    Genre = input.Genre,
    Summary = input.Summary ?? string.Empty
};

var createdBook = await booksService
    .CreateBookAsync(bookDto);
await eventSender.SendAsync(nameof(
    Subscription.OnNewBookAdded), createdBook);

return new AddBookPayload(createdBook);
}
```

Now we just have to expand our `GraphQL` server registration. Navigate to `Program.cs`. Configure Hot Chocolate to `AddMutationType()` and our type extension mutation conventions:

```
services.AddGraphQLServer()
    .AddQueryType<Query>()
    .AddMutationType()
    .AddTypeExtension<BookMutations>()
    .AddSubscriptionType<Subscription>()
    .AddInMemorySubscriptions()
```

8. Let's add more extension methods on the `AddGraphQLServer()` method, enable mutation conventions, and register the custom error interface we created:

```
.AddMutationConventions(applyToAllMutations: true)
.AddErrorInterfaceType<IUserError>();
```

9. Let's test our mutation. Run the API via the `dotnet` CLI or your IDE:

```
dotnet run
```

10. In your web browser, navigate to `http://localhost:5217/graphql`.

In the Banana Cake Pop **Request** window, specify the GraphQL mutation query. We will give the shape of data that will be returned on input as well as a fragment for our error messages:

```
mutation AddNewBook($input: AddBookInput!) {
    addBook(input: $input) {
        book {
            id
            title
            author
        }
        errors {
            ... on BookAlreadyExistsError {
                message
                code
            }
        }
    }
}
```

Let's try passing the following variables:

```
{
    "input": {
        "title": "1984",
        "author": "George Orwell",
        "publicationDate": "1949-06-08T00:00:00Z",
        "isbn": "9780451524935",
        "genre": "Dystopian Fiction",
        "summary": "A dystopian novel about totalitarianism."
    }
}
```

If the book doesn't exist, it will be added.

> **Important note**
>
> The `publicationDate DateTime` value has to be a full ISO 8601 date (since we made the `PublicationDate` property a `DateTime` type).

If the ISBN is not unique in the database, GraphQL will return an error according to our defined custom error per `MutationConvention`. We can change what fields come back simply by changing our mutation in the response window. If we add an `ISBN` field, we can have the GraphQL API return a new field without changing our API code.

How it works...

In this recipe, we implemented a GraphQL mutation to add new books using Hot Chocolate's mutation conventions. We used type extensions to organize our mutation code. Even though we only made one mutation in this recipe, this approach helps organize our GraphQL schema when we have many mutations to add, update, or delete resources.

When we add a new book, the `BookMutations` mutation first checks whether a book with the same ISBN already exists by calling `booksService.BookExistsAsync(input.ISBN)`. If the book does exist, it throws `BookAlreadyExistsException`. We used the `[Error]` attribute to map this exception to a user-friendly error in the GraphQL schema. Thanks to Hot Chocolate's mutation conventions, this error is automatically included in the `errors` field of the mutation's response payload, providing meaningful feedback to the client without exposing internal exception details.

Implementing efficient pagination in GraphQL

In this recipe, we will learn how to add paging to our GraphQL API using Hot Chocolate's built-in paging capabilities. We will implement cursor-based pagination using Hot Chocolate's `[UsePaging]` attribute. The `[UsePaging]` attribute works well with Entity Framework's `IQueryable<T>` to directly work with the database context without having to load extra results into memory. `IQueryable<T>` is so efficient as it enables deferred execution and query composition.

Getting ready

The starter project can be found here: `https://github.com/PacktPublishing/ASP.NET-9-Web-API-Cookbook/tree/main/start/chapter08/Pagination/`.

Note: This recipe uses the `HotChocolate.Data` package, which we installed in the previous recipe and is included in the starter project. This package provides the filtering and sorting capabilities we'll use alongside pagination.

How to do it...

1. We have to add a method to the `BooksRepository` class, which returns `IQueryable<Book>`. Before we can do that, open `IBooksRepository` and define its signature:

    ```
    public interface IBooksRepository {

        ...

            IQueryable<Book> GetBooksAsQueryable();
    }
    ```

2. Implement the method in `BooksRepository.cs`:

    ```
    public IQueryable<Book> GetBooksAsQueryable() {
        return _context.Books.AsNoTracking();
    }
    ```

    This method allows our pagination to work directly with the database context. `AsNoTracking()` improves performance for read-only queries by disabling change tracking. Returning an `IQueryable<T>` type allows for deferred execution.

3. Update `BooksService` to use the new repository method. Define the method in `IBooksService.cs`:

    ```
    public interface IBooksService {
        IQueryable<BookDTO> GetBooks();
    }
    ```

4. Implement the method in `BooksService.cs`:

    ```
    public IQueryable<BookDTO> GetBooks() {
        return _repository.GetBooksAsQueryable()
            .Select(b => new BookDTO
            {
              Id = b.Id,
              Title = b.Title,
              Author = b.Author,
              PublicationDate = b.PublicationDate,
              ISBN = b.ISBN,
              Genre = b.Genre,
              Summary = b.Summary
              });
    }
    ```

5. Now, modify our `Query` class in `Query.cs` to include a paginated books field with filtering:

```
using Books.Models;
using Books.Services;

namespace Books.GraphQL;

public class Query {
    [UsePaging(IncludeTotalCount = true)]
    [UseFiltering]
    public IQueryable<BookDTO> GetBooks([Service] IBooksService
        booksService) {
        return booksService.GetBooks();
    }
}
```

We added the `[UsePaging]` attribute, which is all we need to implement cursor-based paging.

6. Navigate to the `ConfigureServices` method in the `Program.cs` file and add two new extension methods, `AddFiltering()` and `AddSorting()`, to the end:

```
services.AddGraphQLServer()
    .AddQueryType<Query>()
    .AddMutationType()
    .AddTypeExtension<BookMutations>()
    .AddSubscriptionType<Subscription>()
    .AddInMemorySubscriptions()
    .AddMutationConventions()
    .AddErrorInterfaceType<IUserError>()
    .AddFiltering()
    .AddSorting();
```

7. Now let's run our API:

```
dotnet run
```

8. Open your web browser and navigate to Banana Cake Pop at the following URL: `http://localhost:5217/graphql`.

9. Execute the following GraphQL query to return a page of five results with the total count included:

```
query {
    books(first: 5) {
      totalCount
      pageInfo {
              hasNextPage
              endCursor
```

```
        }
      edges {
            cursor
        node {
            id
            title
            author
        }
      }
    }
  }
```

10. To fetch the next page, use the last cursor, `endCursor`, from the previous response. Place that value in the `after` field:

```
query {
    books(First: 5, after: "NA==") {
    ...
```

Now, the next page of results will return after the cursor `"NA=="`. We can also add filtering by simply adding a `where` field:

```
query {
    books(
    first: 10,
    where: {
        author: { startsWith: "Rebeca" }
    }
  )
```

How it works...

We implemented cursor-based paging in GraphQL with the [UsePaging] attribute and enabled filtering with the [UseFiltering] attribute. All it required was a method that interacted with our database context and returned an IQueryable<T> result from our resolver. Hot Chocolate efficiently applied pagination directly at the database level. This approach leveraged deferred execution and query composition, ensuring optimal performance and resource usage.

Filtering and sorting with GraphQL

In this recipe, we will learn how to add filtering and sorting capabilities to our GraphQL API using Hot Chocolate's [UseFiltering] and [UseSorting] attributes. Building on the filtering we implemented in the previous recipe, we'll see how sorting works seamlessly with IQueryable<T> to provide powerful client-side control over data ordering.

Getting ready

The starter project for this recipe can be found here: `https://github.com/PacktPublishing/ASP.NET-9-Web-API-Cookbook/tree/main/start/chapter08/FilteringAndSorting`.

How to do it...

1. Navigate to the `Query.cs` file in the `GraphQL` folder, and update our `Query` class to include filtering and sorting:

```
public class Query {
[UseFiltering]
[UseSorting]
public IQueryable<BookDTO> GetBooks([Service] IBooksService
booksService) {
    return booksService.GetBooks();
  }
}
```

2. Navigate to the `Program.cs` file and add the `.AddFiltering` and `.AddSorting` extension methods to the `AddGraphQLServer` service:

```
public void ConfigureServices(IServiceCollection services) {
    services.AddGraphQLServer()
        .AddQueryType<Query>()
        .AddMutationType()
        .AddTypeExtension<BookMutations>()
        .AddSubscriptionType<Subscription>()
        .AddInMemorySubscriptions()
        .AddErrorInterfaceType<IUserError>()
        .AddFiltering()
        .AddSorting();
}
```

3. Run the API:

```
dotnet run
```

4. Test filtering and sorting in Banana Cake Pop. Navigate to `http://localhost:5217/graphql`. The following query illustrates both sorting and filtering our data:

```
query {
  books(
    where: {
      genre: { eq: "Science Fiction" }
```

```
    },
    order: {
      publicationDate: DESC
    }
  ) {
    id
    title
    author
    publicationDate
  }
}
```

How it works...

By adding the `[UseFiltering]` and `[UseSorting]` attributes to the `GetBooks` method, Hot Chocolate automatically generates filter and sort input types based on your `BookDTO` type. This allows clients to construct complex queries to filter and sort data without additional server-side code.

Distributed GraphQL with Hot Chocolate Fusion

In this recipe, we will explore the most powerful way to stitch schemas in Hot Chocolate v14 – Fusion. GraphQL Fusion represents a modern approach to distributed GraphQL, allowing you to combine multiple GraphQL services into a unified API through a gateway pattern. Unlike traditional schema stitching, Fusion is built from the ground up to support distributed systems and is now backed by the GraphQL Foundation as an open specification for federated GraphQL. The starter project contains two completely independent GraphQL APIs. We will unify the schema of these two independent APIs through a new GraphQL gateway. This makes it easy to combine multiple APIs, even APIs running different tech stacks, into a single GraphQL endpoint to be consumed by clients.

Getting ready

The starter project for this recipe can be found here: `https://github.com/PacktPublishing/ASP.NET-9-Web-API-Cookbook/tree/main/start/chapter08/Fusion`.

This starter project contains two independent GraphQL API projects. Most of the following recipe will take place in the terminal.

How to do it...

1. In the terminal, in the root solution folder, add Fusion to both API projects:

    ```
    cd BooksAPI
    dotnet add package HotChocolate.Fusion
    cd ../Sales
    dotnet add package HotChocolate.Fusion
    cd..
    ```

2. Make sure you are in the `Fusion` folder. Create a tools manifest:

    ```
    dotnet new tool-manifest
    ```

    This will create a `dotnet-tools.json` file in a new `.config` folder.

3. Install the Hot Chocolate Fusion CLI as a required tool:

    ```
    dotnet tool install HotChocolate.Fusion.CommandLine
    ```

4. Configure the Books API subgraph, still in the root `Fusion` folder:

    ```
    dotnet fusion subgraph config set http --url http://
    localhost:5217/graphql -w ./BooksAPI
    ```

5. Configure the Sales API subgraph:

    ```
    dotnet fusion subgraph config set http --url http://
    localhost:5219/graphql -w ./Sales
    ```

6. Update the subgraph names in the generated config files. For the Books API's `subgraph.config.json` file, change the name from `default` to `Books`, and specify the correct port number:

    ```
    {
        "subgraph": "Books",
        "http": {
            "baseAddress": "http://localhost:5217/graphql"
        }
    }
    ```

7. In the `Sales` folder, set the subgraph name to `Sales`:

    ```
    {
        "subgraph": "Sales",
        "http": {
            "baseAddress": "http://localhost:5219/graphql"
        }
    }
    ```

8. In both projects, install the `CommandLine` package so we can export schemas via `dotnet run`:

```
cd BooksAPI
dotnet add package HotChocolate.AspNetCore.CommandLine
cd ../Sales
dotnet add package HotChocolate.AspNetCore.CommandLine
```

9. In the `Program.cs` files of both the `BooksAPI` and `Sales` projects, replace the line `app.Run();` with the following:

```
app.RunWithGraphQLCommands(args);
```

10. Run the following command in the `BooksAPI` directory:

```
dotnet run schema export --output schema.graphql
```

Then, run it again in the `Sales` directory.

11. Install the Hot Chocolate templates. This includes the `Gateway` template we need:

```
dotnet new install HotChocolate.Templates
```

12. Now create the actual gateway:

```
dotnet new graphql-gateway -n Gateway
```

13. Pack the subgraphs:

```
dotnet fusion subgraph pack -w ./BooksAPI
dotnet fusion subgraph pack -w ./Sales
```

This creates the `fsp` files, which will be read by the `compose` command.

14. Now let's compose our actual gateway:

```
dotnet fusion compose -p ./Gateway/gateway.fgp -s ./BooksAPI -s
./Sales
```

15. Now let's run all three services (`BooksAPI`, `Sales`, and the `Gateway` project). You can do this by either adding the gateway to your solution file, and using an IDE to start up all three, or running the following three commands in three separate terminal instances or splits:

```
dotnet run --project BooksAPI
dotnet run --project Sales
dotnet run --project Gateway
```

16. If you open your web browser and navigate to the gateway's port at `http://localhost:5098/graphql`. Banana Cake Pop will open and you can see we have one unified GraphQL API for both projects.

How it works...

GraphQL Fusion combines schema composition and query planning to enable the efficient federation of independent GraphQL APIs. In this recipe, we unified two separate APIs into a single gateway endpoint, demonstrating how Fusion automatically handles schema composition and cross-service relationships. By using a tool manifest file, we ensure all developers on the project use the same version of the Fusion CLI tools, making the gateway configuration process consistent across the team. The gateway intelligently delegates requests to appropriate subgraphs and optimizes query execution, providing clients with a seamless unified API while maintaining the independence of underlying services.

Get This Book's PDF Version and Exclusive Extras

UNLOCK NOW

Scan the QR code (or go to packtpub.com/unlock). Search for this book by name, confirm the edition, and then follow the steps on the page.

Note: Keep your invoice handy. Purchases made directly from Packt don't require an invoice.

9

Deploying and Managing Your WebAPI in the Cloud

In this chapter, we'll explore practical recipes for leveraging .NET in the cloud. We will start off by working with the Azure CLI and enhancing our APIs with external Azure services. We will build an API using an external Azure service (**Azure Maps**) and learn to manage configurations in **Key Vault** so our API can have access to secrets securely once it has been deployed.

We will then learn how to create a custom API gateway using **Yet Another Reverse Proxy** (**YARP**). This gateway setup enables powerful routing and load balancing with distributed systems and servers as a simple alternative to over-complicated microservices. By leveraging YARP's customization, we will achieve a flexible gateway that can handle traffic efficiently. We will also explore creating custom load-balancing policies in YARP.

For the rest of this chapter, we will focus on .NET Aspire. .NET Aspire is quickly becoming the preferred way to orchestrate your .NET deployments. It builds upon lessons learned from Project Tye, which was focused on the command line, and moves everything into C# code by letting you orchestrate your .NET projects directly through an `AppHost`. By leveraging `ServiceDiscovery`, Aspire automatically manages connection strings and enables built-in telemetry and health checks across resources.

In this chapter, we're going to cover the following recipes:

- Building with Azure – core service integration through geolocation
- Azure Key Vault – securing configuration with custom health checks
- Creating an API gateway and custom load balancing policy with YARP reverse proxy
- Migrating a distributed API to .NET Aspire for unified orchestration and monitoring
- Integrating dockerized services with .NET Aspire – an example with Prometheus

Technical requirements

For the recipes in this chapter, you'll need the following:

- **.NET 9 SDK**: The recipes in this chapter are written using .NET 9 features and the latest version of .NET Aspire

- **Azure Subscription**: A free trial subscription will work for following along with the Azure-related recipes

- **Azure CLI**: Required for managing Azure resources from the command line

- **Docker Desktop**: Needed for the Prometheus integration recipe

- **Development HTTPS Certificate**: You'll need to create this using the `dotnet dev-certs` command, which we'll cover in the recipes

Note that while many recipes can be followed using the free tier of Azure services, you will need to provide billing information to create an Azure account. The Azure Maps service used in the first recipe offers a free tier with 5,000 requests per month.

Building with Azure – core service integration through geolocation

In this recipe, we will integrate an Azure-managed external API, specifically using **Azure Maps**, into our Web API. While geolocation is the service of choice for this example, this process is broadly applicable to many Azure services. We are also going to learn how to use `Azure.Identity` for managed authentication. Azure Identity operates differently than the bearer JWT method covered earlier in the book.

We will focus on using the Azure CLI. The Azure CLI is an incredibly powerful tool for resource management. We urge you to explore Azure in the command line even if you are accustomed to deploying via IDE integrations. You will learn how to structure the Web API's settings and services in .NET Core to integrate with a remote Azure service. By the end of this recipe, you will not only have an operational geolocation service but also understand Azure service creation, configuration, and API integration.

Getting ready...

No starter project exists for this recipe, we will be creating a new Web API from scratch. We will be focusing on using the Azure CLI. We will be using a free trial of Azure Maps. The first 5,000 requests are free, but you do need to give Azure your billing information. If you want to follow along, you can create an account on `https://portal.azure.com`. We will skip the most basic steps of account creation, so please create a trial Azure account if you have not already done so.

We will be running and testing our API via the terminal. The testing calls will be made with `Invoke-RestMethod` in PowerShell, but if you prefer, feel free to use Postman or Curl.

How to do it...

1. Link your account to the Azure CLI tool:

    - If you are on Windows you can install the Azure CLI tool via `Chocolatey`:

        ```
        choco install azure-cli
        refreshenv
        ```

    - If you are on Mac, you can install it via `Brew`:

        ```
        brew install azure-cli
        ```

    - On Linux, the Azure CLI is available on various package managers and from here: `https://learn.microsoft.com/en-us/cli/azure/install-azure-cli-linux?pivots=apt`

2. Log in to your account:

    ```
    az login
    ```

    > **Having trouble logging in?**
    > If you have trouble logging into the CLI but can log in to the website. You may need to specify the tenant. The tenant number should be visible when you log in to the Azure portal: `az login -tenant dxxxxxx-exxx-44b8-xxxx-xxxxxxxxxxxx`.

3. Confirm that you have access to your account in the CLI:

    ```
    az account show
    az account list --output table
    ```

4. Create a resource group:

    ```
    az group create --name "MyResourceGroup" --location "<your-location>"
    ```

    Users in North America might use `eastus` or `westus2`, while European users might choose `northeurope` or `westeurope`.

5. Create an Azure Maps account resource.

    In the Azure web portal, search for `Azure Maps` and create a resource. You can select the default options for **Datastore** and **CORS**.

    We can also create the Azure Maps resource via the CLI:

    ```
    az maps account create  --name "GeoGatewayMaps" --resource-group
    "MyResourceGroup" --sku "G2" --kind "Gen2" --accept-tos
    ```

6. Confirm that your Maps account has been set up:

    ```
    az maps account list --output table
    ```

7. To sign into the resource, create a managed identity:

    ```
    az identity create
        --name "MyGeoApiIdentity"
        --resource-group "MyResourceGroup"
    ```

8. Get the keys. We will use `dotnet secrets` to store them for development:

    ```
    az maps account keys list --name "GeoGatewayMaps" --resource-
    group "MyResourceGroup"
    ```

9. Now, create a simple API to test our resource:

    ```
    dotnet new webapi -o mapAPI
    ```

10. Let's navigate to the mapAPI subfolder, In the terminal, initialize user secrets to store our key. In the next recipe, we will integrate Key Vault:

    ```
    cd mapAPI
    dotnet user-secrets init
    ```

11. Store the Maps API key. Use the primaryKey value displayed in the output of the az maps account keys list command from **Step 8**.

    ```
    dotnet user-secrets set "AzureMaps:ApiKey" "<your-primary-key>"
    ```

12. In appsettings.json, create an AzureMaps object and store your BaseUrl:

    ```
    "Logging": {
        "LogLevel": {
            "Default": "Information",
            "Microsoft.AspNetCore": "Warning"
        }
    },
    "AllowedHosts": "*",
    "AzureMaps": {
    ```

```
        "BaseUrl": "https://atlas.microsoft.com/"
    }
}
```

13. Create a dev-cert:

```
dotnet dev-certs https --clean
dotnet dev-certs https --trust
```

14. Create a record for handling the `AzureMapSettings` in a new file called `AzureMapsSettings.cs`:

```
public record AzureMapsSettings
{
    public required string ApiKey { get; init; }
    public required string BaseUrl { get; init; }
}
```

This class will hold our Azure Maps configuration, following the options pattern commonly used in ASP.NET Core applications.

15. Create an interface for the service we will create for interacting with the Azure service. This abstraction also allows us to potentially swap out Azure Maps for another geolocation provider in the future:

```
public interface IGeolocationService
{
    Task<string?> GetCountryCodeAsync(string ipAddress);
}
```

16. Now, create a response model that takes a response from the Azure service in a new file called `AzureMapsResponse.cs`:

```
using System.Text.Json.Serialization;
using System.Text.Json;
using System.Net;

public class AzureMapsResponse
{
    [JsonPropertyName("countryRegion")]
    public required CountryRegion CountryRegion { get; set; }

    [JsonPropertyName("ipAddress")]
    private string _ipAddress = string.Empty;
    public string IpAddress
    {
        get => _ipAddress;
```

```
        set
        {
            if (IPAddress.TryParse(value, out var ip))
            {
                _ipAddress = value;
            }
            else
            {
                throw new JsonException($"Invalid IP address
                format: {value}");
            }
        }
    }
}


public record CountryRegion
{
    [JsonPropertyName("isoCode")]
    public string IsoCode { get; init; } = string.Empty;
}
```

The AzureMapsResponse class maps the JSON response from Azure Maps to a strongly typed C# object. Note that the IP validation is in the setter.

17. Create a new service for interacting with the maps service called AzureMapsGeolocationService.cs. We will not use primary constructor syntax here so we can maintain clear field assignments:

```
public class AzureMapsGeolocationService : IGeolocationService
{
    private readonly HttpClient _httpClient;
    private readonly ILogger<AzureMapsGeolocationService> _
        logger;
    private readonly string _apiKey;

    public AzureMapsGeolocationService(
        HttpClient httpClient,
        IConfiguration configuration,
        ILogger<AzureMapsGeolocationService> logger)
    {
        _httpClient = httpClient;
        _logger = logger;
        _apiKey = configuration["AzureMaps:ApiKey"]
            ?? throw new InvalidOperationException("Azure Maps
                API key not found");
```

```
        _httpClient.BaseAddress = new Uri(
            configuration["AzureMaps:BaseUrl"]                  ??
            "https://atlas.microsoft.com/");
    }
```

18. Now, in the same file, let's implement the `GetCountryCodeAsync` method:

```
public async Task<string?> GetCountryCodeAsync(string ipAddress)
    {
        try
        {
            var response = await _httpClient
                .GetFromJsonAsync<AzureMapsResponse>(
                    $"geolocation/ip/json?api-version=1.0&ip={
                        ipAddress}&subscription-key={_apiKey}");
            _logger.LogInformation(
                "Retrieved location for IP{IP}: {CountryCode}",
                ipAddress, response?.CountryRegion.IsoCode);
            return response?.CountryRegion.IsoCode;
        }
        catch (Exception ex)
        {
            _logger.LogError(
                ex,
                "Failed to get location for IP {IP}",
                ipAddress);
            return null;
        }
    }
}
```

The core of the preceding `GetCountryCodeAsync` method sends an IP address to the Azure Maps service. Instead of token authentication, we sent along our subscription key as a query parameter.

19. In `Program.cs`, let's register the service we made which calls the endpoint:

```
builder.Services.AddHttpClient<IGeolocationService,
AzureMapsGeolocationService>();
```

20. Let's create a minimal API get endpoint. There is no need to create a full controller class for what is only a debugging endpoint. Add the test endpoint between `builder.Build()` and `app.Run()`:

```
app.MapGet("/debug/geo/{ip}", async (string ip,
IGeolocationService geoService) =>
```

```
    {
        var countryCode = await geoService.GetCountryCodeAsync(ip);
        return Results.Ok(new { IP = ip, CountryCode = countryCode
                            ?? "Unknown" });
    });
```

If we call the endpoint with an `ip address`, the service should return an ISO code, as you can see in *Figure 9.1*:

```
C:\my-coding-projects> Invoke-RestMethod -Uri "http://localhost:5289/debug/g
eo/104.22.67.180"

ip              countryCode
--              -----------
104.22.67.180 US
```

Figure 9.1 – Converting an IP address to a country code

How it works...

In this recipe, we set up and registered a new Azure service, assigned it to a resource group, and managed access keys using Azure Identity. Through this process, we learned how our account, resource group, and resource operate together in Azure. Although our geolocation service (which converts an IP address to a country ISO code) is useful on its own, this approach applies to many other Azure services that could be integrated just as easily.

We accomplished almost all of this via the Azure CLI. One advantage of CLI tools is that it is easier to demonstrate repeatable, step-by-step instructions via text rather than manual clicks of the mouse and lots of images. Besides the increased control, the Azure CLI instructions serve as the basis of future automation scripts.

We also established a flexible pattern of using `HttpClientFactory` to register `AddHttpClient<IGeolocationService` and `AzureMapsGeolocationService>` with our service implementation. This code makes it easy to swap out the geolocation provider if we ever need to. To keep it simple in this recipe, we stored our API key using .NET user secrets for development. In the next recipe, we will explore Azure Key Vault.

Azure Key Vault – securing configuration with custom health checks

In this recipe, we'll integrate **Azure Key Vault** to securely store and manage sensitive configuration data, such as API keys. Rather than hardcoding credentials in `appsettings.json`, we'll use Key Vault to centralize our secrets, accessing them directly from Azure when needed.

Since calls to Key Vault can slightly slow down local development, we'll also configure the .NET user-secrets tool to store secrets locally. This is a preferred approach, as it keeps sensitive data out of `appsettings.json` and reduces the risk of accidentally exposing secrets in source control.

To ensure our app can reliably access Key Vault in production, we'll implement custom health checks that monitor connectivity. These checks provide real-time alerts if Key Vault becomes unreachable, preventing us from scratching our heads wondering why we cannot authenticate.

Like the previous recipe, we will use the Azure Maps service as a demonstration. Azure Maps supports multiple authentication methods including Shared Key authentication, Microsoft Entra ID, and **Shared Access Signatures (SAS)**. For this recipe, we'll focus on securing the Shared Key, which provides full access to our Azure Maps account.

Getting ready...

Download the starter project here: `https://github.com/PacktPublishing/ASP.NET-9-Web-API-Cookbook/tree/main/start/chapter09/KeyVault`.

Make sure you have created a `dev-cert`. You should not connect to Azure Key Vault without HTTPS. To create a development HTTPS certificate, open the terminal and enter the following commands:

```
dotnet dev-certs https –clean
dotnet dev-certs https –trust
```

You will also need your Azure subscription ID from when you set up your Azure account. You should be logged into Azure via the CLI with `az login`. If you have any problems logging in, you may need to specify your tenant ID.

How to do it...

1. Install the required packages:

    ```
    dotnet add package Azure.Extensions.AspNetCore.Configuration.
    Secrets
    dotnet add package Azure.Identity
    ```

    We use the `Configuration secrets` package to interact with the Azure service. We then add the `Azure.Identity` package – `Azure.Identity` is the modern way to authenticate with Azure services.

2. Get your Azure user ID:

    ```
    az ad signed-in-user show --query id -o tsv
    ```

3. We will need this ID to make you the `KeyVaultOfficer`.

    The returned string is our object ID. This will be important as the object ID will be used as the `--assignee` parameter, when we set up the `KeyVault`.

4. Get your location.

    Besides the object ID for `assignee`, we will also need our Azure location. You can find that by outputting information on your current group (which you created when you created your account):

    ```
    az group show --name "Luke1" --output table
    ```

5. Make yourself the secrets officer:

    ```
    az role assignment create --assignee "your-objectid" --role
    "Key Vault Secrets Officer" --scope "/subscriptions/your-
    subscriptionid/resourceGroups/Gary1/providers/Microsoft.
    KeyVault/vaults/GeoGatewayKV"
    ```

    Place the object ID value you acquired in *step 2* as the assignee. For `your-subscriptionid`, place the value you got when we first made our subscription.

6. Now, create the actual Key Vault:

    ```
    az keyvault create --name "GeoGatewayKV" --resource-group
    "Luke1" --location "eastus"
    ```

7. Get the keys from the maps account if needed:

    ```
    az maps account keys list --name "GeoGatewayMaps" --resource-
    group "MyResourceGroup"
    ```

8. Finally, set our specific Key Vault secret. This is the primary key for `AzureMaps`, which in the previous recipe was put in `appsettings.json`:

    ```
    az keyvault secret set --vault-name
    "GeoGatewayKV" --name "AzureMapsApiKey" --value
    "CahAP1Ylk0hc03Do3ORaCGgSwi3VgkNGLI1sPEwV3r9
    kjnESbZHIJQQJ99AJACYeBjFxdhjuAAAgAZMP2HCf"
    ```

9. Since connecting to Key Vault on every development server startup can cause a slight delay, we'll set up `user-secrets` to store sensitive data locally for development only:

    I. Now, set up local user secrets for development only:

        ```
        dotnet user-secrets init
        dotnet user-secrets set "AzureMapsApiKey" "your-api-key"
        ```

II.   Update our `Program.cs` file to handle both scenarios:

```
var builder = WebApplication.CreateBuilder(args);
try
{
    if (builder.Environment.IsDevelopment())
    {
        app.MapOpenApi();
        logger.LogInformation("Using development
            configuration with user secrets");
    }
    else
    {
        // Production Key Vault configuration
        string keyVaultName = builder.Configuration[
            "KeyVault:VaultName"
        ] ?? throw new InvalidOperationException(
            "KeyVault:VaultName not found in
            configuration");
        logger.LogInformation(
            "Attempting to connect to Key
            Vault: {KeyVaultName}", keyVaultName);
        var keyVaultUri = new Uri(
            $"https://{keyVaultName}.vault.azure.net/");
        var credential = new DefaultAzureCredential();
        builder.Configuration.AddAzureKeyVault(
            keyVaultUri,credential);
    }
```

III. Note the logging statement at the beginning. Our project will use `user-secrets`, if available, without any additional specifications in our code.

IV.   Still in `Program.cs`, configure the services:

```
builder.Services.Configure<AzureMapsSettings>(options =>
{
    options.ApiKey = builder.Configuration[
        "AzureMapsApiKey"
    ] ?? throw new InvalidOperationException(
        "Azure Maps API key not found");
    options.BaseUrl = builder.Configuration[
        "AzureMaps:BaseUrl"
    ] ?? "https://atlas.microsoft.com/";
});
```

```
        builder.Services.AddHttpClient<IGeolocationService,
            AzureMapsGeolocationService>();
}
catch (Exception ex)
{
    logger.LogError(ex, "Configuration error");
    throw;
}
```

V.   If you swap the logic around at the beginning and move the KeyVault access to the beginning of the Program.cs file, you will notice a slight pause when running the app and trying to connect.

VI.   Let's make sure we add a Healthcheck so we know we are always connected to the AzureKeyVault. First, add the AzureKeyVault:

dotnet add package AspNetCore.HealthChecks.AzureKeyVault

VII.   Register the HealthChecks() middleware before the if/else block, right after our AddHttpClient() service is registered:

```
using Microsoft.Extensions.Diagnostics.HealthChecks;
...
builder.Services.AddHttpClient<IGeolocationService,
AzureMapsGeolocationService>();

builder.Services.AddHealthChecks();
```

VIII.   Then, update Program.cs to add a HealthCheck inside the production setup:

```
builder.Services.AddHealthChecks()
    .AddAzureKeyVault(
        keyVaultUri,
        credential,
        options => options.AddSecret("AzureMapsApiKey"));
```

IX.   Now, add a debug endpoint to make sure we can always access KeyVault:

```
if (app.Environment.IsDevelopment())
{
    app.MapGet("/debug/config", (IConfiguration
        configuration) =>
    {
        return Results.Ok(new
        {
```

```
            KeyVaultConnected = !string.
                IsNullOrEmpty(
                    configuration["AzureMapsApiKey"]),
            KeyVaultName = configuration[
                "KeyVault:VaultName"]
        });
    });
}
```

X. Here, we are using the minimal API. Since this is a developer tool, there is no need to create a full controller.

XI. Finally, create a `HealthChecks` endpoint where we can add a health check for `KeyVault`:

```
app.MapHealthChecks("/health", new HealthCheckOptions
{
    ResponseWriter = async (context, report) =>
    {
        var result = new
        {
            Status = report.Status.ToString(),
            Components = report.Entries.Select(e => new
            {
                Component = e.Key,
                Status = e.Value.Status.ToString(),
                Description = e.Value.Description
            })
        };

        context.Response.ContentType = "application/json";
        await context.Response.WriteAsJsonAsync(result);
    }
});
```

10. Open `appsettings.json` and add the `BaseUrl` and the name of our `KeyVault` value:

```
"AzureMaps": {
  "BaseUrl": "https://atlas.microsoft.com/"
},
"KeyVault": {
  "VaultName": "GeoGatewayKV"
}
```

11. Run our API with the following command:

```
dotnet run
```

12. Test our debug endpoint and the `HealthCheck` endpoint:

```
Invoke-RestMethod -Uri "https://localhost:5000/debug/config"
Invoke-RestMethod -Uri "https://localhost:5001/health"
```

Even though we are in development mode the `HealthCheck` endpoint should return `status=Healthy`.

How it works...

In this recipe, we integrated Azure Key Vault, a powerful and dedicated Azure service, into our resource group to securely store and manage sensitive data. Using Key Vault as an independent service provides enhanced security by centralizing secrets in a protected environment, separate from application code. For local development, we leveraged .NET's `user-secrets` tool, which allows us to store secrets outside of our configuration files, preventing the risk of accidental exposure in source control.

Our application uses `DefaultAzureCredential` to access Key Vault, which provides intelligent credential detection. During local development, it automatically uses your Azure CLI credentials, while in Azure it uses the managed identity of your deployed service. This means you don't need different authentication code for development and production environments.

We also implemented a custom health check that monitors connectivity to Key Vault. This health check gives us immediate feedback if Key Vault becomes unreachable. It also helps us rule out connectivity issues with Key Vault when troubleshooting complex authentication problems.

Creating an API gateway with a YARP reverse proxy and a custom load-balancing policy

In this recipe, we will build a custom API gateway using YARP. We will also create a custom load-balancing policy. Instead of ordinary pre-built load balancing, we will get the geolocation of the incoming request and redirect to the appropriate API based on the clients' region. This API gateway setup is just one of the many ways YARP can be used to handle traffic efficiently, with flexible routing and load-balancing options.

You can use this recipe as a starting point for many practical purposes, such as gradually migrating a monolithic API to a more decentralized structure with independent services. With YARP, you gain fine-grained control over routing, enabling smoother transitions between legacy and modernized services, centralizing authentication, or even dynamically managing rate limiting and security policies within the gateway itself.

Getting ready...

The starter project includes three separate APIs which we will manage via a custom API gateway. Download the starter project from here: `https://github.com/PacktPublishing/ASP.NET-9-Web-API-Cookbook/tree/main/start/chapter09/geolocation`.

This project incorporates the `KeyVault` we created in the *Azure KeyVault – securing configuration with custom health checks* recipe. It also uses a version of the `GeolocationService` we created earlier. If you want to follow along you will have to have a `KeyVault` and Azure Maps resources created in the same resource group (as we did in the previous two recipes).

How to do it...

1. Add the packages for a Yarp reverse proxy:

    ```
    dotnet add package Yarp.ReverseProxy;
    ```

2. Now, let's create the actual custom load-balancing policy.

    This will automatically route requests from one IP address to another route. Create a file called `GeoLoadBalancingPolicy.cs`. Then, import the following namespace and set up the constructor for the `GeoLoadBalancingPolicy` class:

    ```
    namespace YarpGateway.LoadBalancing;

    public class GeoLoadBalancingPolicy : ILoadBalancingPolicy
    {
        private readonly IGeolocationService _geoService;
        private readonly ILogger<GeoLoadBalancingPolicy> _logger;

        public GeoLoadBalancingPolicy(
            IGeolocationService geoService,
            ILogger<GeoLoadBalancingPolicy> logger)
        {
            _geoService = geoService;
            _logger = logger;
        }
    ```

3. Yarp's `ILoadBalancingPolicy` demands that we implement a `Name` property and a `PickDestinationMethod`. Let's implement the logic for the `PickDestinationMethod` now:

    ```
    public string Name => "GeoLoadBalancing";

        public DestinationState? PickDestination(
            HttpContext context,
    ```

```
            ClusterState cluster,
            IReadOnlyList<DestinationState> availableDestinations)
    {
            var clientIp = GetOriginalClientIp(context);
```

4. We will log where we got the IP address from. We will either read the X-Forwarded-For header if the client has been routed through something like a CDN, or we will take the IP address directly from the request:

```
_logger.LogInformation(
            "Processing request from IP {IP} (Remote: {Remote},
Forwarded: {Forwarded})",
            clientIp,
            context.Connection.RemoteIpAddress,
            context.Request.Headers["X-Forwarded-For"].
            ToString());

    var countryCode = Task.Run(async () =>
            await _geoService.GetCountryCodeAsync(clientIp)).
            GetAwaiter().GetResult();

    _logger.LogInformation("IP {IP} resolved to country code
                        {CountryCode}",
            clientIp, countryCode);
```

5. Now, determine the region:

```
var region = DetermineRegion(countryCode);
var destination = availableDestinations.FirstOrDefault(
    d => d.Model.Config.Metadata?
        .GetValueOrDefault("Region") == region);
if (destination == null)
{
    _logger.LogWarning("No destination found for region
        {Region}, using first available", region);
    return availableDestinations.FirstOrDefault();
}
_logger.LogInformation(
    "Routing request to {Destination} for region {Region}",
    destination.Model.Config.Address, region);
    return destination;
}
```

YARP's `LoadBalancing` policies work with `Destination` classes. The `Destination` class has a `Config` property which holds a `DestinationConfig` class. The `MetaData` property of a `DestinationConfig` holds key-value pairs which hold the `"cluster"` group of places that YARP should redirect the request to.

6. Now create a helper method that retrieves the original client of our request. Remove the `X-Forwarded-For` header and retrieve the original IP address:

```
private string GetOriginalClientIp(HttpContext context)
    {
        // Check forwarded headers in order of trust
        var forwardedFor = context.Request.Headers["X-Forwarded-
                        For"].FirstOrDefault();
        if (!string.IsNullOrEmpty(forwardedFor))
        {
            // Get the leftmost IP (original client)
            var ips = forwardedFor.Split(',');
            // Validate IP before using it
            if (IPAddress.TryParse(ips[0].Trim(), out var ip))
            {
                // Don't trust private IPs in X-Forwarded-For
                if (!IsPrivateIpAddress(ip))
                {
                    return ip.ToString();
                }
            }
        }
    }
```

7. Let's finish the method by handling local development gracefully. During local testing, we'll see localhost IPs (`::1` for **IPv6** or `127.0.0.1` for **IPv4**), which can't be geolocated. We'll default them to a US IP, but this won't affect our ability to test different regions using `X-Forwarded-For` headers, as shown in the testing section. We'll also handle cases where the connection IP is unknown:

```
var remoteIp = context.Connection.RemoteIpAddress?.ToString() ??
"unknown";
if (remoteIp == "::1" || remoteIp == "127.0.0.1")
{
    _logger.LogInformation("Local development detected, using
                        default region");
    return "8.8.8.8";
}
return remoteIp;
```

8. Create a helper method to help clean up the private `IsPrivateIpAddress(IPAddress IP)`:

```
private bool IsPrivateIpAddress(IPAddress ip)
{
    // Check if IP is in private ranges
    if (ip.IsIPv4MappedToIPv6)
    {
        ip = ip.MapToIPv4();
    }
    byte[] bytes = ip.GetAddressBytes();
    // Check if it's IPv4 by checking address family
    return ip.AddressFamily ==
        System.Net.Sockets.AddressFamily.InterNetwork &&
        (
            bytes[0] == 10 || // 10.0.0.0/8
            (bytes[0] == 172 &&
                bytes[1] >= 16 &&
                bytes[1] <= 31) || // 172.16.0.0/12
            (bytes[0] == 192 &&
                bytes[1] == 168) // 192.168.0.0/16
        );
}
```

9. Finally, add a helper method that will interpret the ISO country codes returned by the Azure Maps service and route them to our different clusters:

```
private string DetermineRegion(string? countryCode) =>
countryCode switch
    {
        "US" or "CA" or "MX" => "NorthAmerica",
        "GB" or "DE" or "FR" or "IT" or "ES" => "Europe",
        "JP" or "CN" or "KR" or "AU" or "NZ" => "AsiaPacific",
        _ => "Default"
    };
```

10. Now, set up the `Program.cs` class and import the `Yarp` namespaces:

```
using Yarp.ReverseProxy.LoadBalancing;
using YarpGateway.LoadBalancing;
```

11. Register the `LoadBalancing` policy we created, right before where we registered the CORS policy:

```
builder.Services.AddSingleton<ILoadBalancingPolicy,
GeoLoadBalancingPolicy>();
```

12. Now, register the `AddReverseProxy` service. We will use `builder.Configuration.GetSection` to load cluster and route configurations from the `ReverseProxy` property section of `appSettings.json`:

```
builder.Services.AddReverseProxy()
.LoadFromConfig(builder.Configuration.
GetSection("ReverseProxy"));
```

13. Now, create a minimal API endpoint to debug the route IP:

```
app.MapGet("/debug/route/{ip}", async (string ip,
    IGeolocationService geoService) =>
{
    var countryCode = await geoService.
    GetCountryCodeAsync(ip);
    return Results.Ok(new
    {
        Ip = ip,
        CountryCode = countryCode,
        Region = countryCode switch
        {
            "US" or "CA" or "MX" =>
                "NorthAmerica","GB" or "DE"
            or "FR" or "IT" or "ES" =>
                "Europe","JP" or "CN"
                or "KR" or "AU" or "NZ" =>
                    "AsiaPacific",
                    _ => "Default"
        }
    });
});
```

14. Finally, add a debug endpoint that returns the required routing information:

```
app.MapGet("/debug/routing", async (
    HttpContext context,
    IConfiguration config,
    IGeolocationService geoService) =>
{
    var ip = context.Request.Headers["X-Forwarded-For"].
            FirstOrDefault()
        ?? context.Connection.RemoteIpAddress?.ToString()
        ?? "unknown";

    var countryCode = await geoService.
```

```
                                 GetCountryCodeAsync(ip);
            var region = countryCode switch
            {
                "US" or "CA" or "MX" => "NorthAmerica",
                "GB" or "DE" or "FR" or "IT" or "ES" => "Europe",
                "JP" or "CN" or "KR" or "AU" or "NZ" or "HK" =>
                "AsiaPacific",
                _ => "Default"
            };
```

15. Format and return the results:

```
            return Results.Ok(new
            {
                TestIP = ip,
                CountryCode = countryCode,
                Region = region,
                ExpectedPort = region switch
                {
                    "NorthAmerica" => 5010,
                    "Europe" => 5020,
                    "AsiaPacific" => 5030,
                    _ => 5010 // default to NA
                }
            });
        app.MapOpenApi();
```

16. Add the YARP configuration to `appsettings.json`:

```
    {
      // ... existing configuration ...

      "ReverseProxy": {
        "Routes": {
          "api-route": {
            "ClusterId": "apiCluster",
            "Match": {
              "Path": "/{**catch-all}"
            }
          }
        },
        "Clusters": {
          "apiCluster": {
            "LoadBalancingPolicy": "GeoLoadBalancing",
            "Destinations": {
```

```
      "na-api": {
        "Address": "https://localhost:5011",
        "Metadata": {
          "Region": "NorthAmerica"
        }
      },
      "eu-api": {
        "Address": "https://localhost:5021",
        "Metadata": {
          "Region": "Europe"
        }
      },
      "ap-api": {
        "Address": "https://localhost:5031",
        "Metadata": {
          "Region": "AsiaPacific"
        }
      }
    }
   }
  }
 }
}
```

17. Test the application. Run the YARP project we just built, along with the three other API projects. You can do this in multiple terminal splits, or via Visual Studio.

    The following tests will use `Invoke-RestMethod`, but feel free to use Postman or curl. We can pass an IP address to get the region:

    ```
    Invoke-RestMethod -Uri "https://localhost:5001/debug/
    route/8.8.8.8"
    ```

    This IP address should return US and a region of North America. `176.31.84.249` should return FR for France and a region of Europe.

18. We can now test our app by calling a normal endpoint in our main Books API. We can forward the endpoint and then watch it being forwarded to our different APIs based on the `X-Forwarded-For` header. If `X-Forwarded-For` is not present – such as the client not going through a CDN but directly accessing the API – it will be read from the HTTP context. The following code will route to the Europe API:

    ```
    Invoke-RestMethod -Uri "https://localhost:5001/api/books/1"
    -Headers @{
        "X-Forwarded-For" = "176.31.84.249"
    }
    ```

Change X-Forwarded-For to 8.8.8.8 and watch the North America API receive the request (it will log to the console).

How it works...

In this recipe, we built a custom API gateway using YARP, integrating a reverse proxy with a custom load-balancing policy that directs requests based on geolocation. This setup provides fine-grained control over request routing and opens the door to a wide range of YARP features.

With YARP, we can configure local clusters, customize ports, and control IPs, offering flexibility for various deployment needs. For example, we could enhance our gateway further by using YARP's transforms to add or remove headers, such as stripping additional forwarding headers or controlling HTTP method overrides. Additionally, YARP enables advanced functionality such as custom rate limiting policies, centralized authentication, and even security enforcement at the gateway level rather than at individual endpoints.

There are many, many practical use cases for this pattern: we could manage the migration from a legacy .NET Framework API to a modern .NET project, redirecting traffic from the old to the new site only – as the new site is completed. We could even manage authentication entirely within the gateway project and use YARP to route secured traffic as needed.

Using YARP in this way offers a convenient alternative to third-party solutions such as Azure API Manager or Azure Front Door, bringing powerful and customizable gateway features directly into the C# environment.

Migrating a distributed API to .NET Aspire for unified orchestration and monitoring

In this recipe, we'll migrate an existing distributed API project to .NET Aspire, transforming multiple independent services into a unified system with centralized orchestration and monitoring. While .NET Aspire is often introduced with new projects, this approach shows how Aspire can seamlessly integrate with existing APIs, making it an ideal choice for projects ready to modernize or scale. By moving our distributed API to Aspire, we gain the ability to orchestrate services directly in C#, manage service discovery with ease, and monitor health states through a built-in dashboard.

Getting ready...

If you are going to use Visual Studio, it is critical that you have the latest version as we do not want Visual Studio to be using .NET 8 Aspire templates and not .NET 9.

It also is critical that you are not using .NET 8 Aspire templates and workloads. Running the following command in your terminal will make sure that .NET 8 Aspire templates will be replaced with .NET 9:

```
dotnet new install Aspire.ProjectTemplates::9.0.0 --force
```

Mixing .NET 8 and .NET 9 Aspire can lead to frustrating troubleshooting issues.

Download the starter project from here: `https://github.com/PacktPublishing/ASP.NET-9-Web-API-Cookbook/tree/main/start/chapter09/AddAspire`.

> **Note**
> The web API projects in the starter project have been slightly modified from the previous recipe.
> APIs that use a separate `Startup.cs` class do not reliably work with .NET Aspire's Service
> Discovery. It is essential for service discovery that your API only has a `Program.cs` file.

How to do it...

1. Create the app host project and add it to our solution:

    ```
    dotnet new aspire-apphost -o Geolocation.AppHost
    dotnet sln add ./Geolocation.AppHost/Geolocation.AppHost.csproj
    ```

    `AppHost` is where we orchestrate and configure our distributed application – all in C# code.

2. Create the `ServiceDefaults` project and add it to our solution:

    ```
    dotnet new aspire-servicedefaults -o Geolocation.ServiceDefaults

    dotnet sln add .\Geolocation.ServiceDefaults\Geolocation.ServiceDefaults.csproj
    ```

3. Add a reference of each project to `AppHost`:

    ```
    dotnet add ./Geolocation.AppHost/Geolocation.AppHost.csproj
    reference ./YarpGateway/YarpGateway.csproj
    ```

4. We also need our `AppHost` to have a reference to each project:

    ```
    dotnet add ./Geolocation.AppHost/Geolocation.AppHost.csproj
    reference .\Europe\Europe.csproj
    dotnet add ./Geolocation.AppHost/Geolocation.AppHost.csproj
    reference .\AsiaPacific\AsiaPacific.csproj
    dotnet add ./Geolocation.AppHost/Geolocation.AppHost.csproj
    reference .\NorthAmerica\NorthAmerica.csproj
    ```

5. If you open `AppHost csproj`, you should see a reference to each of our four projects:

    ```
    <ItemGroup>
      <ProjectReference Include="..\YarpGateway\YarpGateway.
      csproj" />
      <ProjectReference Include="..\Europe\Europe.csproj" />
      <ProjectReference Include="..\AsiaPacific\AsiaPacific.
      csproj" />
      <ProjectReference Include="..\NorthAmerica\NorthAmerica.
      csproj" />
    </ItemGroup>
    ```

6. In each of the four individual projects, add a reference to our `ServiceDefaults` project:

    ```
    dotnet add ../YarpGateway/YarpGateway.csproj reference ../
    Geolocation.ServiceDefaults/Geolocation.ServiceDefaults.csproj
    ```

    Note that this reference is the opposite of the previous: many-to-one. Each one of our projects has one single reference to the `ServiceDefaults` project.

7. Repeat for each of our APIs:

    ```
    dotnet add ..\AsiaPacific\AsiaPacific.csproj reference ..\
    Geolocation.ServiceDefaults\Geolocation.ServiceDefaults.csproj
    dotnet add ..\Europe\Europe.csproj reference ..\Geolocation.
    ServiceDefaults\Geolocation.ServiceDefaults.csproj
    dotnet add ..\NorthAmerica\NorthAmerica.csproj reference ..\
    Geolocation.ServiceDefaults\Geolocation.ServiceDefaults.csproj
    ```

    You will see a confirmation message like this for each one:

    ```
    Reference `..\Geolocation.ServiceDefaults\Geolocation.
    ServiceDefaults.csproj` added to the project.
    ```

8. Each of the three API's `csproj` files should now include a reference like so:

    ```
    <ItemGroup>
      <ProjectReference Include="..\Geolocation.ServiceDefaults\
      Geolocation.ServiceDefaults.csproj" />
    </ItemGroup>
    ```

9. Open the `Program.cs` file in the YARP project. Right before the `LoadBalancing` policy is registered and after our logger is created, add service defaults:

    ```
    builder.AddServiceDefaults();
    builder.Services.AddSingelton<ILoadBalancingPolicy,
    GeoPolicy>();
    ```

10. Now, open the `Program.cs` file of each of our API projects. On the line after the `WebApplication` builder is created, register our service defaults:

```
var builder = WebApplication.CreateBuilder(args);
builder.AddServiceDefaults();
```

> **Note**
>
> This will only work if you have correctly added a reference to the ServiceDefaults project in each API per *step 6*.

11. Now that we have service discovery enabled, setting up Aspire Apphost should be easy. Open the `AppHost/Program.cs` file:

```
var builder = DistributedApplication.CreateBuilder(args);

builder.AddProject<Projects.YarpGateway>("gateway");

builder.Build().Run();
```

12. Let's fill out this `Program.cs` file further. We now need to add `WithReference` so the dashboard works correctly:

```
var builder = DistributedApplication.CreateBuilder(args);

var naApi = builder.AddProject<Projects.NorthAmerica>("na-api");
var euApi = builder.AddProject<Projects.Europe>("eu-api");
var apApi = builder.AddProject<Projects.AsiaPacific>("ap-api");

builder.AddProject<Projects.YarpGateway>("gateway")
    .WithReference(naApi)
    .WithReference(euApi)
    .WithReference(apApi);

builder.Build().Run();

builder.AddProject<Projects.YarpGateway>("gateway");

builder.Build().Run();
```

13. If you run the solution file in Visual Studio or run the Geolocation.AppHost project via the CLI – a nice dashboard will be available via your web browser on localhost, as shown in *Figure 9.2*:

Figure 9.2 – The Aspire dashboard

We can click on a resource for further information. Notice the `Health State` property. We didn't need to set up health checks – Aspire automatically runs basic health checks in the background:

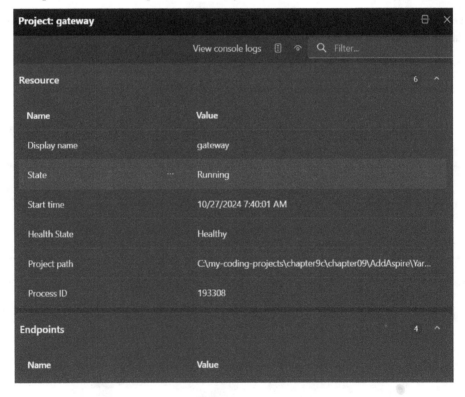

Figure 9.3 – Notice the Health State resource

How it works...

In this recipe, we migrated our distributed API project to .NET Aspire by setting up an `AppHost` to configure and orchestrate the entire system, with Service Discovery enabled for each API service. `AppHost` serves as the primary hub for orchestrating services in a distributed environment, allowing us to configure and manage the entire API network from one central location. Meanwhile, Service Discovery (which is enabled in each project via middleware) provides a way for individual services to locate each other without hardcoding connection strings or URLs, streamlining the setup and enhancing flexibility.

Additionally, we retained our custom YARP configuration, to preserve the load-balancing policy created in earlier recipes. .NET Aspire also offers an integrated YARP solution that works seamlessly with the platform, offering additional customization options if needed. .NET Aspire also automatically runs health checks on all resources in the background, saving us from having to write health checks for each distributed resource.

Integrating dockerized services with .NET Aspire – an example with Prometheus

Most Aspire examples focus on using services with native Aspire integrations, and the community has provided many popular .NET libraries as Aspire-compatible NuGet packages. In this recipe, however, we'll take a different approach by setting up Prometheus. Prometheus is a powerful monitoring tool that provides persistent telemetry data suitable for production, in contrast to Aspire's temporary telemetry. We will set up Prometheus in a separate Docker container and integrate it into our Aspire project. Although Aspire is primarily designed to minimize reliance on Docker, adding containerized services allows us to extend Aspire's capabilities, orchestrating a broader range of tools and services within the same environment.

Getting ready...

This recipe requires that you have Docker installed. We recommend Docker Desktop. Make sure the Docker Desktop service is running and available on your machine.

You can download the starter project from `https://github.com/PacktPublishing/ASP.NET-9-Web-API-Cookbook/tree/main/end/chapter09/Prometheus` or just continue from the previous recipe.

How to do it...

1. Add the Prometheus exporter package to the Aspire `ServiceDefaults` project. In the `Geolocation.ServiceDefaults` folder run:

```
dotnet add package OpenTelemetry.Exporter.Prometheus.AspNetCore
```

2. In the `ServiceDefaults` project's `Extensions.cs` file, enable the Prometheus exporter:

```
public static TBuilder ConfigureOpenTelemetry<TBuilder>(this
TBuilder builder) where TBuilder : IHostApplicationBuilder
{
// existing code
    builder.Services.AddOpenTelemetry()
        .WithMetrics(metrics =>
        {
            metrics.AddAspNetCoreInstrumentation()
                .AddHttpClientInstrumentation()
                .AddRuntimeInstrumentation()
                .AddPrometheusExporter(); // Add this line
        })
// method continues
```

3. Add the Prometheus exporter configuration to the `AddOpenTelemetryExporters` method:

```
private static TBuilder AddOpenTelemetryExporters<TBuilder>(this
TBuilder builder) where TBuilder : IHostApplicationBuilder
{
    var useOtlpExporter = !string.IsNullOrWhiteSpace(builder.
    Configuration["OTEL_EXPORTER_OTLP_ENDPOINT"]);

    if (useOtlpExporter)
    {
        builder.Services.AddOpenTelemetry().UseOtlpExporter();
    }

    builder.Services.AddOpenTelemetry()
        .WithMetrics(metrics => metrics.
        AddPrometheusExporter(options =>
            options.DisableTotalNameSuffixForCounters = true));

    return builder;
}
```

4. Update the `MapDefaultEndpoints` method in `Extensions.cs` to expose the Prometheus scraping endpoint:

```
public static WebApplication MapDefaultEndpoints(this
WebApplication app)
{
    // Enable the Prometheus metrics endpoint
    app.MapPrometheusScrapingEndpoint();
```

```
    // Health check endpoints
    if (app.Environment.IsDevelopment())
    {
        app.MapHealthChecks("/health");
        app.MapHealthChecks("/alive", new HealthCheckOptions
        {
            Predicate = r => r.Tags.Contains("live")
        });
    }

    return app;
}
```

5. Create the Prometheus configuration. First, create a `prometheus` folder in your solution directory, then create a `prometheus.yml` file inside. In `scrape_configs`, add a target for the port of each of our three APIs and the YARP API gateway:

```yaml
global:
  scrape_interval: 15s

scrape_configs:
  - job_name: 'aspire'
    static_configs:
      - targets: ['host.docker.internal:5000']
```

6. In the AppHost's `Program.cs` file, configure the Prometheus container on the line immediately after the builder variable is created:

```
var builder = DistributedApplication.CreateBuilder(args);
builder.AddContainer("prometheus", "prom/prometheus")
    .WithBindMount("../prometheus", "/etc/prometheus",
        isReadOnly: true)
    .WithHttpEndpoint(port: 9090, targetPort: 9090);
```

7. Open our gateway's `appsetting.json` file. Replace `localhost` with `*` so Kestrel can listen on all interfaces:

```
"Kestrel": { "Endpoints": { "Http": { "Url": "http://*:5000" }
```

8. Run the AppHost's project:

```
dotnet run --project Geolocation.AppHost
```

9. Test that the endpoint is ready for Prometheus integration:

```
Invoke-RestMethod "http://localhost: 5000/metrics"
```

10. Now, make some requests through the gateway to generate traffic using the dynamically created port number visible in the Aspire dashboard:

```
Invoke-RestMethod -Uri "http://localhost:5000/api/books/1"
-Headers @{"X-Forwarded-For" = "176.31.84.249"}
```

11. Visit the Prometheus UI (`http://localhost:9090`) and confirm the active connections to our gateway in the expression bar with the following commands:

```
kestrel_active_connections
http_server_request_duration_seconds_count
```

How it works...

In this recipe, we've added persistent telemetry to our Aspire application using Prometheus. While Aspire's dashboard provides excellent real-time monitoring capabilities, its telemetry data only exists for the current session. By integrating Prometheus, we gain historical telemetry data that persists across sessions, enabling long-term monitoring and trend analysis. We focused on collecting metrics from our gateway service, but the same approach could be applied to any of our APIs by adding the `MapDefaultEndpoints()` call to their `Program.cs` files.

Prometheus serves as an excellent foundation for more advanced monitoring solutions. While this recipe demonstrates basic metrics collection, Prometheus data can be visualized using tools such as Grafana. Also, we configured our own Docker container and added it to Aspire. Aspire integration capabilities for custom containers let you extend Aspire's functionality beyond built-in services, allowing you to incorporate any containerized tool in your distributed application.

Learn more on Discord

To join the Discord community for this book – where you can share feedback, ask questions to the authors, and provide solutions to other readers – scan the QR code or visit the link:

`https://packt.link/aspdotnet9WebAPI`

10

The Craft of Caching

Caching is a crucial optimization technique for any web application, but the variety of caching approaches can be overwhelming. This chapter starts with client-side caching strategies, where we will explore both manual HTTP header manipulation and ASP.NET Core's ResponseCache middleware. These initial recipes focus on putting the burden on the client. The server effectively offloads storage responsibilities to the client while maintaining control over cache validation and invalidation.

As we progress, the chapter shifts focus to server-side distributed caching using Redis. Thanks to .NET Aspire's seamless Redis integration, implementing distributed caching becomes surprisingly straightforward. We will explore output caching middleware for simple response caching, IDistributedCache for fine-grained control, and finally, .NET 9's new HybridCache. This innovative addition to the framework combines the speed of in-memory caching with the reliability of distributed storage.

In this chapter, we're going to cover the following recipes:

- Manual client-side response caching with HTTP headers
- Validating client-side cache with Last-Modified headers
- Client-side ETag cache validation with the ResponseCache attribute
- Output caching with Aspire Redis
- Server-side caching with IDistributedCache and Redis via .NET Aspire
- Using the new HybridCache library to simplify distributed caching

Technical requirements

For the recipes in this chapter, you'll need the following:

- **.NET 9 SDK**: We will be installing the needed packages as we go.
- **Docker Desktop**: This is required for running Redis containers through .NET Aspire.

- All projects in this chapter are hooked up to an Aspire solution. Most can be run either by starting the solution and using the Aspire dashboard, or you can run the main API project from the command line. If you are going to run from the command line, we recommend running the `AppHost` project and the `BookAPI` project from separate terminal splits, rather than running the solution file.

- All recipes in this chapter come with a special web page client to better see the effects of the different caches we will explore. In each starter project, you can open the client with `test-cache.html`, as shown in *Figure 10.1*:

Figure 10.1 – Books API cache demonstration

Manual client-side response caching with HTTP headers

While ASP.NET Core provides comprehensive response caching middleware, sometimes, manually setting cache headers is the quickest solution. This approach lets you implement caching on specific endpoints without modifying the application's middleware pipeline while maintaining direct control over caching behavior at the controller level. It also helps us better understand how HTTP caching works before we explore the framework's abstractions. In this recipe, we'll implement the simplest form of HTTP caching: telling the client (browser) to cache a response for a fixed duration.

Getting ready

Download the starter project here: `https://github.com/PacktPublishing/ASP.NET-9-Web-API-Cookbook/tree/main/start/chapter10/ManualResponseCache`.

Open the included demo web client: simply open the `test-client.html` file in your web browser.

How to do it...

1. Open the `BooksController.cs` file and, in the `GetBooks` method, manually set a `Cache-Control` header on the line right before the controller returns `Ok(pagedResult.Items)`:

    ```
    Response.Headers.CacheControl = "max-age=60, private"
    ```

    We are sending two important instructions to the browser: `max-age=60` tells the browser to keep the cached response for 60 seconds and `private` indicates that only this browser (user-agent) should cache the response, not any intermediate proxies and not the server itself.

2. Run the Web API, either by running the full solution with Aspire or simply running the `BooksAPI` project. Press the **Fetch Books (Cacheable)** button. The first request takes 5 seconds to respond. If you press the button again within 60 seconds, you will see a **Cache HIT** icon, as shown in *Figure 10.2*:

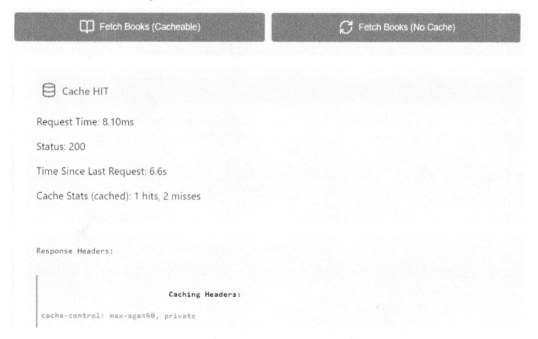

Figure 10.2 – Books API cached result

How it works...

In this recipe, we instructed only the client to cache the response. We avoided storing any cached data whatsoever on our server. We didn't have to worry about multiple server instances or a distributed cache store. We used the modern `Cache-Control` header instead of the deprecated `Pragma` and `Expires`. The main advantage of this approach is its simplicity – we are letting the browser handle all caching without any server-side caching infrastructure. The browser won't contact our server at all during the caching period. The trade-off is that we have no way to invalidate the cache if data changes before the 60-second window expires.

Validating client-side cache with Last-Modified headers

When implementing client-side caching, we often need to invalidate cached data when the server's content changes. In this recipe, we'll implement cache validation using HTTP's `Last-Modified` header mechanism. The client will record the last time it received new data. The server will record the last time new data was added. By comparing these timestamps, clients ensure they are receiving updates when new data is added, all without storing cached data on the server.

Getting ready

Download the starter project here: `https://github.com/PacktPublishing/ASP.NET-9-Web-API-Cookbook/tree/main/start/chapter10/IfModifiedResponseCache`.

Open the included web client, `test-cache.html`, in your web browser.

How to do it...

1. Open the `services` folder and create a new file called `IModificationTracker.cs`. In this interface, we are going to define a contract for two methods:

    ```
    namespace Books.Services;

    public interface IModificationTracker
    {
        DateTime? LastModified { get; }
        void SetModified();
    }
    ```

2. Create a file called `ModificationTracker.cs` and implement the `LastModified` and `SetModified` methods, which serve as a simple explicit getter and setter:

    ```
    namespace Books.Services;

    public class ModificationTracker : IModificationTracker
    ```

```
{
    private DateTime? _lastModified = DateTime.UtcNow;

    public DateTime? LastModified => _lastModified;

    public void SetModified()
    {
        _lastModified = DateTime.UtcNow;
    }
}
```

3. Now, open `Program.cs` and register our new service as a dependency injection container. We will make the `Singleton` service lifetime so it remains alive for as long as the server instance is active:

    ```
    builder.Services.AddSingleton<IModificationTracker,
    ModificationTracker>();
    ```

4. Now, open the `IBooksService.cs` file. We need to define a `GetLastModifiationTimeAsync` method that will register when our new resource is created. Add the method definition to the bottom:

    ```
    public interface IBooksService
    {
    ... // removed for space
        Task<DateTime?> GetLastModificationTimeAsync();
    ```

5. Open the `BooksService` file, import the new `Singleton` service we registered, and initialize it in the constructor:

    ```
    public class BooksService : IBooksService
    {
        private readonly IBooksRepository _repository;
        private readonly IModificationTracker _tracker;

        public BooksService(IBooksRepository repository,
                            IModificationTracker tracker)
        {
            _repository = repository;
            _tracker = tracker;
        }
    ...
    ```

6. On the next line, implement the `GetLastModificationTimeAsync` method, which will retrieve the time we added a resource:

```
public Task<DateTime?> GetLastModificationTimeAsync()
{
    return Task.FromResult(_tracker.LastModified);
}
```

7. Scroll down to the `CreateBookAsync` method. On the line after we call the `CreateBookAsync` method, set the last modified value:

```
public async Task<BookDTO> CreateBookAsync(BookDTO bookDTO)
{
  ... // removed for space

    var result = await _repository.CreateBookAsync(book);

    _tracker.SetModified();

    return new BookDTO
```

8. Open `BooksController.cs` and scroll down to the `[HttpPost]` endpoint. The only thing we have to add here is that we are going to specify a `"no-store"` header. On the line after `CreateBookAsync` is called, set a `cache-control` header:

```
Response.Headers.CacheControl = "no-store";
```

> **Note on CORS**
>
> For the standard caching headers, we do not have to modify our **CORS (Cross-Origin Resource Sharing)** `.WithExposedHeaders` method in `Program.cs`. CORS will let the ordinary caching headers through by default. The custom pagination header this API uses, `"X-Pagination"`, is registered with CORS as it is non-standard.

9. In the same `BooksController.cs` file, navigate to the paginated `[HttpGet]` endpoint, the `GetBooks` action method. We are going to return a `304 Not Modified` status code to inform the client to use its cached data. Let's add an additional `ProducesResponseType` attribute to comply with Open API standards:

```
[HttpGet]
[EndpointSummary("Paged Book Information")]
[EndpointDescription("This returns all the books from our SQLite
database, using EF Core")]
[ProducesResponseType(StatusCodes.Status200OK, Type =
typeof(IReadOnlyCollection<BookDTO>))]
[ProducesResponseType(StatusCodes.Status304NotModified)]
```

```
[ProducesResponseType(StatusCodes.Status500InternalServerError)]
public async Task<IActionResult> GetBooks([FromQuery] int
pageSize = 10, [FromQuery] int lastId = 0)
```

10. Let's start creating our caching logic at the very top of the `try` block. The first thing we will do is retrieve the timestamp of the last time a new book was added:

```
var lastModified = await _service.
GetLastModificationTimeAsync();
```

11. On the next line, set the `last-modified` header:

```
Response.Headers.LastModified = lastModified?.ToString("R");
```

This header gives the client the timestamp of when this data was last modified. After the request, the client is supposed to send this timestamp in its own `if-modified-since` header.

12. On the next line, let's set the cache headers to return regardless of the response:

```
Response.Headers.CacheControl = "no-cache, private";
Response.Headers.Vary = "Accept, Accept-Encoding, Query";
```

We use `"no-cache, private"` instead of `"max-age"` because we want the browser to always check with the server using `If-Modified-Since`, while still allowing it to cache the response.

13. Let's start implementing our caching logic. Compare the timestamps. First, ensure both times are in UTC format for accurate comparison:

```
if (Request.Headers.IfModifiedSince.Count > 0 && lastModified.
    HasValue)
{
    var ifModifiedSince = Request.GetTypedHeaders()
        .IfModifiedSince?.UtcDateTime.ToUniversalTime();
    var lastModifiedUtc = lastModified.Value
        .ToUniversalTime();
```

Notice we made sure to convert both datetimes to universal time so we are sure to be comparing the same things.

14. Create rounded versions of both timestamps to ensure reliable comparison. `DateTime` comparisons in .NET are precise to the tick level, which can cause false negatives when comparing timestamps from different sources:

```
if (ifModifiedSince.HasValue)
        {
                    var ifModifiedSinceRounded = new DateTime(
                        ifModifiedSince.Value.Year,
```

```
                    ifModifiedSince.Value.Month,
                    ifModifiedSince.Value.Day,
                    ifModifiedSince.Value.Hour,
                    ifModifiedSince.Value.Minute,
                    ifModifiedSince.Value.Second,
                    DateTimeKind.Utc);

        var lastModifiedRounded = new DateTime(
            lastModifiedUtc.Year,
            lastModifiedUtc.Month,
            lastModifiedUtc.Day,
            lastModifiedUtc.Hour,
            lastModifiedUtc.Minute,
            lastModifiedUtc.Second,
            DateTimeKind.Utc);

    var comparison = DateTime.Compare(lastModifiedRounded,
        ifModifiedSinceRounded);
```

We need to round the date times by assigning the time values to the second, with the new `DateTime` object. If we don't, there can be extra ticks left in either date time, and the comparison can be inaccurate.

`DateTime.Compare` returns 0 for two equal `DateTime` objects and a value less than 0 if the first `DateTime` is before the second:

```
var comparison = DateTime.Compare(lastModifiedRounded,
ifModifiedSinceRounded);
if (comparison <= 0)
{
    return StatusCode(StatusCodes.Status304NotModified);
}
```

We are testing whether the resource on the server (last modified) was changed before the browser was updated. If so, we tell the client they are free to use a cached version. Note that the equality check is critical here. If the same client is calling this `GetBooks` endpoint repeatedly before anything new is added, the `last-modified` and `if-modified-since` values will be the same.

15. Run the application. Use the web client to post a new book, as shown in *Figure 10.3*:

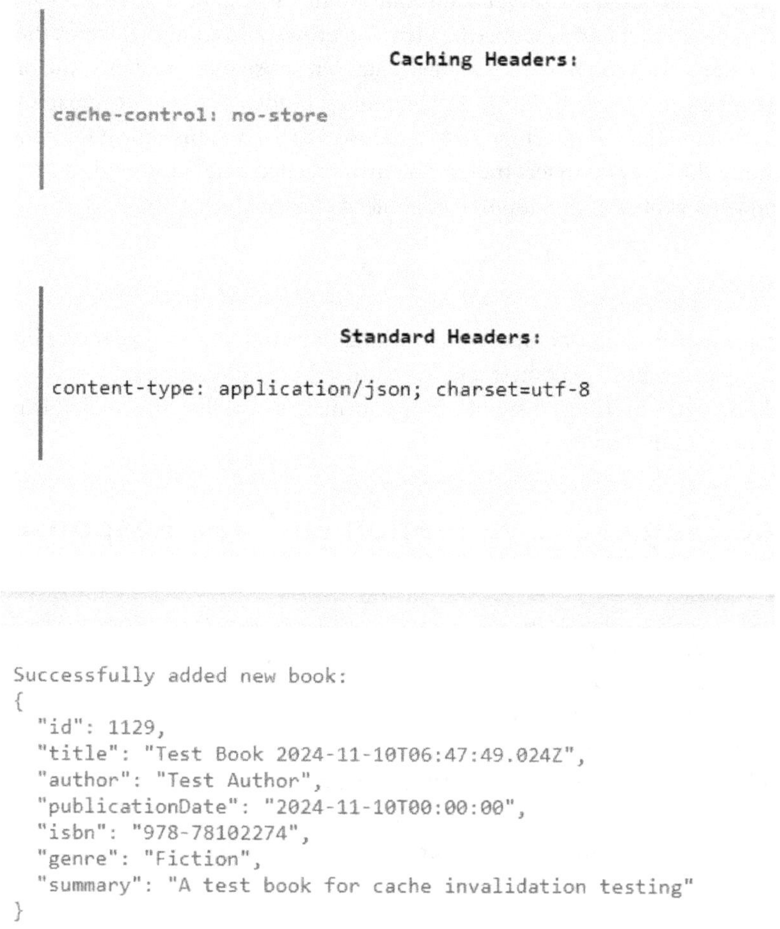

Caching Headers:

```
cache-control: no-store
```

Standard Headers:

```
content-type: application/json; charset=utf-8
```

```
Successfully added new book:
{
    "id": 1129,
    "title": "Test Book 2024-11-10T06:47:49.024Z",
    "author": "Test Author",
    "publicationDate": "2024-11-10T00:00:00",
    "isbn": "978-78102274",
    "genre": "Fiction",
    "summary": "A test book for cache invalidation testing"
}
```

Figure 10.3 – Adding a new book from the web client

Go back and forth between the blue **Fetch Books (Cacheable)** button and adding new books. You should see that after the first fetch, a cached response is returned for the Books endpoint. If you add a new book, by pressing the green **Add New Book** button, the cache is invalidated.

How it works...

In this recipe, we implemented HTTP cache validation using the Last-Modified header, an alternative to **ETag** validation.

When a new resource is added, the server tracks the last time it was modified but does not store any cached data. On GET requests, the server sends out the timestamp of when the resource was last modified as a Last-Modified response header. The browser (user agent) stores the timestamp from this header along with the normal response data. On subsequent requests, the browser then sends this timestamp as an If-Modified-Since request header. The server compares the response with its last modification time. It returns a 304 Not Modified status code if the content has not changed, informing the browser to feel free to display its cached data, or it sends a 200 OK status code with the updated content if the resource has indeed changed.

There's more...

While this example uses in-memory timestamp tracking (limiting it to a single server instance), you could store the last-modified timestamp in your database for distributed scenarios. Even with this database check, you will still gain significant performance benefits, by avoiding expensive data queries when content hasn't changed.

Client-side ETag cache validation with the ResponseCache attribute

While ASP.NET Core's ResponseCache attribute provides a convenient way to manage HTTP cache headers, it primarily handles header generation rather than actual caching logic. In this recipe, we'll combine the attribute's header management with our own ETag-based cache validation. This approach gives us fine-grained control over cache invalidation while using the attribute to handle basic cache headers. The ResponseCache attribute's Location property might suggest server-side caching capabilities, but it only affects header generation. By implementing our own ETag generation and validation, we can achieve proper client-side caching with reliable cache invalidation when content changes.

Getting ready

Download the starter project here: https://github.com/PacktPublishing/ASP.NET-9-Web-API-Cookbook/tree/main/start/chapter10/ResponseCacheMiddleware.

How to do it...

1. Open the Program.cs file and, on the line after var builder, register our in-memory cache:

```
public static void Main(string[] args)
{
    var builder = WebApplication.CreateBuilder(args);
    builder.Services.AddMemoryCache();
```

2. On the next line, register the ASP.NET Core `ResponseCache`:

    ```
    builder.Services.AddResponseCaching();
    ```

3. Let's modify our CORS policy to expose ETags. ETags are usually considered a standard caching header, but our client may restrict it due to CORS:

    ```
    builder.Services.AddCors(options =>
    {
        options.AddDefaultPolicy(builder =>
        {
            builder.AllowAnyOrigin()
            .AllowAnyHeader()
            .AllowAnyMethod()
            .WithExposedHeaders("X-Pagination", "X-Books-
                                Modified", "ETag");
        });
    });
    ```

4. Toward the bottom of the file, add the `ResponseCaching` middleware at the very beginning of the pipeline:

    ```
    var app = builder.Build();
    ...
    app.UseResponseCaching();
    ```

> **Note**
>
> The response cache middleware must be placed after `UseCors`. CORS middleware needs to add necessary headers (such as *Access-Control-Allow-Origin*) to the response. This way, the response caching middleware can cache the complete response, including those CORS headers.

5. Now, open the `BooksController.cs` file. At the top of the file, import the namespace for the memory cache and HTTP headers:

    ```
    using Microsoft.Extensions.Caching.Memory;
    using Microsoft.Net.Http.Headers;
    ```

6. Set up `IMemoryCache`:

    ```
    public class BooksController : ControllerBase
    {
        private readonly IBooksService _service;
        private readonly IMemoryCache _cache;
        private readonly ILogger<BooksController> _logger;
    ```

```
public BooksController(
    IBooksService booksService,
    IMemoryCache cache,
    ILogger<BooksController> logger)
{
    _service = booksService ?? throw new
        ArgumentNullException(nameof(booksService));
    _cache = cache ?? throw new
        ArgumentNullException(nameof(cache));
    _logger = logger;
}
...
```

7.   Place the ResponseCache attribute – with a very short duration of 3 seconds. We will also use the ResponseCacheLocation enum to specify that the cache location should only be set on the client:

```
[ResponseCache(Duration = 3, Location = ResponseCacheLocation.
Client)]
```

8.   Next, at the top of the try block, we are going to try to retrieve an ETag with the key of BooksETag from the memory cache. If it does not exist, we are going to create it:

```
string? etag;
if (!_cache.TryGetValue("BooksETag", out etag))
{
    var cacheOptions = new MemoryCacheEntryOptions()
        .SetSlidingExpiration(TimeSpan.FromMinutes(5))
        .SetAbsoluteExpiration(TimeSpan.FromHours(24));
    etag = $"\"{Guid.NewGuid():n}\"";
    _cache.Set("BooksETag", etag, cacheOptions);
```

9.   On the next line, let's check whether or not the browser's request includes the if-none-match caching header. If it does, compare it to the ETag stored in the memory cache. If they match, we'll be returned the 304 Not Modified HTTP status code and tell the browser to use the cached version:

```
if (Request.Headers.IfNoneMatch.Count > 0)
{
    var requestETag = Request.Headers.IfNoneMatch.First();
    if (requestETag == etag)
    {
        return StatusCode(StatusCodes.Status304NotModified);
    }
};
```

10. Now, if the ETag does not match, we return our result normally. Scroll down to right before `return Ok(pagedResult.Items);`. However, this time, we make sure to send the generated ETag to the client:

```
Response.Headers.Append("X-Pagination", JsonSerializer.
Serialize(paginationMetadata, options));
Response.GetTypedHeaders().ETag = new
EntityTagHeaderValue(etag);

    return Ok(pagedResult.Items);
```

11. Now, scroll down to the `CreateBook` method, which is our `HttpPost` endpoint. After a book is created, we will replace the ETag in `IMemoryCache` with the new ETag header:

```
var createdBook = await _service.CreateBookAsync(bookDto);
_cache.Set("BooksETag", $"\"{Guid.NewGuid():n}\"");
Response.Headers.CacheControl = "no-store";
```

12. Start the API and open the `test-client.html` page. Press the **Fetch Books (Cacheable)** button.

The first time you make a request, the cache will miss. If you press the button multiple times, you should see the ETag remains the same and the cache is now hit.

13. Now. press the green **Add New Book** button. The next time you press **Fetch Books (Cacheable)**, the cache will miss and you will perform a full reload. Also notice that the ETag is now different, as shown in *Figure 10.4*:

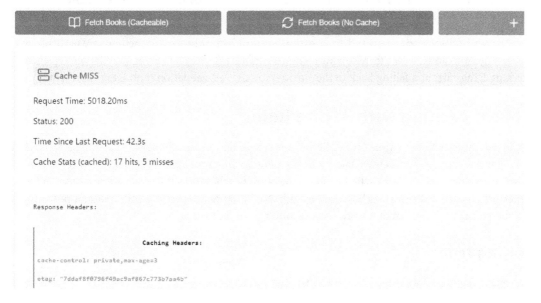

Figure 10.4 – Cache miss due to client and server ETag not matching

How it works...

The `ResponseCache` attribute acts as a filter that intercepts and manipulates response headers – nothing more. Even its most distinctive feature, `VaryByQueryKeys`, simply adds appropriate `Vary` headers to the response. Understanding the limitations of `ResponseCache` led us to implement our own ETag-based cache validation system while still leveraging the middleware's header management capabilities.

Our implementation stores and manages ETags in `IMemoryCache` on the server side, but this isn't for caching responses – it's purely for validation. While we register the `ResponseCache` middleware, we don't use its caching capabilities since that would require setting `Cache-Control` to `'public'` – instead, we're implementing a client-side caching strategy. When the browser makes a request, it includes its stored ETag in the `If-None-Match` header. Our server compares this with the current ETag stored in memory. If they match, we return a `304 Not Modified` status, telling the browser its cached copy is still valid. When content changes (such as when a new book is added), we generate a new ETag, automatically invalidating any cached responses on the client side. This approach gives us precise control over cache invalidation while still benefiting from the `ResponseCache` middleware's header management. The result is a practical caching solution that combines the simplicity of the `ResponseCache` header management with the precision of ETag-based cache validation.

See also

You can find the `ResponseCache` middleware source code here: `https://github.com/dotnet/aspnetcore/blob/main/src/Middleware/ResponseCaching/src/ResponseCachingMiddleware.cs`.

The `ContentIsNotModified` and `TryServeCachedResponseAsync` methods are particularly noteworthy. You can see how the middleware implements the HTTP specification's validation sequence, checking ETags first and falling back to the `Last-Modified` validation if no ETag is present.

Output caching with Aspire Redis

While response caching focuses on HTTP header manipulation and client-side caching, ASP.NET Core's output caching middleware takes a fundamentally different approach. Instead of relying on browsers to store and validate cached content, the output cache stores the complete response on the server side. When combined with Redis through .NET Aspire integration, this creates a powerful distributed caching solution that works across multiple server instances.

Getting ready

This recipe requires Docker Desktop to be installed and running.

It is essential that you are always installing Aspire packages for .NET 9 not for .NET 8.

The starting project can be found here: `https://github.com/PacktPublishing/ASP.NET-9-Web-API-Cookbook/tree/main/start/chapter10/OutputCacheRedis`.

How to do it...

1. Navigate to the `BooksAPI` project folder and install the necessary NuGet package. Open your terminal and install the `Aspire Redis OutputCaching` package:

```
dotnet add package Aspire.StackExchange.Redis.OutputCaching
```

2. Set up the .NET Aspire `AppHost` project:

    I. Navigate to the `AppHost` project. This project will configure the Redis resource.

    II. Install the necessary NuGet package in the app host project:

```
dotnet add package Aspire.Hosting.Redis
```

3. Configure the Redis resource in the app host. Open the `Program.cs` file in the app host project and configure the Redis resource:

```
using Projects;

var builder = DistributedApplication.CreateBuilder(args);
var cache = builder.AddRedis("cache");
```

4. Now, instruct Aspire to load the main `BookAPI` project with the Redis cache provider we just configured:

```
builder.AddProject<Books>("BookAPI")
    .WithExternalHttpEndpoints()
    .WithReference(cache);

await builder.Build().Run();
```

5. Navigate back to the `BooksAPI` project. In this project, install the Redis output caching package:

```
dotnet add package Aspire.StackExchange.Redis.OutputCaching
```

6. In `Program.cs`, add the Redis output cache:

```
public static void Main(string[] args)
    {
        var builder = WebApplication.CreateBuilder(args);

        builder.AddRedisOutputCache(connectionName: "cache");
        builder.AddServiceDefaults();
```

> **Note**
>
> The `connectionName` parameter `"cache"` must match the name we defined when calling `AddRedis` in the Aspire app host's `Program.cs` file. This connection name is how Aspire links the Redis service to our API.

7. Let's register the output cache middleware. This middleware must be placed in the pipeline after CORS and after routing or the output cache will not work:

    ```
    var app = builder.Build();

    app.UseCors();
    app.UseRouting();
    app.UseOutputCache();
    app.UseWebSockets();
    app.MapControllers();
    ```

8. Open the `BooksController.cs` file. At the top of the file, import the `OutputCaching` namespace:

    ```
    using Microsoft.AspNetCore.OutputCaching;
    ```

9. Apply the `OutputCache` attribute to the `GetBooks` action method, our main `HttpGet` endpoint:

    ```
    [OutputCache(Duration = 60, Tags = new[] { "GetBooks" })]
    public async Task<IActionResult> GetBooks([FromQuery] int
    pageSize = 10, [FromQuery] int lastId = 0)
    {
    ```

    We also added a `"GetBooks"` tag. Unlike ETags used in HTTP caching, output cache tags are server-side labels that let us invalidate specific cached entries. We'll use this tag to clear the cache when data changes.

10. Let's navigate to the `HttpPost` method and do exactly that. When a new resource is created, we will evict the cache entries tagged with the `GetBooks` tag:

    ```
    try
    {
        var createdBook = await _service.CreateBookAsync(bookDto);
        var outputCache = HttpContext.RequestServices.
            GetRequiredService<IOutputCacheStore>();
        await outputCache.EvictByTagAsync("GetBooks", HttpContext.
            RequestAborted);

        return CreatedAtAction(nameof(GetBookById),
            new { id = createdBook.Id }, createdBook)
    ```

We use the `EvictByTagAsync` to remove cache entries tagged with the `"GetBooks"` tag, ensuring that clients receive updated data on the next request.

11. Start the app host and the API project. Either run the solution file in your IDE or open two terminals. In both the `BookAPI` folder and the `AppHost` project folder, run `dotnet run`.

    The Aspire dashboard should open in your web browser. It is essential that Docker Desktop is running in the background. On the Aspire dashboard, you should see both the cache and the `BookAPI` project running. *Figure 10.5* shows both running correctly:

Figure 10.5 – The Aspire dashboard

12. Open the `test-client.html` page.

    Press the **Fetch Books (Cacheable)** button. The first time you make a request, the cache will miss. If you press the button multiple times, you should see the cache is hit. If you add a new book via the green **Add New Book** button and then try to fetch again, the cache will miss and you will perform a full reload.

> **Note**
>
> Unlike our previous recipe, you won't see `cache-control` headers in the response. That's because the output cache operates entirely server-side – there's no need to coordinate with the client's cache since all caching decisions are made by our server using Redis.

How it works...

Output cache middleware intercepts and caches server responses in Redis, eliminating the need to execute action methods for identical requests. Unlike the response cache, which coordinates with browser caching through HTTP headers, the output cache handles everything on the server side. When we add a new book, `EvictByTagAsync` clears cached entries tagged with `"GetBooks"`, ensuring fresh data on subsequent requests. Since we're not using ETags or client-side cache validation, the client always receives a response from the server, but the server uses caching to improve performance.

Best of all, by configuring Redis as the cache store through Aspire, the cache entries are stored in a centralized location, making them accessible to all server instances of the application.

Server-side caching with IDistributedCache and Redis via .NET Aspire

Unlike previous recipes that focused on HTTP caching headers, IDistributedCache provides direct control over server-side caching. When combined with Redis through .NET Aspire, we can cache specific data objects and share them across multiple server instances. This approach is particularly useful when you need fine-grained control over what gets cached and for how long.

Getting ready

Ensure that Docker Desktop is installed and running on your machine.

As we go through this recipe, make sure to install the Aspire packages for .NET 9, not for .NET 8.

Download the starter project here: `https://github.com/PacktPublishing/ASP.NET-9-Web-API-Cookbook/tree/main/start/chapter10/DistributedCacheRedis`.

How to do it...

1. Set Up the .NET Aspire AppHost project:

    I.   Navigate to the AppHost project, which will configure the Redis resource.

    II. Add the Redis hosting package:

    ```
    dotnet add package Aspire.Hosting.Redis
    ```

    III. Navigate to the BooksAPI project and add the Redis nuget package:

    ```
    dotnet add package Aspire.StackExchange.Redis
    ```

> **Note**
> If you open the csproj file, the version numbers should match the Aspire.AppHost.Sdk version you're using.

2. Now, we need to configure the Redis resource in the app host. Open the Program.cs file in the AppHost project and configure the Redis resource:

    ```
    using Projects;

    var builder = DistributedApplication.CreateBuilder(args);
    ```

```
var cache = builder.AddRedis("cache");

builder.AddProject<Books>("BooksAPI")
       .WithExternalHttpEndpoints()
       .WithReference(cache);

await builder.Build().RunAsync();
```

The `AddRedis("cache")` method creates a Redis instance, while `WithReference(cache)` makes it available to our `BooksAPI` project.

3.   Let's configure the `BooksAPI` project to use Redis via Aspire. In the `BooksAPI` project, open `Program.cs` and add the Redis distributed cache:

```
var builder = WebApplication.CreateBuilder(args);

// Add Redis Distributed Cache
builder.AddRedisClient(connectionName: "cache");
builder.Services.AddServiceDefaults();
```

4.   Now. register `IDistributedCache` and `IConnectionMultiplexer`:

```
builder.Services.AddStackExchangeRedisCache(options =>
{
    options.Configuration = builder.Configuration
        .GetConnectionString("cache");
});
builder.Services.AddSingleton<IConnectionMultiplexer>(sp =>
{
    var configuration = builder.Configuration
        .GetConnectionString("cache");
    return ConnectionMultiplexer.Connect(configuration);
});
```

5.   We now need to implement caching in `BooksController`. Open `BooksController.cs` and add the necessary namespaces:

```
using Microsoft.Extensions.Caching.Distributed;
using StackExchange.Redis;
```

6. Inject `IDistributedCache` into the controller. Let's update the `BooksController` constructor to include `IDistributedCache`:

```
public class BooksController : ControllerBase
{
    private readonly IBooksService _service;
    private readonly IDistributedCache _cache;
    private readonly ILogger<BooksController> _logger;

    public BooksController(
        IBooksService booksService,
        IDistributedCache cache,
        ILogger<BooksController> logger)
    {
        _service = booksService ?? throw new
            ArgumentNullException(nameof(booksService));
        _cache = cache ?? throw new
            ArgumentNullException(nameof(cache));
        _logger = logger ?? throw new
            ArgumentNullException(nameof(logger));
    }
```

7. Modify the `GetBooks` method to use caching. At the top of the `try` block, generate a unique cache key based on the pagination parameters:

```
public async Task<IActionResult> GetBooks([FromQuery] int
pageSize = 10, [FromQuery] int lastId = 0)
{
    try
    {

        string cacheKey = $"GetBooks_{pageSize}_{lastId}";
```

8. On the next line, attempt to retrieve the cached data:

```
PagedResult<BookDTO>? pagedResult = null;

string? cachedData = await _cache.GetStringAsync(cacheKey);

if (!string.IsNullOrEmpty(cachedData))
{
    _logger.LogInformation("Fetching books from cache.");
    pagedResult = JsonSerializer.Deserialize<
        PagedResult<BookDTO>>(cachedData);
```

```
            if (pagedResult == null)
            {
                _logger.LogWarning("Cached data was invalid.
                                    Fetching from database.");
            }
        }
```

We declare `pagedResult` as nullable and try to retrieve serialized data from the cache. If we find cached data, we deserialize it into the `PagedResult<BookDTO>` type. The null check after deserialization helps us handle potential serialization issues gracefully.

9. If we don't retrieve any data from the cache, we will then proceed to fetch the books from the database, as normal. The 5-second delay is left in to simulate a demanding query/server load:

```
    if (pagedResult == null)
        {
            _logger.LogInformation("Fetching books from
                                    database.");

            await Task.Delay(5000);

            pagedResult = await _service.GetBooksAsync(pageSize,
                    lastId, Url);

            var serializedData = JsonSerializer.
                                 Serialize(pagedResult);

            var cacheOptions = new DistributedCacheEntryOptions
            {
                AbsoluteExpirationRelativeToNow = TimeSpan.
                    FromMinutes(5)
            };
```

10. We need to store this new response data in our distributed cache. On the next line, store the response data in the cache before returning the result:

```
    await _cache.SetStringAsync(cacheKey, serializedData,
    cacheOptions);
        }

            // Add the pagination metadata to the response headers
            var options = new JsonSerializerOptions
            {
                Encoder = System.Text.Encodings.Web.
    JavaScriptEncoder.UnsafeRelaxedJsonEscaping
            };
```

11. Now, return our data with the pagination headers. We return our data in the same way, regardless of whether it was cached or retrieved from the database:

```
var paginationMetadata = new
        {
            pagedResult.PageSize,
            pagedResult.HasPreviousPage,
            pagedResult.HasNextPage,
            pagedResult.PreviousPageUrl,
            pagedResult.NextPageUrl,
        };

        Response.Headers.Append("X-Pagination", JsonSerializer.
        Serialize(paginationMetadata, options));

        return Ok(pagedResult.Items);
}
```

Note that we create one `pagedResult` at the beginning and load it with either a result from the cache or the database. Only when we have the result ready do we then add the pagination metadata.

12. Let's work on a way to invalidate our cache. Let's create a helper method that scans the Redis cache store. This method should remove any cached data that has a key beginning with `"GetBooks"`:

```
private async Task InvalidateGetBooksCacheAsync()
{
    var connectionMultiplexer = HttpContext.RequestServices
        .GetRequiredService<IConnectionMultiplexer>();
    var server = connectionMultiplexer.GetServer(
        connectionMultiplexer.GetEndPoints().First());

    foreach (var key in server.Keys(pattern: "GetBooks_*"))
    {
        await _cache.RemoveAsync(key);
    }
}
```

This method uses Redis's pattern matching to find and remove all cached entries that start with `"GetBooks_"`. This ensures that when new books are added, all paginated results are refreshed, regardless of their page size or last ID parameters.

13. Finally, let's modify our POST endpoint, the CreateBook action method, to invalidate our cache. All we have to do is call our helper method right before returning. On the line after we create the book, call the InvalidateGetBooksCacheAsync method:

```
try
    {
        var createdBook = await _service.
                        CreateBookAsync(bookDto);

        // Invalidate cache entries related to GetBooks
        await InvalidateGetBooksCacheAsync();

        return CreatedAtAction(nameof(GetBookById),
            new { id = createdBook.Id }, createdBook);
    }
```

14. Run our application. Either run the solution file in an IDE or run dotnet run from the terminal in both the BooksAPI project directory and the AppHost project directory.

15. Open the test-client.html file.

> **Note**
>
> If we repeatedly press the blue **Fetch Books (Cacheable)** button, we retrieve a cached result. If we add a new book with the green **Add New Book** button, the cache is invalidated.

There is one other thing to point out about our client. Even when using the blue **Fetch Books (No Cache)** button, we are receiving cached data from the backend. While this button sends a cache-control: no-cache header, our server-side distributed cache operates independently of HTTP headers. The IDistributedCache service makes caching decisions without considering these HTTP headers. If we wanted to respect HTTP cache headers, we would need to explicitly check them in our controller logic.

How it works...

IDistributedCache with Redis provides a fundamentally different approach to caching when compared to response or output caching. Instead of relying on HTTP headers to coordinate with client browsers, we're storing serialized data objects directly in Redis. When a request arrives, we generate a unique cache key based on the pagination parameters, allowing us to cache different *pages* of results separately.

The real power comes from Redis's pattern-matching capabilities. When we add a new book, the `InvalidateGetBooksCacheAsync` method uses the pattern of `"GetBooks_*"` to find and remove all cached entries, ensuring that subsequent requests receive fresh data. This is more flexible than the tag-based approach often used with output caching, as we can invalidate specific cache entries based on complex patterns.

Unlike response cache or output cache middleware, which integrate with HTTP's caching mechanism, this approach operates independently of HTTP headers. That's why even requests marked with `'no-store'` or `'no-cache'` headers still receive cached responses – we're making caching decisions at the data access level, not the HTTP level.

Using the new HybridCache library to simplify distributed caching

The new `HybridCache` library in ASP.NET Core combines the benefits of in-memory caching (`IMemoryCache`) and distributed caching (`IDistributedCache`) into a single, easy-to-use API. When data is requested, `HybridCache` first checks the fast local memory cache, falling back to a distributed cache if needed. The distributed cache can work with any `IDistributedCache` implementation as a backplane, enabling cache synchronization across multiple server instances. It provides features such as cache stampede protection, serialization abstractions, and automatic handling of multi-level caching. In this recipe, we'll integrate `HybridCache` into our `Books` API to optimize performance and simplify caching logic.

Getting ready

Ensure you have the .NET 9 SDK installed, as `HybridCache` is available starting from .NET 9.

Ensure that Docker Desktop is installed and running on your machine as we will use Redis via Aspire.

The starter project can be found here: `https://github.com/PacktPublishing/ASP.NET-9-Web-API-Cookbook/tree/main/start/chapter10/HybridCacheRedis`.

How to do it....

1. Set up `AppHost` to host Redis by navigating to the `Books.AppHost` folder and installing Redis:

    ```
    dotnet add package Aspire.Hosting.Redis
    ```

2. In the app host's `Program.cs` file, register the `redis` cache, and provide it to the `BooksAPI` project:

    ```
    using Projects;

    var builder = DistributedApplication.CreateBuilder(args);
    ```

```
var cache = builder.AddRedis("cache");

builder.AddProject<Books>("BookAPI")
       .WithExternalHttpEndpoints()
       .WithReference(cache);

builder.Build().Run();
```

3. Navigate to the BooksAPI folder and install the following packages:

    ```
    dotnet add package Microsoft.Extensions.Caching.
    Hybrid  --prerelease
    dotnet add package Aspire.StackExchange.Redis.DistributedCaching
    ```

    These packages install HybridCache. They also allow us to register IDistributedCache
    with Aspire's Redis integration.

4. Because HybridCache does not yet support wildcard pattern matching for cache keys (such
    as "GetBooks_*"), we will implement a simple key tracking service to maintain a list of
    active cache keys. Create a new file called ICacheKeyTracker.cs in the Services
    folder. Create an interface for a new service that will track keys:

    ```
    namespace Books.Services;

    public interface ICacheKeyTracker
    {
        void TrackKey(string key);
        IReadOnlyCollection<string> GetKeys();
        void Clear();
    }
    ```

5. Now, create a CacheKeyTracker.cs file. Implement the service that will keep track of
    what unique keys we created in a HashSet. First, instantiate our objects and implement the
    method for adding keys:

    ```
    namespace Books.Services;

    public class CacheKeyTracker : ICacheKeyTracker
    {
        private readonly HashSet<string> _keys = new();
        private readonly object _lock = new();

        public void TrackKey(string key)
        {
            lock (_lock)
    ```

```
    {
        _keys.Add(key);
    }
}
```

6. On the next line, implement the methods for getting and clearing keys:

```
public IReadOnlyCollection<string> GetKeys()
{
    lock (_lock)
    {
        return _keys.ToList();
    }
}

public void Clear()
{
    lock (_lock)
    {
        _keys.Clear();
    }
}
}
```

7. Navigate to the `Program.cs` file, still in the `BooksAPI` folder. At the top of `Program.cs`, import the `Extensions` namespace for using `HybridCache`:

```
using Microsoft.Extensions.Caching.Hybrid;
```

8. Still in `Program.cs`, register our custom service for managing cache keys, right after we create the builder:

```
var builder = WebApplication.CreateBuilder(args);

builder.Services.AddSingleton<ICacheKeyTracker,
CacheKeyTracker>();
```

9. On the next line, configure `HybridCache`. Since this feature is in preview, we need to disable the `EXTEXP0018` warning:

```
#pragma warning disable EXTEXP0018
builder.Services.AddHybridCache(options =>
{
    options.MaximumPayloadBytes = 1024 * 1024;
    options.DefaultEntryOptions = new HybridCacheEntryOptions
    {
```

```
            Expiration = TimeSpan.FromMinutes(5),
            LocalCacheExpiration = TimeSpan.FromMinutes(2)
        };
    });
    #pragma warning restore EXTEXP0018
```

This registers the Aspire-provided Redis client. It also registers `DistributedCache`, which will serve as the L2 cache for `HybridCache`. Finally, we register `HybridCache` itself.

Why not just use AddStackExchangeRedisCache?

We could use `'builder.Services.AddStackExchangeRedisCache(options => { options.Configuration = "127.0.0.1:58477"; });'`, and directly register it with an IP address. However, we're using Aspire to manage Redis, so it's better to keep configurations consistent and use Aspire's methods.

---

10. In `BooksController`, import the `HybridCache` namespace:

```
    using Microsoft.Extensions.Caching.Hybrid;
```

11. Adjust the controller to work with `HybridCache` and the service we created for tracking keys:

```
    public class BooksController : ControllerBase
    {
        private readonly IBooksService _service;
        private readonly HybridCache _cache;
        private readonly ICacheKeyTracker _keyTracker;
        private readonly ILogger<BooksController> _logger;

        public BooksController(
            IBooksService booksService,
            HybridCache cache,
            ICacheKeyTracker keyTracker,
            ILogger<BooksController> logger)
        {
            _service = booksService ?? throw new
                ArgumentNullException(nameof(booksService));
            _cache = cache ?? throw new
                ArgumentNullException(nameof(cache));
            _keyTracker = keyTracker ?? throw new
                ArgumentNullException(nameof(keyTracker));
            _logger = logger ?? throw new
                ArgumentNullException(nameof(logger));
        }
```

12. Modify the `GetBooks` method to use `HybridCache` and assign a cache key when generated. For this endpoint, we will implement custom cache options that override the default caching options:

```
[HttpGet]
public async Task<IActionResult> GetBooks([FromQuery] int
pageSize = 10, [FromQuery] int lastId = 0)
{
    try
    {
        string cacheKey = $"GetBooks_{pageSize}_{lastId}";

        _keyTracker.TrackKey(cacheKey);
        var cacheEntryOptions = new HybridCacheEntryOptions
        {
            // L2 cache expiration
            Expiration = TimeSpan.FromMinutes(3),
            // L1 cache expiration
            LocalCacheExpiration = TimeSpan.FromMinutes(1)
        };
```

13. On the next line, modify where we retrieve books from the service, to first try to fetch from our cache:

```
var pagedResult = await _cache.GetOrCreateAsync(
    cacheKey,
    async token =>
    {
        _logger.LogInformation("Fetching books from database.");
        await Task.Delay(5000, token); // Simulate delay
        return await _service.GetBooksAsync(pageSize, lastId,
                                            Url);
    },
    cacheEntryOptions,
    cancellationToken: HttpContext.RequestAborted);
```

The rest of the `GetBooks` method remains the same.

14. Invalidate the cache when a new book is added. Navigate to our POST endpoint, the `CreateBook` method, in the same file. If there are any tags created, clear the cache of all tags. `HybridCache` does allow us to pass a collection:

```
[HttpPost]
public async Task<IActionResult> CreateBook([FromBody] BookDTO
bookDto)
{
    if (!ModelState.IsValid)
```

```
    {
        return BadRequest(ModelState);
    }
    try
    {
        var createdBook = await _service.
                            CreateBookAsync(bookDto);
        var keys = _keyTracker.GetKeys();
        if (keys.Any())
        {
            await _cache.RemoveAsync(keys);
        }
    }
```

How it works...

HybridCache combines two levels of caching: a short-lived in-memory cache (L1) and a longer-lived distributed Redis cache (L2). When we set LocalCacheExpiration to 2 minutes and Expiration to 5 minutes, we get the best of both worlds – extremely fast local memory access for frequently accessed data, with Redis providing a broader distributed cache layer.

Unlike IDistributedCache, which requires working directly with byte arrays and handling serialization, HybridCache provides a simpler API with built-in serialization support. It also prevents cache stampede by ensuring only one concurrent caller for a given key executes the data retrieval, while other callers wait for that result.

At the time of this writing, one of the most anticipated features of HybridCache – tag-based cache invalidation – is not yet implemented. Tags would provide functionality similar to the OutputCache tag system, allowing groups of related cache entries to be invalidated together. This feature is particularly important as it addresses a key limitation of IDistributedCache, which has no built-in way to group related cache entries. To work around this limitation, we implemented a key tracking service to maintain a list of active cache keys, allowing us to invalidate related entries when data changes.

Currently, FusionCache, an open source third-party library, is the first production-ready implementation of HybridCache. FusionCache has released an implementation of the HybridCache abstract class and is easy to integrate. FusionCache also includes many more features than HybridCache, such as fail-safe mechanisms, soft/hard timeouts, and eager refresh. Best of all, FusionCache does indeed support tagging, unlike the current version of HybridCache.

For performance optimization, HybridCache avoids unnecessary byte[] allocations by using IBufferDistributedCache, which is supported in both Redis and SQL Server caching packages. You can further optimize performance by marking cached types as sealed or applying the [ImmutableObject(true)] attribute, allowing HybridCache to safely reuse object instances.

See also

- FusionCache: `https://github.com/ZiggyCreatures/FusionCache`

11
Beyond the Core

In modern distributed systems, communication patterns fall into two main categories: **North-South traffic** (communication between external clients and your backend services) and **East-West traffic** (inter-service communication within your system). This chapter focuses on East-West traffic patterns in .NET distributed applications.

We will begin with fundamental gRPC communication in .NET Aspire, showing how to manually configure and implement service-to-service calls. The journey will continue with bidirectional streaming via pure gRPC, showcasing how to handle real-time updates without additional overhead. We will then transition to implementing similar communication patterns using **Distributed Application Runtime** (**Dapr**). While Aspire handles service orchestration, Dapr provides production-ready implementations of common microservices patterns through its sidecar architecture. Specifically, we will explore Dapr's **publish/subscribe** (**pub/sub**) messaging and state management.

Though .NET Aspire is still maturing (our recipes aren't completely free of having to write YAML), its integration with Dapr offers a glimpse of the future of .NET distributed applications. These recipes progress from basic service-to-service communication to sophisticated patterns, illustrating both the power and current limitations of these emerging technologies. Each approach – whether pure gRPC or Dapr-based – presents its own advantages for different scenarios.

In this chapter, we're going to cover the following recipes:

- Microservice communication via gRPC and .NET Aspire
- Implementing bidirectional streaming with gRPC in .NET Aspire
- Implementing real-time updates with Dapr pub/sub in .NET Aspire
- Sharing state between services with Dapr state stores

Technical requirements

For the recipes in this chapter, you'll need the following:

- **.NET 9 SDK**: Please make sure you are using the latest .NET 9 SDK, which is available here: `https://dotnet.microsoft.com/en-us/download/dotnet/9.0`.

- **Aspire**: Most of these recipes use the latest Aspire templates. Download them via Visual Studio, installing the `Aspire.ProjectTemplates` NuGet package available at `https://www.nuget.org/packages/Aspire.ProjectTemplates` or via the terminal by executing the following dotnet CLI command:

  ```
  dotnet new install Aspire.ProjectTemplates
  ```

- **Go**: We will be using a CLI tool created with Go. If you are following along with Windows, having the Go compiler installed in order to compile this CLI tool is the easiest way to install it. However, you can also just clone the Docker container. macOS users can install it via Homebrew. The project website lists other options: `https://github.com/fullstorydev/grpcurl`.

  Once you have Go installed, installing the `grpcurl` tool is easy via the terminal:

  ```
  go install github.com/fullstorydev/grpcurl/cmd/grpcurl@latest
  ```

  For Windows users, make sure that `%USERPROFILE%\go\bin` is added to your path.

Microservice communication via gRPC and .NET Aspire

Returning and receiving data from the client is one thing, but what if our API needs to talk to another API or other backend service? That's where gRPC comes in – the industry standard for passing messages between backend services (East-West traffic). We will leverage .NET Aspire orchestration and service discovery, while retaining the lower-level control of inter-service message communication, by setting up our own gRPC channel. This channel will pass messages between `BooksAPI` and a new `InventoryService` whenever a new book is created.

Getting ready

The starter project for this recipe can be found here: `https://github.com/PacktPublishing/ASP.NET-9-Web-API-Cookbook/tree/main/end/chapter11/gRPCAspire`.

It is recommended that you have the `grpcurl` CLI tool installed in your terminal per the *Technical requirements* section of this chapter. While we'll use PowerShell to test our REST endpoints, we'll need `grpcurl` specifically for testing our gRPC services.

How to do it...

1. Create a new `InventoryService` API project:

   ```
   dotnet new webapi -o InventoryService
   ```

2. In the new service project, create a `Protos` folder. In this new `Protos` folder, create a file named `inventory.proto`. In the `inventory.proto` file, the first thing we have to define is what version of the **Protocol Buffers (Protobuf)** syntax we are going to be using:

   ```
   syntax = "proto3";
   ```

3. Next, define the C# namespace for the code, which will be generated from this Protobuf file:

   ```
   option csharp_namespace = "InventoryService.Grpc";
   ```

4. Define the `Protobuf` specification. We will first define a unary call for initializing the stock inventory. Then, we will define streaming for monitoring stock levels:

   ```
   service Inventory {
       rpc InitializeInventory (
           InitializeInventoryRequest
       ) returns (InitializeInventoryResponse);

       rpc MonitorStock (StockRequest)
           returns (stream StockUpdate);
   }
   ```

5. Now that we have our unary and stream service defined, let's define four gRPC types of messages this service can receive:

   ```
   message InitializeInventoryRequest {
       int32 book_id = 1;
       string isbn = 2;
       int32 initial_stock = 3;
   }

   message InitializeInventoryResponse {
       bool success = 1;
       string inventory_id = 2;
   }

   message StockRequest {
       int32 book_id = 1;
   }
   ```

```
message StockUpdate {
    int32 current_stock = 1;
    string location = 2;
    int64 timestamp = 3;
}
```

> **Note**
>
> If you are used to working with arrays in .NET, where indexing starts at 0, you will have to adjust your thinking when working with `Protobuf`. `Protobuf` uses 1-based indexing, unlike many programming languages (such as C#/.NET) that use 0-based indexing – indexes that start at 0. This means that in a `.proto` file, the first field is assigned the number 1, the second field the number 2, and so on. During serialization and deserialization, the `Google.Protobuf Nuget` package – which we will install later in this recipe – automatically handles type conversion, mapping these fields to their .NET equivalents.

6. Let's install the necessary NuGet package to add gRPC functionality to our project:

    dotnet add package Grpc.AspNetCore

7. Let's add the gRPC reflection package. This is not strictly necessary for our gRPC service to run but it will make debugging much easier:

    dotnet add package Grpc.AspNetCore.Server.Reflection

8. Let's modify the `InventoryService.csproj` profile file to convert our `Protobuf` file into a `Grpc` server:

    ```
    <ItemGroup>
        <Protobuf Include="Protos\inventory.proto"
    GrpcServices="Server" />
    </ItemGroup>
    ```

    Notice that `GrpcServices` is set to `Server` and not `Client`.

9. Open the `InventoryService\Program.cs` file. We are going to explicitly tell the web host to open our gRPC on port `5003` if not defined by Aspire. We are going to specify that we want to use the `Http2` spec, as gRPC is part of the HTTP2 spec:

    ```
    builder.WebHost.ConfigureKestrel(options =>
    {
        var port = builder.Configuration
            .GetValue<int?>("Ports:gRPC") ?? 5003;
        options.ListenLocalhost(port, o => o.Protocols =
            Microsoft.AspNetCore.Server.Kestrel.Core.HttpProtocols.
                Http2);
    });
    ```

10. On the next line, add the gRPC service:

    ```
    builder.Services.AddGrpc();
    ```

11. Next, enable gRPC reflection:

    ```
    builder.Services.AddGrpcReflection();
    ```

    This service is not strictly necessary for our gRPC channel to send or receive messages; however, it will make testing a lot easier.

12. Map our gRPC service. On the line after `var app = builder.Build();`, register `InventoryServiceImplementation`:

    ```
    var app = builder.Build();
    app.MapGrpcService<InventoryServiceImplementation>();
    ```

13. Now, we will define the C# service that will interact with our `Protobuf` file. Still in the `inventoryService` project, create a folder called `Services`. In that folder, create a new file called `InventoryServiceImplementation.cs`. In the `InventoryServiceImplementation.cs` file, let's import the namespaces we will need:

    ```
    using Grpc.Core;
    using InventoryService.Grpc;
    ```

    We first bring in the main `Grpc` library via `Grpc.Core`. We then import the `InventoryService.Grpc` namespace, which was defined via the `csharp_namespace` property on the second line of our `Protobuf` file, `inventory.proto`.

14. Next, let's import a logger into our service via a primary constructor:

    ```
    namespace InventoryService.Services;

    public class InventoryServiceImplementation
    (ILogger<InventoryServiceImplementation> logger)
        : Inventory.InventoryBase
    {
    ```

15. Now, let's set up the ability to receive a request. `InitializeInventory` will receive one of our `Protobuf` messages and return a GUID for a new book inventory when it receives a message from the other project:

    ```
    public override Task<InitializeInventoryResponse>
    InitializeInventory(
        InitializeInventoryRequest request,
        ServerCallContext context)
    {
        logger.LogInformation(
    ```

```
            "Initializing inventory for Book {BookId} with ISBN
            {ISBN}, Initial Stock: {Stock}",
            request.BookId,
            request.Isbn,
            request.InitialStock);

        var inventoryId = Guid.NewGuid().ToString();

        logger.LogInformation(
            "Created inventory record {InventoryId} for Book
            {BookId}",
            inventoryId,
            request.BookId);

        return Task.FromResult(new InitializeInventoryResponse
        {
            Success = true,
            InventoryId = inventoryId
        });
    }
}
```

Note

`InitializeInventoryRequest` was a message type we defined in the `inventory.proto` file. `ServerCallContext` is the context of the communication being passed by gRPC.

---

16. Set up `BooksAPI` to send a message. We are going to send a unary message when a new book is added to our `Inventory` service over a gRPC channel. The first thing we have to do is install the three NuGet packages required to create a gRPC client:

```
dotnet add package Grpc.Net.ClientFactory
dotnet add package Grpc.Tools
dotnet add package Google.Protobuf
```

ClientFactory versus Client

When setting up gRPC clients in .NET, you'll encounter two main packages: `Grpc.Net.Client` and `Grpc.Net.ClientFactory`. While `Grpc.Net.Client` provides basic gRPC client functionality, `Grpc.Net.ClientFactory` offers additional features for dependency injection scenarios. The `ClientFactory` package includes `Grpc.Net.Client` as a dependency and integrates with .NET's dependency injection system. In our Aspire-based application, we use `Grpc.Net.ClientFactory` because it works seamlessly with the dependency injection system and provides better integration with service discovery. This allows us to register our gRPC client with a single line.

---

17. Next, create an identical `Protos` folder in the `BooksAPI` project. Copy the `inventory.proto` file over from `Inventory.Service`. This needs to be the exact same file as in our `InventoryService` project. It is crucial that the `inventory.proto` file in the `BooksAPI` project is identical to the one in `InventoryService` to prevent any serialization or deserialization issues.

18. Reference the `Protobuf` file in the project file. To use the `Protobuf` file to define our gRPC file, we need to add the gRPC file to our `inventory.proto` file in our `csproj` file:

```
<ItemGroup>
    <Protobuf Include="Protos\inventory.proto"
    GrpcServices="Client" />
</ItemGroup>
```

Unlike our `InventoryService.csrpoj` file, we define `GrpcServices` as `Client` and not `Service`.

19. Register the gRPC client in the dependency injection container. Open the `Program.cs` file and add `GrpcClient` to use port `5003`:

```
builder.Services.AddGrpcClient<Inventory.
InventoryClient>(options =>
{
    options.Address = new Uri("http://localhost:5003");
})
```

> **Note**
>
> Unlike the server-side implementation that required creating a full service class, the client-side implementation is much simpler. We only need to register the client and then use it directly in our controllers.

20. On the next line, further configure the channel to stay open and use HTTP2:

```
.ConfigureChannel(channel =>
{
    var handler = new SocketsHttpHandler
    {
        EnableMultipleHttp2Connections = true,
        KeepAlivePingDelay = TimeSpan.FromSeconds(60),
        KeepAlivePingTimeout = TimeSpan.FromSeconds(30),
        PooledConnectionIdleTimeout = Timeout.InfiniteTimeSpan
    };
    channel.HttpHandler = handler;
});
```

21. Inform our HTTP Post endpoint to send a message when a new book is added. Open the `BooksController` file. Let's import the `InventoryService` namespace:

```
using InventoryService;
```

This is the C# namespace defined in our `protobuf` file.

22. In the constructor, import our gRPC client:

```
[ApiController]
public class BooksController : ControllerBase
{
    private readonly IBooksService _service;
    private readonly Inventory.InventoryClient _inventoryClient;
    private readonly ILogger<BooksController> _logger;

    public BooksController(
            IBooksService booksService,
            Inventory.InventoryClient inventoryClient,
            ILogger<BooksController> logger)
    {
        _service = booksService ?? throw new
            ArgumentNullException(nameof(booksService));
        _logger = logger;
        _inventoryClient = inventoryClient;
    }
```

23. Next, let's modify our HTTP Post to send a gRPC message after the model is validated and a new book is created. Add the following after the model is validated:

```
public async Task<IActionResult> CreateBook([FromBody]
BookDTO bookDto)
{
    if (!ModelState.IsValid)
    {
        return BadRequest(ModelState);
    }
    try
    {
        _logger.LogInformation("Creating new book with ISBN:
        {ISBN}", bookDto.ISBN);
        var createdBook = await _service.
        CreateBookAsync(bookDto);
        _logger.LogInformation(
            "Book created successfully with ID: {BookId}",
            createdBook.Id);
```

```
        var response = await _inventoryClient
            .InitializeInventoryAsync(
                new InitializeInventoryRequest
                {
                    BookId = createdBook.Id,
                    Isbn = createdBook.ISBN,
                    InitialStock = 10
                });

        _logger.LogInformation(
                "Inventory initialized successfully.
                InventoryId: {InventoryId}",
                    response.InventoryId);
        return CreatedAtAction(nameof(
            GetBookById), new { id = createdBook.Id },
            createdBook)
    }
    catch (Exception ex)
```

24. Next, let's set up Aspire. We'll use Aspire to set up our HTTP ports. gRPC is supported in Aspire, but we still had to do a fair amount of manual setup:

   I.   First, we need to add the Aspire AppHost. Using the Aspire templates, add an AppHost for our projects:

   ```
   dotnet new aspire-apphost -o BooksAPI.AppHost
   ```

   II. Add the service defaults:

   ```
   dotnet new aspire-servicedefaults -o BooksAPI.
   ServiceDefaults
   ```

   III. Configure the AppHost. Add our gRPC server to the AppHost\Program.cs file:

   ```
   var builder = DistributedApplication.CreateBuilder(args);
   var inventory = builder.AddProject<Projects.
   InventoryService>("inventory")
       .WithEndpoint(
           endpointName: "grpc",
           callback: endpoint =>
           {
               endpoint.Port = 5003;
               endpoint.UriScheme = "http";
               endpoint.Transport = "http2";
               endpoint.IsProxied = false;
   ```

```
        }
    );
```

IV. Now, add the `BooksAPI` project:

```
var books = builder.AddProject<Projects.BooksAPI>("books")
    .WithReference(inventory)
    .WithHttpEndpoint(
        name: "api",
        port: 5011,
        isProxied: false
    );
builder.Build().Run();
```

V. We now need to add `Project` references. Add our two projects to the app host. In the `AppHost` folder, add references to both `BooksAPI` and the gRPC inventory service:

```
dotnet add reference ..\BooksAPI\BooksAPI.csproj
dotnet add reference ..\InventoryService\InventoryService.
csproj
```

VI. Now, in each of our two projects (`BooksAPI` and `InventoryService`), add references to `ServiceDefaults` (individual projects add a reference to the Aspire `ServiceDefaults`, *not* the other way around):

  i. In the `BooksAPI` folder, add a reference to the `ServiceDefaults` folder:

```
dotnet add reference ..\BooksAPI.ServiceDefaults\
BooksAPI.ServiceDefaults.csproj
```

  ii. In the `InventoryService` folder, add a reference to the `ServiceDefaults` project:

```
dotnet add reference ..\BooksAPI.ServiceDefaults\BooksAPI.
ServiceDefaults.csproj
```

VII. Register `ServiceDefaults` in the dependency injection container of the `Program.cs` file of `InventoryService`:

```
var builder = WebApplication.CreateBuilder(args);
builder.AddServiceDefaults();
```

VIII. In the `BooksAPI/Program.cs` file, add `ServiceDefaults`:

```
var builder = WebApplication.CreateBuilder(args);
builder.AddServiceDefaults();
builder.Services.AddControllers();
...
```

25. Either run the solution file in Visual Studio or run the `AppHost` project:

```
cd BooksAPI.AppHost
dotnet run
```

26. List all gRPC services exposed by the server:

```
grpcurl -plaintext localhost:5003 list
```

27. Describe a specific method:

```
grpcurl -plaintext localhost:5003 describe Inventory.
InitializeInventory
```

28. Describe the request message type:

```
grpcurl -plaintext localhost:5003 describe
InitializeInventoryRequest
```

29. Now, try to actually send the message of a new book being created. See whether we can send a mock *book added* call:

```
grpcurl -plaintext -d '{"bookId": 1, "isbn": "test-
isbn", "initialStock": 10}' localhost:5003 Inventory.
InitializeInventory
```

30. Now, we can see that our gRPC channel is open and working, straight from the terminal, as shown in *Figure 11.1*:

```
C:\my-coding-projects> grpcurl -plaintext -d '{"bookId": 1, "isbn": "test-is
bn", "initialStock": 10}' localhost:5003 Inventory.InitializeInventory
{
  "success": true,
  "inventory_id": "2dd4ba27-4a3c-4a02-a2c8-7f848b1eadd4"
}
C:\my-coding-projects>
```

Figure 11.1 – Hello gRPC

31. Let's see whether a message comes back when we add a new book. Let's add a new book and then check the Aspire log to see whether a gRPC message came back:

   I.   Let's add a new book to the API and then make sure a gRPC message was sent. Create a new book object in PowerShell:

```
$body = @{
    title = "Test Book"
    isbn = "1234567890"
    author = "Test Author"
    publishDate = "2024-01-01"
```

```
            genre = "Fiction"
            summary = "A test book"
     } | ConvertTo-Json
```

II.   Now, send the request:

```
Invoke-RestMethod -Method Post -Uri "http://localhost:5011/
api/books" -ContentType "application/json" -Body $body
```

The `grpcurl` and `PowerShell` tests are for different things. The `grpcurl` test is testing the service directly.

32. In the Aspire logs, we can see that our system is still working. We can see the new ID created by `InventoryService` and received via gRPC. If you navigate to the Aspire dashboard in your web browser and open the log for `books`, you should be able to find the following entry:

```
95   2024-11-24T17:49:54 info: Books.Controllers.BooksController[0]
96   2024-11-24T17:49:54      Inventory initialized successfully. InventoryId: 4454c8ad-9ecb-4a90-ac88-a05da493c7bf
```

Figure 11.2 – BooksAPI receives a gRPC message

How it works...

We set up microservices communication using gRPC over HTTP2 using Aspire. The current state of gRPC support in Aspire requires some manual configuration. That's why we had to explicitly configure `HTTP/2` transport and ports in the `Program.cs` file of `InventoryService`. You might notice a warning in the Aspire dashboard about overriding addresses – this occurs because we are using both Aspire's endpoint management and explicit Kestrel configuration. We leveraged Aspire's service discovery capabilities, even though we're managing the gRPC-specific configuration manually.

We implemented `BooksAPI` as the gRPC client and `InventoryService` as the gRPC server. This design decision reflects a common pattern in microservices where one service (`BooksAPI`) needs to notify another service (`InventoryService`) about events – in this case, when a new book is added. When `BooksAPI` creates a new book, it uses the generated gRPC client to send a message to `InventoryService`, which processes the request and returns an inventory ID over the `HTTP/2` connection.

When we build our projects, the `Grpc.Tools` package processes our `.proto` file and generates strongly typed C# classes. Notice how we specified different `GrpcServices` values in each project's `.csproj` file – `"Server"` for `InventoryService` and `"Client"` for `BooksAPI`. This tells the `protobuf` compiler to generate different code for each project – server-side implementation classes for `InventoryService` and client-side calling code for `BooksAPI`.

Implementing bidirectional streaming with gRPC in .NET Aspire

You are not limited to only sending messages one at a time and in a one-way direction. You can implement a bidirectional streaming gRPC service. This will enable both the client and server to send streams of messages to each other independently within a single call. This is particularly useful for real-time applications where both parties need to continuously exchange data.

Getting ready

The starter project for this recipe can be found here: `https://github.com/PacktPublishing/ASP.NET-9-Web-API-Cookbook/tree/main/end/chapter11/gRPCBidirectional`.

How to do it...

1. Let's modify the `Protobuf` file in both the `BooksAPI` and `InventoryService` projects to modify the `MonitorStock` method for bidirectional streaming. Let's designate `StockRequest` as able to receive a stream and not just return a stream:

    ```
    service Inventory {
        rpc InitializeInventory (
            InitializeInventoryRequest
        ) returns (InitializeInventoryResponse);
        rpc MonitorStock (
            stream StockRequest
        ) returns (stream StockUpdate);
    }
    ```

    The `stream` keyword before both the request (`StockRequest`) and response (`StockUpdate`) indicates that both the client and server can communicate independently simultaneously.

2. Still in the `inventory.proto` file, let's update the `StockUpdate` message to include `book_id`:

    ```
    message StockUpdate {
        int32 book_id = 1;
        int32 current_stock = 2;
        string location = 3;
        int64 timestamp = 4;
    }
    ```

    Ensure that both the `BooksAPI` project and `InventoryService` project have the exact same `inventory.proto` files to prevent serialization issues.

3. Inside the `InventoryService` project, let's implement the `MonitorStock` method. We'll start by defining the method signature that handles bidirectional streaming:

```
public override async Task MonitorStock(
    IAsyncStreamReader<StockRequest> requestStream,
    IServerStreamWriter<StockUpdate> responseStream,
    ServerCallContext context)
```

4. Inside the method, let's use `await foreach` to continuously read incoming stock monitoring requests:

```
{
    await foreach (var stockRequest in requestStream.
        ReadAllAsync())
    {
        _logger.LogInformation(
            "Received stock request for Book ID: {BookId}",
            stockRequest.BookId);
```

5. Now, we will simulate sending multiple stock updates for each request:

```
for (int i = 0; i < 5; i++)
    {
        var stockUpdate = new StockUpdate
        {
            BookId = stockRequest.BookId,
            CurrentStock = 100 - i * 10,
            Location = "Warehouse A",
            Timestamp = DateTimeOffset.UtcNow
                .ToUnixTimeSeconds()
        };

        await responseStream.WriteAsync(stockUpdate);
        _logger.LogInformation(
            "Sent stock update: {Stock}",
            stockUpdate.CurrentStock);

        await Task.Delay(1000);
    }
}
```

6. After we receive a stream of `StockRequest` messages from the client, we will respond with a stream of `StockUpdate` messages:

```
logger.LogInformation(
    "Received stock request for Book ID: {BookId}",
    stockRequest.BookId);

for (int i = 0; i < 5; i++)
{
    var stockUpdate = new StockUpdate
    {
        BookId = stockRequest.BookId,
        CurrentStock = 100 - i * 10,
        Location = "Warehouse A",
        Timestamp = DateTimeOffset.UtcNow
            .ToUnixTimeSeconds()
    };
```

We are simulating stock updates by just sending multiple `StockUpdate` messages for each `StockRequest`. If we wanted to, we could stream our database data or anything else.

7. Update `BooksController` to consume the streaming data. In the `BooksAPI` project, open the `BooksController.cs` file and add the `Grpc.Core;` namespace to the top of the file:

```
using Grpc.Core;
```

8. Now, let's add two new endpoints to `BooksController`. Set up the GET request to consume streaming data:

```
[HttpGet("{id}/stock")]
[EndpointSummary("Monitor stock levels for a book")]
[EndpointDescription(
    "Streams stock updates for a specific book ID.")]
[ProducesResponseType(StatusCodes.Status200OK)]
[ProducesResponseType(StatusCodes.Status500InternalServerError)]
 public async Task<IActionResult> MonitorStock(int id)
    {
        try
        {
            _logger.LogInformation("Starting stock monitoring
                for Book ID: {BookId}", id);

            var call = _inventoryClient.MonitorStock(new
                StockRequest { BookId = id });
```

9. Place the received updates in a collection of stock updates and return each update:

```
var stockUpdates = new List<StockUpdate>();
await foreach (var update in call.ResponseStream.
    ReadAllAsync())
    {
        _logger.LogInformation("Received stock
            update for Book ID: {BookId} - Stock:
                {Stock}, Location: {Location},
                Timestamp: {Timestamp}",
                id, update.CurrentStock, update.Location,
                update.Timestamp);

        stockUpdates.Add(update);
    }

    return Ok(stockUpdates);

}
```

10. Let's catch any gRPC errors separately from our normal endpoint exceptions:

```
catch (RpcException rpcEx)
    {
    _logger.LogError(rpcEx,
        "gRPC error while monitoring stock for Book ID:
        {BookId}", id);
    return StatusCode(500, "An error occurred while
        monitoring stock levels.");
    }
    catch (Exception ex)
    {
        _logger.LogError(ex, "An error occurred while
            monitoring stock for Book ID: {BookId}", id);
        return StatusCode(500, "An error occurred while
            monitoring stock levels.");
    }
    }
}
```

We now have an endpoint that handles server-side streaming, receiving stock updates for a single BookId.

11. Next, let's make another endpoint that monitors the total stock with bidirectional streaming:

```
[HttpGet("api/stock/monitor")]
public async Task MonitorStock(
    CancellationToken cancellationToken)
{
    using var call = _inventoryClient
        .MonitorStock(cancellationToken: cancellationToken);
```

12. On the next line, start a task to send stock requests:

```
_ = Task.Run(async () =>
{
    for (int bookId = 1; bookId <= 3; bookId++)
    {
        var stockRequest = new StockRequest {
            BookId = bookId };
        await call.RequestStream.WriteAsync(
            stockRequest);
        _logger.LogInformation("Sent stock request for
            Book ID: {BookId}", bookId);
        await Task.Delay(1000); // Simulate delay
    }
    await call.RequestStream.CompleteAsync();
});
```

13. On the next line, let's receive the stock updates:

```
await foreach (var stockUpdate in call.ResponseStream.
ReadAllAsync(cancellationToken))
{
    _logger.LogInformation(
        "Received stock update for Book ID: {BookId},
        Stock: {Stock}",
        stockUpdate.BookId, stockUpdate.CurrentStock);
}
```

With the `RequestStream.WriteAsync` method, the client sends multiple `StockRequest` messages and concurrently receives `StockUpdate` messages. It uses `Task.Run` to send requests without blocking the receiving of responses.

14. Let's test our new bidirectional implementation. First, let's test the basic bidirectional streaming:

```
grpcurl -plaintext -d '{"book_id": 1}' localhost:5003 Inventory/
MonitorStock
```

This should show you multiple stock updates for book ID 1, with decreasing stock values. The `grpcurl` test will show live updates one at a time.

15. Now, let's test our new GET endpoint. We should be able to see the stream of gRPC data collected by our endpoint and returned to us over REST. Unlike the previous `grpcurl` command, this will show all updates together in a collected format:

```
Invoke-RestMethod -Uri "http://localhost:5011/api/books/1/stock"
-Method Get
```

16. Because `grpcurl` lacks support for bidirectional streaming tests, let's use `Invoke-RestMethod` to test monitoring multiple books:

```
Invoke-RestMethod -Uri "http://localhost:5011/api/books/monitor"
-Method Get
```

How it works...

In this recipe, we implemented bidirectional streaming with gRPC, which allows both the client and server to send multiple messages over a single long-lived connection. In the Protobuf definition, the `inventory.proto` file, we added the `stream` keyword to both the request and response types in `MonitorStock`, indicating that both sides can send multiple messages. In `InventoryService`, the `MonitorStock` method uses `IAsyncStreamReader` to read incoming requests and `IServerStreamWriter` to send responses. This pattern allows for true bidirectional communication – the service can receive new monitoring requests while simultaneously sending stock updates.

We then created two different GET endpoints with two different approaches to consuming streaming gRPC:

- A single endpoint (GET `/api/books/{id}/stock`) that collects all streamed updates and returns them as a single REST response.

- A more complex endpoint (GET `/api/books/monitor`) that implements true bidirectional streaming. This endpoint both sends and receives messages concurrently.

Implementing real-time updates with Dapr pub/sub in .NET Aspire

In this recipe, we'll implement real-time updates and interservice communication using Dapr's pub/sub capabilities. While traditional service-to-service communication often relies on direct HTTP calls or message queues that require complex configuration, Dapr with Aspire simplifies this by providing a pub/sub abstraction that's cloud-agnostic and requires minimal setup. Best of all, thanks to Aspire, we don't need the traditional YAML files for Dapr configuration

Getting ready

Make sure Docker Desktop is installed and running.

Install the Dapr CLI. For Windows, you can install it via WinGet:

```
winget install Dapr.CLI
```

Other ways to install the Dapr CLI can be found here: https://docs.dapr.io/getting-started/install-dapr-cli/.

The starter project for this recipe can be found here: https://github.com/PacktPublishing/ASP.NET-9-Web-API-Cookbook/tree/main/start/chapter11/DaprAspire.

How to do it...

1. We will need to establish the Dapr CLI for Dapr to work with while we are working on our local machine. In the terminal, type the following:

    ```
    dapr init
    ```

2. In the BooksAPI.AppHost folder, install the Aspire version of Dapr into the AppHost project:

    ```
    dotnet add package Aspire.Hosting.Dapr
    ```

3. Still in the AppHost project, install Redis, as Dapr will use this as the default message broker:

    ```
    dotnet add package Aspire.StackExchange.Redis
    ```

4. Add the main Dapr package for AspNetCore integration in the BooksAPI folder:

    ```
    dotnet add package Dapr.AspNetCore
    ```

5. Navigate to the InventoryService folder and install the package there as well.

6. Open the Program.cs file in the AppHost folder and import the **Aspire Hosting Dapr** library we installed in *step 1*:

    ```
    using Aspire.Hosting.Dapr;
    ```

7. Import the namespaces required for working with our dependency injection container:

    ```
    using Microsoft.Extensions.Configuration;
    using Microsoft.Extensions.DependencyInjection;
    ```

8. Set up Aspire to provide a Dapr pub/sub component:

    ```
    var pubsub = builder.AddDaprPubSub("pubsub");
    ```

9. Now, set up the `InventoryService` project with a Dapr sidecar. If we are publishing our app, set it to use `https`:

```
var inventory = builder.AddProject<Projects.
InventoryService>("inventory")
    .WithDaprSidecar(new DaprSidecarOptions
    {
        AppId = "inventory",
        AppProtocol = builder.ExecutionContext.IsPublishMode ?
                    null : "https",
        AppPort = 5001
    })
    .WithExternalHttpEndpoints()
```

10. On the next line, add a reference to our `pubsub` component:

```
    .WithReference(pubsub);
```

11. Now, register our independent books API with a Dapr sidecar. This will include a reference to the `pubsub` component and a reference to `BooksAPI`:

```
var books = builder.AddProject<Projects.BooksAPI>("books")
    .WithDaprSidecar(new DaprSidecarOptions
    {
        AppId = "books",
        AppProtocol = builder.ExecutionContext.IsPublishMode ?
                    null : "https",
        AppPort = 5011
    })
    .WithExternalHttpEndpoints()
    .WithReference(pubsub)
    .WithReference(inventory);
```

12. We need to configure Aspire to work with our local instance of Dapr. First, open PowerShell and register the Dapr CLI path as an environment variable:

```
[Environment]::SetEnvironmentVariable("DAPR_CLI_PATH", "C:\dapr\
dapr.exe", "User")
```

If `C:\dapr\dapr.exe` is not your path to Dapr, you can look for it in PowerShell, like so:

`Get-Command dapr`

13. Continue in our app host's `Program.cs` file. Register the `DAPR_CLI_PATH` environment variable we defined with Aspire:

```
if (builder.Configuration.GetValue<string>("DAPR_CLI_PATH") is {
} daprCliPath)
```

```
    {
        builder.Services.Configure<DaprOptions>(options =>
        {
            options.DaprPath = daprCliPath;
        });
    }

    builder.Build().Run();
```

This code is currently necessary because Aspire doesn't automatically detect the Dapr CLI in your system PATH. This is a known limitation being tracked in issue #2219. You'll need this configuration for both local development and CI/CD environments.

14. Let's also register the Dapr dashboard service, so we can use the Dapr dashboard alongside the Aspire dashboard:

```
Var daprDashboard = builder.AddExecutable("dapr-dashboard",
"dapr", ".", "dashboard")

    .WithHttpEndpoint(port: 8080, targetPort: 8080, name: "dapr-
dashboard-http", isProxied: false)

    .ExcludeFromManifest();
```

15. In the BooksAPI/Models folder, create a file called StockUpdate.cs. Fill in the StockUpdate class:

```
namespace Books.Models;

public record StockUpdate(
    int BookId,
    int CurrentStock,
    string Location,
    long Timestamp);
```

16. In the InventoryService folder, create a Models folder. Create a file called StockUpdate.cs here as well and create an identical StockUpdate record but with a different namespace:

```
namespace InventoryService.Models;

public record StockUpdate(
    int BookId,
    int CurrentStock,
    string Location,
    long Timestamp);
```

17. Update the `Program.cs` file of `InventoryService` to work with Dapr. Aspire's `AppHost` does the heavy lifting so all we have to add are the service defaults. We will also import `DaprClient`, which will represent the object we push our `pubsub` updates to:

```
builder.AddServiceDefaults();

builder.Services.AddControllers();
builder.Services.AddDaprClient();
var app = builder.Build();

app.UseCloudEvents();
app.MapSubscribeHandler();
app.MapControllers();

app.Run();
```

We also register the cloud events and subscription handler middleware.

18. Create a new `Controllers` folder and create a file called `InventoryController.cs`. In this file, let's create a new controller:

```
using Dapr.Client;
using Microsoft.AspNetCore.Mvc;
using InventoryService.Models;

namespace InventoryService.Controllers;

[ApiController]
[Route("[controller]")]
public class InventoryController(
    DaprClient daprClient,
    ILogger<InventoryController> _logger) : ControllerBase
```

Notice that we passed in `DaprClient` via a primary constructor.

19. Now, let's create one endpoint. This REST endpoint takes a POST request and sends a message to `DaprClient`:

```
[HttpPost("monitor/{bookId}")]
public async Task<IActionResult> PublishStockUpdates(int bookId)
```

20. Let's fill in the action method. We will create a collection of possible book stock levels:

```
{
    var scenarios = new[]
    {
        (stock: 100, location: "Main Warehouse"),
```

```
        (stock: 75, location: "Store Front"),
        (stock: 50, location: "Online Fulfillment"),
        (stock: 25, location: "Reserve Stock"),
        (stock: 10, location: "Last Units Warning")
};
```

21. Now, let's put that information into a series of `update` objects and publish those updates to `daprClient`:

```
foreach (var scenario in scenarios)
    {
        var update = new StockUpdate(
            BookId: bookId,
            CurrentStock: scenario.stock,
            Location: scenario.location,
            Timestamp: DateTimeOffset.UtcNow
                        .ToUnixTimeSeconds());

        await daprClient.PublishEventAsync(
            "pubsub", "stockupdates", update);
```

22. Let's log what happened to the Aspire dashboard. We will simulate a delay and return a message to the client:

```
_logger.LogInformation(
            "Published stock alert: Book {BookId} has {Stock}
                                    units in {Location}",
            bookId, scenario.stock, scenario.location);

        await Task.Delay(1000);
    }

    return Ok("Stock updates published");
}
```

23. Now, let's set up `BooksAPI` to receive the message. Open the `BooksAPI\Program.cs` file and, on the line after we register the books service, register `DaprClient`:

```
builder.Services.AddScoped<IBooksService, BooksService>();
builder.Services.AddDaprClient();

var app = builder.Build();
```

24. At the end of the middleware pipeline, register our cloud events and subscription handler, right after where `UseHttpsRedirection` is registered:

```
app.UseHttpsRedirection();
app.UseCloudEvents();
app.MapSubscribeHandler();
```

25. Now, let's add a special POST endpoint that can receive our pub/sub messages. First, let's import the namespace required to interact with the Dapr client:

```
using Dapr;
```

26. At the bottom of the file, let's define a new endpoint. This will be a POST method that receives the message from the Dapr client:

```
[Topic("pubsub", "stock-updates")]
[HttpPost("stock-updates")]
public IActionResult HandleStockUpdate([FromBody] StockUpdate
update)
    {
```

27. Dapr places our `update` message inside the `StockUpdate` parameter. Let's read the message and return the relevant stock level:

```
var alertLevel = update.CurrentStock switch
        {
            <= 10 => "CRITICAL",
            <= 25 => "LOW",
            <= 50 => "MODERATE",
            _ => "HEALTHY"
        };
```

28. Let's log the request:

```
_logger.LogInformation(
        "Stock Alert [{Level}]: Book {BookId} has {Stock}
                                units in {Location}",
        alertLevel,
        update.BookId,
        update.CurrentStock,
        update.Location);
```

29. Finally, we'll return the update to the client:

```
return Ok(new
    {
        bookId = update.BookId,
```

```
            stock = update.CurrentStock,
            location = update.Location,
            alertLevel,
            timestamp = DateTimeOffset.FromUnixTimeSeconds(update.
                    Timestamp)
    });
```

30. Let's test this with our CLI tools. We can start the application by navigating to the `AppHost` project and executing the following command:

    dotnet run

    Your operating system may pop a message up asking whether Dapr is trustworthy.

31. With the Dapr CLI, let's make sure that we can publish events:

    ```
    dapr publish --publish-app-id inventory
    --pubsub pubsub --topic stock-updates --data
    "{\"bookId\":1,\"currentStock\":100,\"location\":
    \"Test\",\"timestamp\":1234567890}"
    ```

    That command should return `"Event published successfully"`.

32. Call the Dapr subscription manually, to make sure the subscription ability is active:

    ```
    $response = Invoke-RestMethod -Uri "http://localhost: 51312/
    dapr/subscribe" -Method Get
    $response | ConvertTo-Json
    ```

    The response may appear empty as it indicates no active subscription. The preceding port of `51312` might be the wrong port on your machine. While we configured the application ports (`5001`/`5011`), the Dapr sidecar ports are dynamic, so be sure to check your Aspire dashboard for the correct HTTP port.

33. Let's trigger the subscription:

    ```
    Invoke-RestMethod -Uri "http://localhost:49567/inventory/
    monitor/1" `
        -Method Post `
        -ContentType "application/json"
    ```

34. Next, let's check the stock levels of one of our books:

    ```
    Invoke-RestMethod -Uri "http://localhost:51991/api/books/stock-
    updates" `
        -Method Post `
        -ContentType "application/json" `
        -Body '{"bookId": 1, "currentStock": 100,
                "location": "Warehouse A"}'
    ```

Besides the response, we can also check the logs and telemetry on the Aspire dashboard. Moreover, we can also visit the **dapr** dashboard at `http://localhost:8080`, as shown in *Figure 11.3*:

Figure 11.3 – The dapr dashboard

How it works...

The `Aspire.Hosting.Dapr` package enables us to configure Dapr directly in our `AppHost` project using C# code instead of YAML files. The `'AddDaprPubSub'` method sets up a pub/sub component that both services can reference. Under the hood, it also configures Redis as the default message broker. Each service gets its own Dapr sidecar through `'WithDaprSidecar()'`, which acts as a proxy for pub/sub communication. `InventoryService` publishes stock updates using `DaprClient`, while `BooksAPI` subscribes to these updates using the `'[Topic]'` attribute.

`MapSubscribeHandler()` in `BooksAPI` is crucial – it tells Dapr about our subscriptions when the service starts, enabling the Dapr sidecar to route messages to the correct endpoints. When a message is published to the `"stock-update"` topic, Dapr delivers it to our subscribed endpoint automatically, handling all the serialization and delivery mechanics.

Sharing state between services with Dapr state stores

Let's say you need to share the state between different microservices in your ASP.NET Core application using Dapr's state store functionality. We can modify Dapr's state store to use a shared key prefix strategy. This enables multiple services to access the same state data.

Getting ready

Make sure Docker Desktop is installed and running.

Install Redis. Windows users can install Redis via the following:

```
choco install redis
```

Dapr must be installed. After you clone the project, to install the latest Dapr runtime binaries, run the following:

```
dapr init
```

The starter project can be found here: `https://github.com/PacktPublishing/ASP.NET-9-Web-API-Cookbook/tree/main/start/chapter11/DaprStore`.

How to do it...

1. Install the Redis package in each of our two APIs. In both the `BooksAPI` folder and the `InventoryService` folder, run the following:

   ```
   dotnet add package Aspire.StackExchange.Redis
   ```

2. In the `BooksAPI.AppHost` folder, create a sub-folder called `Components`. In this directory, create a file called `statestore.yaml` and fill in the following YAML code:

   ```yaml
   apiVersion: dapr.io/v1alpha1
   kind: Component
   metadata:
     name: statestore
   spec:
     type: state.redis
     version: v1
     metadata:
     - name: redisHost
       value: localhost:6379
     - name: redisPassword
       value: ""
     - name: actorStateStore
       value: "true"
     - name: keyPrefix
       value: "name"
   ```

   This changes the default `keyPrefix` strategy for our Dapr store component.

3. In the `BooksAPI.AppHost` folder, open the `Program.cs` file and configure our store on the line after pubsub:

    ```
    var pubsub = builder.AddDaprPubSub("pubsub");
    var stateStore = builder.AddDaprStateStore("statestore", new
    DaprComponentOptions
    {
        LocalPath = "components/statestore.yaml"
    });
    ```

    Unfortunately, the `DaprComponentOptions` class can only take a path for further configuration. That is why we created our `.yaml` file as opposed to passing options directly in `AppHost`.

4. In `InventoryController`, let's create an endpoint that saves a message:

    ```
    [HttpPost("test-stock/{bookId}")]
    public async Task<IActionResult> TestStockUpdate(int bookId)
    {
        var random = new Random();
        var stock = random.Next(1, 101);
        var locations = new[] { "Main Warehouse", "Store Front",
            "Online Fulfillment", "Reserve Stock" };
        var location = locations[random.Next(locations.Length)];

        var update = new StockUpdate(
            BookId: bookId,
            CurrentStock: stock,
            Location: location,
            Timestamp: DateTimeOffset.UtcNow.ToUnixTimeSeconds());
    ```

5. On the next line, we have to be careful that we explicitly convert the object to JSON:

    ```
    var jsonData = JsonSerializer.Serialize(update);
        var metadata = new Dictionary<string, string>
        {
            { "contentType", "application/json" }
        };
    ```

6. Next, save to the store and return a result to the client:

    ```
    await daprClient.SaveStateAsync(
            "statestore",
            $"book-{bookId}-stock",
            jsonData,
            metadata: metadata);


        _logger.LogInformation(
    ```

```
    "Saved stock update: Book {BookId} has {Stock} units
        in {Location}",
    bookId, stock, location);

return Ok(new {
    message = "Stock update saved",
    update = update
});
```

7. Navigate to the `BooksController.cs` file inside the `BooksAPI` project folder and create a new endpoint to read the log:

```
[HttpGet("stock-log/{bookId}")]
public async Task<IActionResult> GetStockLog(int bookId)
{
    var stateKey = $"book-{bookId}-stock";

    try
    {
        var stockUpdate = await _daprClient
            .GetStateAsync<StockUpdate>(
                "statestore",
                stateKey);

        if (stockUpdate == null)
            return NotFound($"No stock log for book {bookId}");

        return Ok(stockUpdate);
    }
    catch (Exception ex)
    {
        _logger.LogError(ex, "Error retrieving stock log");
        return StatusCode(500);
    }
}
```

8. Let's test our shared state functionality between `InventoryService` and `BooksAPI` in the terminal. First, create a stock update:

```
Invoke-RestMethod -Uri "http://localhost:49567/inventory/test-
stock/5" -Method Post
```

Finally, retrieve a stock log from the books service:

```
Invoke-RestMethod -Uri "http://localhost:51991/api/books/stock-
log/5" -Method Get
```

How it works...

Dapr's state store typically prefixes keys with the application ID (e.g., `inventory||` or `books||`), isolating the state between services. By setting `keyPrefix: "name"` in the component configuration, we tell Dapr to use the state store name as the prefix instead (`statestore||`). This enables both services to access the same state using the same key.

The inventory service saves stock updates with explicit JSON content type metadata to ensure proper serialization. The books service can then retrieve these updates using the same key structure, as both services share the same state store prefix. This shared state approach is particularly useful for scenarios where multiple services need consistent access to the same data – saving us the trouble of having to implement complex synchronization mechanisms.

12
Unlock Your Exclusive Benefits

Your copy of this book includes the following exclusive benefit:

- ☁ Next-gen Packt Reader
- 📄 DRM-free PDF/ePub downloads

Follow the guide below to unlock them. The process takes only a few minutes and needs to be completed once.

Unlock this Book's Free Benefits in 3 Easy Steps

Step 1

Keep your purchase invoice ready for *Step 3*. If you have a physical copy, scan it using your phone and save it as a PDF, JPG, or PNG.

For more help on finding your invoice, visit `https://www.packtpub.com/unlock-benefits/help`.

> **Note**
>
> If you bought this book directly from Packt, no invoice is required. After *Step 2*, you can access your exclusive content right away.

Step 2

Scan the QR code or go to `packtpub.com/unlock`.

On the page that opens (similar to *Figure 12.1* on desktop), search for this book by name and select the correct edition.

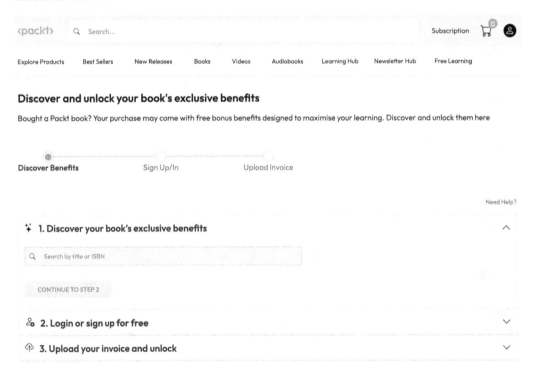

Figure 12.1: Packt unlock landing page on desktop

Step 3

After selecting your book, sign in to your Packt account or create one for free. Then upload your invoice (PDF, PNG, or JPG, up to 10 MB). Follow the on-screen instructions to finish the process.

Need help?

If you get stuck and need help, visit
`https://www.packtpub.com/unlock-benefits/help`
for a detailed FAQ on how to find your invoices and more. This QR code will take you to the help page.

Note

If you are still facing issues, reach out to `customercare@packt.com`.

Index

packtpub.com

Subscribe to our online digital library for full access to over 7,000 books and videos, as well as industry leading tools to help you plan your personal development and advance your career. For more information, please visit our website.

Why subscribe?

- Spend less time learning and more time coding with practical eBooks and Videos from over 4,000 industry professionals

- Improve your learning with Skill Plans built especially for you

- Get a free eBook or video every month

- Fully searchable for easy access to vital information

- Copy and paste, print, and bookmark content

At www.packtpub.com, you can also read a collection of free technical articles, sign up for a range of free newsletters, and receive exclusive discounts and offers on Packt books and eBooks.

Other Books You May Enjoy

If you enjoyed this book, you may be interested in these other books by Packt:

C# 13 and .NET 9 – Modern Cross-Platform Development Fundamentals – Ninth Edition

Mark J. Price

ISBN: 978-1-83588-122-4

- Discover the new features of .NET 9, including more flexible params and new LINQ like CountBy and Index

- Leverage the new ASP.NET Core 9 features for optimized static assets, OpenAPI document generation, and HybridCache

- Utilize the native AOT publish capability for faster startup and reduced memory footprint

- Build rich web user interface experiences using Blazor in ASP.NET Core 9

- Integrate and update databases in your applications using Entity Framework Core 9 models

- Query and manipulate data using LINQ

- Build powerful services using Minimal APIs

Real-World Web Development with .NET 9

Mark J. Price

ISBN: 978-1-83588-038-8

- Build web applications using ASP.NET Core MVC with well-structured, maintainable code
- Develop secure and scalable RESTful services using Web API and OData
- Implement authentication and authorization for your applications
- Test and containerize your .NET projects for smooth deployment
- Optimize application performance with caching and other techniques
- Learn how to use and implement Umbraco CMS

Packt is searching for authors like you

If you're interested in becoming an author for Packt, please visit `authors.packtpub.com` and apply today. We have worked with thousands of developers and tech professionals, just like you, to help them share their insight with the global tech community. You can make a general application, apply for a specific hot topic that we are recruiting an author for, or submit your own idea.

Share Your Thoughts

Now you've finished *ASP.NET Core 9 Web API Cookbook*, we'd love to hear your thoughts! Scan the QR code below to go straight to the Amazon review page for this book and share your feedback or leave a review on the site that you purchased it from.

`https://packt.link/r/1835880355`

Your review is important to us and the tech community and will help us make sure we're delivering excellent quality content.

Learn more on Discord

To join the Discord community for this book – where you can share feedback, ask questions to the authors, and provide solutions to other readers – scan the QR code or visit the link:

`https://packt.link/aspdotnet9WebAPI`

www.ingramcontent.com/pod-product-compliance
Lightning Source LLC
Chambersburg PA
CBHW080618060326
40690CB00021B/4739